ROUTLEDGE LIBRARY EDITIONS:
ETHICS

Volume 7

ETHICS FOR UNBELIEVERS

ETHICS FOR UNBELIEVERS

AMBER BLANCO WHITE

Taylor & Francis Group
LONDON AND NEW YORK

First published in 1949 by Routledge & Kegan Paul Ltd

This edition first published in 2021
by Routledge
2 Park Square, Milton Park, Abingdon, Oxon OX14 4RN

and by Routledge
52 Vanderbilt Avenue, New York, NY 10017

Routledge is an imprint of the Taylor & Francis Group, an informa business

© 1949 Amber Blanco White
© 2020 Dusa McDuff

All rights reserved. No part of this book may be reprinted or reproduced or utilised in any form or by any electronic, mechanical, or other means, now known or hereafter invented, including photocopying and recording, or in any information storage or retrieval system, without permission in writing from the publishers.

Trademark notice: Product or corporate names may be trademarks or registered trademarks, and are used only for identification and explanation without intent to infringe.

British Library Cataloguing in Publication Data
A catalogue record for this book is available from the British Library

ISBN: 978-0-367-85624-3 (Set)
ISBN: 978-1-00-305260-9 (Set) (ebk)
ISBN: 978-0-367-49901-3 (Volume 7) (hbk)
ISBN: 978-1-00-304806-0 (Volume 7) (ebk)

Publisher's Note
The publisher has gone to great lengths to ensure the quality of this reprint but points out that some imperfections in the original copies may be apparent.

Disclaimer
The publisher has made every effort to trace copyright holders and would welcome correspondence from those they have been unable to trace.

ETHICS
FOR UNBELIEVERS

by
AMBER BLANCO WHITE

LONDON
ROUTLEDGE & KEGAN PAUL LTD.

First Published in England
by ROUTLEDGE & KEGAN PAUL LTD.
Broadway House, 68-74 Carter Lane
London, E.C.4
1948

This book is dedicated to my husband, without whose insistence and encouragement during the last eight years it would never have been finished.

*Owing to production delays
this book was not published
until* 1949

THIS BOOK IS PRODUCED IN COMPLETE
CONFORMITY WITH THE AUTHORIZED
ECONOMY STANDARDS

*Printed in Great Britain
By W. & J. Mackay & Co., Ltd., Chatham*

LIST OF CHAPTERS

CHAPTER	PAGE
Foreword	vi
1. Introductory	1
2. Revealed Moral Codes	12
3. The Conventional View of Conscience	26
4. The Origin of Conscience	37
5. The Nature of Conscience	47
6. The Moral Code of the Individual	59
7. Communal Codes (1)	75
8. Communal Codes (2)	90
9. The Philosophers (1) Confucius and the Greeks	105
10. The Philosophers (2) The Value of Pleasure	123
11. Methods and Criteria of a Scientific System of Ethics	136
12. The Good Man	150
13. The Good Society (1)	170
14. The Good Society (2)	182
15. Sexual Morality	197
16. Conclusion	218

FOREWORD

The system of psychology upon which this essay is based is that of Freud. I think that is made clear in the text. But it should perhaps be mentioned that in one particular I have departed from his doctrine without saying so. That is, I have treated the moral code of the individual and his conscience or Super-Ego as two separate things, different in kind though of course closely connected. When I first advanced this theory in my book *Worry in Women* it had not, so far as I know, been adopted by any Freudian, though it seems to me implicit in many of their judgments. Nor does it appear in the writings of any moralist, since those who recognise the existence of the conscience have believed it to be an organ which tells us what is right and what is wrong. My reasons for the course I have taken are, I hope, made clear in Chapters 3—6. And I can now say that Dr. Ernest Jones, in his review of my book in *The International Journal of Psycho-Analysis* took no objection to the distinction drawn. This I think he must have done had it not seemed to him obvious. All other descriptions of the human mind are restatements of psycho-analytical findings or simple deductions from them.

AMBER BLANCO WHITE

1948.

CHAPTER I

INTRODUCTORY

The purpose of this book is to discuss the desirability, the nature and the validity of a scientific system of morals, and then whether, and upon what basis, such a system could be built. No apology for this attempt should be necessary at the present time; there can seldom have been a greater need for thought upon ethical problems.

In the first place most men are agreed that unless the human race can change its accustomed behaviour, can become more friendly and less prone to quarrel, its future will be unpleasant and possibly short. But apart from this immediate threat, wherever we look and whatever form our interests may take we find ourselves confronted by unsolved moral controversies. They embitter politics, complicate economic issues, divide the generations and disturb our daily lives. Instances could be given by the dozen. Is the motive of private profit good or evil? Should men be killed because they have acted upon sincerely held but now unpopular opinions? How far should states interfere with the personal lives of their citizens? What are the duties of the powerful among nations to the weak, the rich to the poor, the civilised to the primitive? How far does the taking of a job involve an obligation to work one's best?

All these, in whole or in part, are matters of right and wrong, and all have given rise to acute disagreement. Another crop of vexed questions springs from a world-wide decline in the power of the father over his family, and of men over women. These two changes are undermining the old foundations of family life and disrupting the traditional sexual codes. Never before have very large numbers of people asked themselves such questions as: " Have I a right to keep Henry, if I can, or ought he to go back to his wife and family now that the war is over? " The problem has arisen often enough, but rarely the moral doubt. " Why should I listen to father? I'm sure I never asked to be born! " is also a modern attitude. And since a challenge to the authority of the father induces scepticism towards the claims of all established authorities, subversive social and political factors are concurrently strengthened. It may be added that from whatever source rebellion springs it tends to include in its attack the moral assumptions of the ruler.

Again, we have just emerged from a ferocious war which was brought about in part by the deepest possible disagreement as to moral values and the purpose of human life. The ideals of the victors triumphed with their arms—or so it seemed for a time. But superior force cannot refute moral doctrines even though, for a time, it may render them unattractive.

Problems such as these have always emerged in turbulent ages, but many people find them now especially difficult to solve. This is not because they are more complex than they were in the past, but because opinion upon the attribution of good and bad has seldom, if ever, been so confused and divergent. Whereas each community used to possess a moral code which it took for granted and by which it measured not only its own affairs but those of the world at large, the habit of our time is to criticise not only the accepted moral doctrines but the bases of morality itself. Multitudes are now asking : " Why should I try to do right ? " "Am I not entitled to be happy if I can ? " : " Why should I not look out for myself when all the others do ? " : " Why should we love our enemies when it only makes them despise us ? " Guidance on such matters is sought from the mouths even of itinerant Brains Trusts.

It is sought because outside the churches, recognised or self-styled, and the folds of one or two ideologies, there exists no accepted system of morals to which men can turn, nor any body of principle from which they could form one for themselves. In this country at any rate it seems to be widely held that Christ was the best man who ever lived, and Socrates (or my father, or the king, or some other personal hero) the second best, and that Christian ethics on the whole are good although Christians only too often are not. After this the more thoughtful minds are influenced by scraps from the teachings of Darwin, Marx, Plato and Mill, even when none of these authors has been read, and by vague ideas such as : " You ought to help others if you can" : " We all have a right to lead our own lives and make our own mistakes " : " It is wrong to want things too much " : " If you want a thing badly enough you can get it " : " Morals are a matter of climate " : " You can always find out what you ought to do if you only try hard enough".

Nor are these states of mind confined to the self-taught.

Nothing can be, on occasion, more bemusing than a sound classical education superimposed upon a sound religious training. Nor are our minds made clearer by the claims of specialists who think exclusively in terms of their own subjects—economists pressing purely economic solutions, biologists stressing biological forces, and historians pointing to those of the morals of history which happen to be clear to themselves. In short there exists in the minds of many thoughtful people a confusion as to theory which is tolerable only because it does not preclude a high standard of behaviour in ordinary life. The young people who champion moral anarchy and ridicule all conventional moral values are often kind, reliable, hardworking and anxious to be good citizens—in many ways more civilised than their forebears. Frequently beneath the fierceness lies considerable distress and a strong desire to clear their minds. Again and again one finds that the lack of moral standards is causing acute anxiety. "I feel adrift in life": "There ought to be a purpose in life, and yet when I try to make sure what it is I don't get anywhere": "I keep asking myself, 'Why should I do any of this? Why not clear out and do just as I please? Of course one cannot do just what one pleases, but I should like to have a clear explanation of why not." These attitudes seem to be typical and widespread.

Their main causes are generally recognised—the spread of reading, the growth of science and its immense prestige, and knowledge of foreign cultures. Educated men and women have always shown interest in ethical theories. Now the interest has spread, but often in an atmosphere of cynicism towards everything which the authorities want one to believe.

Science in one form or another concerns and must continue to concern an increasing proportion of our populations. And science even when badly taught demands some accuracy of mind, some respect for facts and the placing of some value upon evidence. Both its spirit and what it teaches are found by millions, rightly or wrongly, to be incompatible both with the dogmas of the churches and with the religious attitude to life. Statements by eminent churchmen that this incompatibility is an illusion are accepted by very few scientists. But science is taught so much as a collection of facts, as a number of separate examination subjects, and so little as a discipline, that its moral lessons are but dimly seen if they are seen at all. Nor do the branches usually studied provide the data needed for sound constructive thinking in the field of Ethics. Up to the present therefore science has acted rather as a

A*

solvent than as a contributing factor to the steadying of moral values. It will be necessary later to examine the form which this contribution might take.

As for clashes between cultures, it is admitted nowadays that men of other creeds and races can hold beliefs which are neither benighted, depraved nor inspired by devils even though they differ from those of the Atlantic peoples. The mood of the moment, indeed, seems to be one of self-disparagement; and though the noble savage is no longer admired as he was in the eighteenth century, eastern mystics of various descriptions seem to have taken his place. Fashions such as that for an idealised Buddhism are of but passing importance: what matters is that the moral notions of every century, school and clime are to be found in the lucky-bag of popular literature, and that most of those who dip into it have no means of judging the value of their prize.

If these statements are largely true of the industrial peoples, the rest of the world seems to be faring even worse. The impact of the machine civilisations upon less powerful groups is an anxiety to all who are interested in more primitive communities or responsible for their welfare.

That this state of affairs exists would, I think, be generally admitted. It is also a matter of general anxiety. And in this country the solution proposed for the whole problem is to bring the nation back to religion. The churches claim that their interpretation of life gives it both a meaning and a purpose. They offer moral codes respected by all and familiar for nearly two thousand years. They buttress these codes by absolute sanctions which need for their acceptance only a sufficiency of faith. They hold out mercy to the evil-doer who sincerely repents, and the comfort of God's grace to guide his footsteps in the way of salvation. With these goes, of course, the promise of eternal life, now hardly shadowed by the fear of a physical hell. Religion, in short, should bring light out of darkness, order out of chaos, and the splendour of righteousness out of original sin. Further, the argument runs, if all this be rejected, what is left? If morality be not the observance of the will of God, what is it?

If these statements were exact, if these promises could be believed, no more would remain to be said. If they were even acceptable, if there seemed any likelihood of a general return to the old ways, those who still disagreed could do little but observe the results of that return. But if the claims of the churches with regard to morals are erroneous, or even if a mass reconversion is improbable, then it must be desirable that we should find if we can a non-supernatural basis for morality.

It falls outside the scope of this book to discuss at length the chances of a general return to orthodox Christian beliefs.[1] Great and well directed efforts have been made during the last few years to influence opinion in this direction. They have had some success. All wars and periods of misery produce overwhelming desire for relief from the various anxieties which they engender, and these in their turn are apt to lead to the acceptance of religious doctrines. It is known, for instance, that there has been a close inverse correlation all through their history between the prosperity of the Chinese people and the popularity of religion in China. The increase in church attendance which occurred during the late war may turn out to be partly of this nature. If so, it will decline again when the pressing fears caused by the war begin to be forgotten—on condition, of course, that they are not replaced by others as terrible. Even if this supposition is wrong, very large numbers of people have not yet joined in the movement, and no obvious ground exists for supposing that they will do so.

Indeed it is precisely because the return to a religious system of belief involves the acceptance of the Church's outlook upon morals that the way of return is barred to many minds. Men will believe almost anything if they want to believe it badly enough, but what is thought—truly or falsely—to be the narrowness, intolerance and lack of understanding shown by churchmen towards " modern problems " acts as a strong deterrent to belief. Even those who feel that " there may be something in it " do not consult the vicar about their personal difficulties. This is not always due to intellectual scruples, since fortune-tellers and astrologers may be consulted instead. The stars are felt to be impartial, apostles of High Thises-and-Thats in tune with the modern world, and the old woman who reads the crystal more kindly and sympathetic than the parish priest.

There are reasons therefore for supposing that the official remedy will fail, and even the chance of such a failure makes it worth while to examine the claim that religion is the only, or even the best, source and support of human virtue. No belief has been

[1] If any reader will go through the Book of Common Prayer, extract from the three Creeds, the thirty-nine Articles and the Catechism, the beliefs which he is expected to hold and proclaim on pain of damnation, and then tabulate and compare them—and if he will then discuss them with any fair sample of his fellow-countrymen—he will understand the extent of the problem.

more firmly held by the majority of mankind; nevertheless it may prove to be wrong. A great deal more will be said on the subject in the body of this book, but the one or two examples given below will show, perhaps, that the onus of proof lies upon those who maintain that there is any necessary connection between goodness and piety.

In the first place, although lofty moral standards based upon love towards God and man have been recognised in Europe for many centuries, few will doubt today that the problem of bringing them into effect has still to be solved. This is not because the standards were rejected; on the contrary they were during most of that time implicitly believed. Only a handful of devil-worshippers dared to think them wrong. They were accepted, but they did not work. The ages of faith were also ages of violence, persecution, treachery, crime and oppression of the poor. It is during the recent period of decline in faith that we have seen the growth of what is called the social conscience. The causes which produced this apparent paradox will be discussed later, as will the frenzy of cruelty we have witnessed during the last few years.

To pass from the community to the individual: Wherever in England or America statistical inquiries have been made into the religious background of delinquent children, it has been found that a higher percentage of them come from definitely religious schools and homes. The evidence is far from complete, but all of it agrees. In those English towns for which figures are available the Council schools produce the smallest proportion of unsatisfactory children, the schools of the Protestant churches come next, and the Catholic schools produce the highest proportion. It is customary to explain these facts away by saying that the children who attend church schools are poorer than the Council pupils. In some cases this is true, but it seems also to be true that poverty, taken by itself, is not a cause of crime in children. Dr. Cyril Burt, in his standard work *The Young Delinquent* says that the outstanding feature in juvenile delinquency is "the narrow religious home". After this come sudden falls in the standard of living,[1] bad heredity and mental deficiency, and emotional disturbances caused by deaths, divorces and the appearance of rivals in the family circle. This again seems paradoxical, but again its causes can be clearly shown.

To give only one more example: Few disinterested observers are prepared to say that church people are more virtuous on the

[1] This is borne out by the appalling increase in thieving during the late war.

whole than agnostics. As a rule the fact is admitted and then the reply is made that unbelievers are still under the influence of Christian doctrine and by it protected from wickedness.

In so far as the standards of communities are in question, there is something in this argument. The moral codes of Europe and America are strongly influenced by the traditions of the Christian churches. But when we come to individuals—to the question of why John Smith is as honest as Geoffrey Brown—the matter becomes one of living up to one's standards as well as of the standards themselves. In this sphere the argument quoted would only be true if agnostics refrained from vice only because they followed the example given by the Christians round them. Then one might say with truth that the one goodness depended on the other.

Agnostics, in fact, do nothing of the sort. The average agnostic is far more likely to charge church-people with betraying their own profession, with being censorious, hypocritical and so forth, than to take them for his model. On the contrary, a weak point in his moral system is often a desire to flout and shock the orthodox so that the sight of their respectability makes him worse and not better. Unbelievers are on the whole a critical class, and they accept the Christian code, or part of it, because it seems to them good on its merits. And they do, therefore, confront us with the fact that a great many people can achieve a normal degree of goodness without the aid of any supernatural sanction.

Believers often feel, of course, that this is unfair. Only a divine being could have produced the Christian code, which they believe to be unique and superior to all others. Therefore the least that one should do if one makes use of it is to admit these facts and one's own indebtedness. But this reasoning is based upon ignorance of the fact that the principal moral doctrines of Christianity —certainly those which are most widely influential today—were enunciated by Confucius five hundred years before the birth of Christ.[1] And Confucius, even though he probably believed in Heaven, also held that it does not concern itself with the behaviour of human beings.

All these facts indicate that we have no obvious reason for believing that the population of this country would be more virtuous if they were more religious. Their manner of sinning

---

[1] The words "Thou shalt love thy neighbour as thyself" occur in Leviticus, which reached its present form about 400 B.C. Every clergyman must be aware of this yet it remains part of the Church's teaching that they represent an exclusively Christian contribution to morals.

might be different, but that is not the same thing, nor necessarily an improvement. To say this is not to deny that many find help in religion, and under its wing lead better lives than they would otherwise have done.[1] Nor does it prevent us from admitting that when Christianity made its appearance its moral codes were a great advance upon those then current in the Roman Empire. But the question at issue is not now whether we shall embrace a new and untried gospel of love and fellowship and eternal life. It is whether a return to a system of dogmas which are intellectually unconvincing, and the bosom of churches whose histories are none too reassuring, would produce closer obedience to a code of morals with which most of us have been familiar all our lives.

As soon as we ask this question we see that it leads to another —whether this code is exactly what is needed, and the present doctrines of the churches always as useful as they ought to be in solving the moral issues which cause most anxiety today.

Upon both these questions much more will of course be said. But before leaving the subject here it may be as well to remember that Britain is not the only country in the world, nor Christianity the only religion. What is needed at the moment is not so much an increase in the goodness of any one nation— though that is desirable—as an increase in good will, just dealing and wisdom all the world over. And short of a sudden conversion to Christian doctrine of all the peoples of the earth, a general return to religion will not secure this end. For the more pious each race becomes the more closely will it cling, in theory, to its traditional morality, and the more difficult it will become, therefore, to reconcile conflicting beliefs and claims. Moral feelings based upon religion are of all things the most difficult to change when confronted by different feelings based upon a different faith. The tendency of a human being in this situation is to rally to his own group and suspect all others. Nobody needs to be reminded how often this has led to misunderstanding, suspicion, hatred and war. A timely example is the gulf which divides Moslems and Hindus in India.

It has often been argued that the points upon which the great religions differ do not matter. The forms of religion may vary but its spirit does not. Every creed preaches at least the importance of duty and, as for the rest, God makes known to each race as much of the truth as it is capable of understanding at each particular stage in its development.

[1] For further discussion on this point see Chapter. 6, page 71.

It seems hardly necessary to argue that this comfortable haze reveals nothing. Those who find comfort in what they call " Progressive Revelation " shut their eyes to the events of the past and even to the present teachings of the various faiths. For what does this doctrine involve ? That whatever is taught by a church is part of the truth ? That whatever morals a community may have are the best of which they are capable ? If so, why seek to convert or reform or give moral instruction to any group or sect ? Why try to interfere with the caste system in India ? Why not admire the religious customs of the Aztecs and the worshippers of Baal ? Why take objection to religious persecution ? All these things are believed in as commanded by God. If right and wrong are to have any content at all besides the mere performance of what has been taught as a duty, then we must believe that many moral dogmas have been horribly mistaken and are witnesses to nothing but the ferocity of man.

For all these reasons, and for many others, there seems to be a growing feeling that we should look again, as have many of the greatest moralists in the past, for a system of morality which does not depend upon religion. In practice numbers of men and women manage their lives well enough without such a system. But though the individual who has been set a good example may often live up to it without supernatural sanctions, it cannot but be dangerous to leave all those who reject religious dogmas to the chances and haphazard encounters of life. A consistent body of belief which is logically defensible seems to be one of the needs of the time.

To secure it, we must solve three problems. The first is to discover ends and purposes for moral effort which are likely to appeal to the majority of mankind and arouse their sense of duty. That is to say, we need effective moral ideals. The second problem is to find a standard by which divergent moral beliefs can be judged, so that we may fairly say of them that one is better or more useful than another. The third is to evolve a serviceable code, or series of codes, which give an adequate foundation for conduct, no matter where or by whom it is needed.

Modern psychology has shown that it is unnecessary to add what would formerly have been thought of as the most urgent requirement—that is, the creation of a sense of duty. All but lunatics and idiots possess a sense of duty, and the task of parents and educators is not to bring it into existence but to allow it to develop normally and attach it to suitable goals.[1]

These statements assume that some system of ethics is both necessary and binding, an assumption which also needs examination.

The beginnings of a universal moral code exist already. All human groups agree that some human impulses need regulation. The desire to kill one's neighbour is one of them ; another is the desire to ravish his wife. Different communities differ greatly about the best methods of dealing with murderous impulses and controlling the sexual instincts, but none is willing to leave them to the momentary feelings of the individual. The reason is simple— life in groups is possible only if based upon some degree of order. How strict that degree should be is another open question.

These rudiments of agreement are, of course, far from the coherent body of principle which is rapidly becoming more and more desirable. And it may as well be said at once that no attempt is made in this book to elaborate such a system. I am neither endowed nor equipped for the task and not such a fool as to attempt it. Freud, in a letter to Otto Rank which the latter quotes in his *Thirty Years with Freud*, wrote that on the basis afforded by modern psychology it should be possible to work out a scientific moral code. But it seems improbable that this will be done successfully by any one man, or even group, or as a deliberate exercise. Factors such as climate and differences in outlook due to long tradition will continue to influence morals for centuries to come. Even the most fervent believer in Christian marriage would not insist that the practice of the Church of England should be imposed on the Japanese as part of the Peace Settlement.

Agreement as to desirable behaviour, becoming more detailed, will more probably extend through the growth of a common respect for scientific method and increased recognition of the relevant facts. When it does we shall find ourselves dealing not so much with lists of disconnected maxims and particular sins and virtues as with common purposes and the knowledge of how human beings are likely to react to various stimuli. We know already, for instance, that if we do not want children to lie we must not only teach them the importance of truth both by precept and example, but refrain from putting them into positions which will in practice lead to lying. Lies are the weapons of the fearful and the oppressed, and most of us realise that if children are to

[1] Cf. Ch. 9.

be truthful they must neither be frightened nor made to suffer unduly.

Information of this sort is accepted and used for various reasons but in the main either because it is found to work, or because it is taught by men and women who are respected and loved. A good deal of it exists; it is increasing in amount and being more or less gradually assimilated. Whether we think of it in this light or not it will act as a strong influence on morals, at least in the direction of making them more effective.

With regard to the matter of sanctions the scientific moralist is in a strong position. If he chooses to make use of the available material he can give a definite answer to the questions: "What is morality?"; "Why should I do right?"; "How am I to judge between these different values?" and "What is the purpose of life?" And while giving these answers he can clear the ground of several false beliefs—among them some which have, to many, made virtue seem almost synonymous with frustration and unhappiness.

In the sphere of ultimate moral ideals—the first of the problems mentioned as needing solution—a statement which satisfies one man rouses contempt in another. But we are at least able, for the first time, to see why this is so—information which is much more important that it may seem at first sight. To know the causes of disagreement is the first step towards overcoming as much of it as possible. In short we possess nowadays a technique for dealing with ethical problems which was not available to the sages and philosophers of the past, and one which should enable us to improve on their results. For it we are indebted partly to the use of scientific concepts, and partly to a vast increase in our knowledge of human nature.

To give the more important of these relevant facts; to answer the questions quoted above and to encourage discussion of moral problems from this new angle, is the purpose of what I have written. If the book begins with a good deal of destructive criticism, that is due to the fact that even where sound conclusions have been reached, wrong grounds have been given for them, or they have been based upon invalid reasoning. Some of these errors are bars to all advance, especially the belief that morality is the handmaid of religion. While this is felt no progress can be made, and for this reason our inquiry begins by examining the most widely accepted vehicle of moral laws, the revealed ethical code.

CHAPTER 2

REVEALED MORAL CODES

Mankind in general, once it has emerged from slavery to custom, believes that morality is a code of behaviour imposed by a god or gods, a code which men would not have evolved for themselves, and to which they are by nature refractory. To do right, in fact, is to please one's god, to obey him and do his will. And so widespread is this attitude that apart from the followers of Confucius, a few groups of philosophers, and now a growing but still comparatively small body of scientists, not one man in a million has doubted its truth. Even those who cannot bring themselves to accept the dogmas of religion often do not know where to look for an alternative sanction for morality.

If the beliefs of human beings were determined by reason the theory of its divine origin would have provoked a great deal more criticism than it has. For many of the gods made by man in his own image have possessed few of the virtues which they themselves are supposed to have enjoined. They were admitted to be bloodthirsty, greedy, immoral and deceitful—in fact perfectly capable of providing their followers with an ethical system devised in a drunken orgy. It is difficult to imagine less suitable arbiters of right and wrong, or, from a moral point of view, a less convincing sanction. Whatever else it may be it can hardly be right to serve and obey stupid, dissolute and ferocious beings. Indeed in primitive tribes to please the gods is thought of as sensible rather than as moral. " If anyone annoys the spirits they will destroy the crops with thunderstorms" gives a practical basis for obedience, especially if those who fail to obey are regularly punished by the tribe. But it is a train of thought and feeling which has little to do with morality as generally conceived. Appeasement may be wise, but it is only incidentally a virtue.

As men and their ideas about their gods developed this type of difficulty lessened. Raging, revengeful deities, such as Baal or even the God of the prophet Jeremiah, ceased to fulfil the ideals of mankind. Great teachers arose who preached that the source of morality must itself be perfect—an attractive belief, though accepted in its entirety only by a few. Large numbers of Christians are still haunted by the bogy of a cruel revengeful God, even when they think themselves certain that God is Love. A great deal of twisted thinking has resulted from the effort to reconcile these two conceptions of Godhead. But no Christian or Buddhist or Moslem would deny that God is perfect.

In consequence of this change in outlook the religions with perfect gods are confronted by what is known as the problem of evil—that is, the onus of explaining how the wickedness and misery which we see around us can be permitted by, and have proceeded from, a God who is at once all-powerful, all-loving and all-wise. But so strong and deep is the demand for an absolute and unshakable basis for morality that even this tormenting problem is preferred to the admission of any weakness of imperfection in the Deity. Neither Christians nor Moslems are willing to believe in a god who would like to have made a better universe but was unable to do so. Still less would they be prepared to worship one in whose nature there is any admixture of evil.

The other great religions do not seem to feel any need at all for consistency. The Brahma of the Buddhists is at one moment Infinite Stillness and apparently empty of attributes, and then we find this negation appearing to the Buddha and begging him to preach his new method of salvation. As for Brahminism and Hindoism, all one can say is that trying to make sense of them is a sterile method of approach.

The majority of mankind have been disturbed by neither of these dilemmas. It took a Socrates to point out that considering what the gods were like, goodness could not consist in pleasing them. The rest of the world went on with a policy of appeasement on the one hand and on the other an attempt to be as virtuous as they could. It was not thought necessary to distinguish between these activities. Believers were assisted not only by man's infinite capacity for unreason, but by the fact that in most communities the moral code was far more sensible and enlightened than the gods. This is a fact of great significance, though it is only of recent years that we have been able to understand and explain it.

In the meantime, as nations became more civilised and their gods less vicious and incalculable, the moral code took on greater importance and the need for sacrifice in material form was felt to be less and less urgent.

Youths and maidens are no longer driven into fiery furnaces as an act of official worship, though Jews have been gassed in millions to ease the delusions of Hitler. Christians have ceased to mutilate themselves with official approval and Hindus are prevented by the police from throwing themselves under the wheel of Juggernaut. The vast tributes that flowed into the coffers of churches, the mountains of burnt offerings, have dwindled until this once enormous sphere of human behaviour may come down to putting threepence into the plate and giving up sweets in Lent. Morality is no longer regarded principally a matter of buying off the vengeance of one's God : it is the performance of His will by obedience to His word.

The will of God is generally supposed to be ascertainable in two ways : through some sacred text revealed of old to a prophet or succession of prophets, and through the conscience of the individual. Different religions, and different sects belonging to the same religion, place a very different degree of emphasis upon these two factors. Some, like the Catholic Church, claim both the first and the last word upon all moral questions ; other allow a large amount of latitude. They believe that a man's conscience must be his ultimate guide. But in spite of this belief the sacred texts are held to have divine authority and any wide deviation from their accepted interpretation is regarded with suspicion, if not prohibited by law.

To the difficulties inherent in this double basis for ethics it will be necessary to return. This chapter deals with some of the more important consequences that follow from founding one's moral ideas upon a revealed moral code.

Such a system has important advantages. So long as the religious beliefs in question hold their authority, it helps to remove morality from the realm of controversy. It provides an absolute sanction, which has been supported until recently by belief in heaven and hell. It gives the moral code the place which it ought to hold as a stabilising feature in life. Rapid changes in moral values are always risky and disturbing things.

Further, the text of the code itself is as a rule familiar to every member of the community, and associated with important sources of emotion. It binds together those who accept it, and because it finds an echo in their hearts, it can often be used to restrain the tyrant and confound the tempter. These are extremely valuable functions.

But revealed codes have their disadvantages, and some of these are grave.

The first, and perhaps the greatest, is that they are difficult to modify. In theory this need not be so. Many religious thinkers accept the doctrine that what is absolute is obedience to God's will, and that His requirements will naturally differ in detail as the circumstances of life on this planet change.

But this, in one sentence, strips from morality precisely that absolute quality which men on the whole most desire it to possess. Such a doctrine may be sensible but it throws upon the shoulders of human beings just the burden which they seek to escape—that of determining for themselves the validity of the ethical ideas which happen to be orthodox at any given moment. Were Christ, Mahomet, Buddha, Socrates, true prophets, or did they all deserve to be executed, as two of them were? Does the new sect possess the root of the matter, or should it be put to the sword? Some of the most cruel wars and persecutions in history have sprung from disagreement over these questions.

Until recently the usual solution found by the individual was to evade the problem. On the one hand he liked to believe that morality, down to its smallest details, is absolute, and immutable —as it was in the past, is now, and ever shall be. At the same time he avoided the necessity of facing the fact that changes in moral values do occur, by accepting the moral leadership of his church. The church was the guardian of morality and he its faithful servant. It was for his pastors to reconcile what they were telling him and his generation with what had been preached to his forefathers.

This system is felt as natural, and in static periods works without much friction. Such changes as occur need not be violent, and can often be accepted without any realisation that they have taken place. Students of past moralities are few, and so long as the church in question neither falls into a corruption so vile that it shocks the average man, nor presses reforms upon a reluctant flock, the bulk of its followers hardly notice what is going on.

In fact the history of morals is a history of constant change. If we take only the Christian churches—since they are the most familiar—we find that celibacy and the monastic life used to be exalted above marriage; that freedom of conscience was denied, dissidents burned at the stake in the name of morality, and the heathen converted by force. Men who did not leave a portion of their money to the Church were believed to be doomed to hell, but one could buy off years in purgatory if one left the money for masses. When the printing press made copies of the scriptures available these ideas were discarded by much of Christendom, but only after a series of bloody wars. Theories about property, usury,

Sunday observance, the sinfulness of war and the functions of the saints. have varied in different places and at different times. There have been bitter conflicts about such subjects as salvation by faith and salvation by works and the use of the confessional, to say nothing of the amount of mercy to be shown to different types of sinners. All these problems have a direct bearing on morals. And the bitter conflicts which arose while the doctrines of Christianity were being slowly determined through the Dark and the early Middle Ages, were thought by their participants to be of the highest moral import. But through it all how many even of the more learned churchmen questioned their belief that religion provided them with a stable, unequivocal and absolute moral standard?

In spite of all these and many other matters in which opinions have fluctuated from one extreme to the other, the main objection to the governance of morals by the churches has been, as I have said, that on the whole their judgments adapted themselves too slowly to changing circumstances. In many things, though not in all, they have been the opponents of enlightenment where they should have been its champions.

The reasons for this are not difficult to see. The first and the most intractable is that a revealed code, being of a divine origin, is absolute and unchangeable except through further revelation. It is deeply revered, and is felt by those to whom it has been taught as the rock upon which their own moral integrity is based. To alter it may distress them unendurably. If an upright man believes that he does his duty only because he must obey the will of God, he is likely to form two conclusions, both of which are natural though neither is true. The first is: "If it were not for my belief in God I should not try to do my duty," and the second: "All performance of duty depends upon belief in its divine origin." The existence in very large numbers of heathen, infidels and atheists who also try to do their duty should show him that this reasoning is false, but of course it does not. Therefore he will tend to oppose a strenuous resistance to anything which seems to him likely to weaken the particular moral code in which he has been brought up. If change is to be admitted, where will it stop? If women are not to be veiled from the eyes of men, or prostitutes whipped through the streets, or girls who have lost their virtue driven from the estate, what will become of female chastity? If the state is to interfere between parent and child, what of the sanctity of family life? A code taught as absolute is sacred as a whole, and to imperil any part of it is to threaten the whole structure of morals.

These conclusions may not be clearly or even consciously entertained, but the feelings to which they give rise will not be less powerful on that account. Therefore any attempt by religious leaders to move with the times means running the risk of widespread distress and scandal among the faithful, or even of a split within the church. Perhaps the majority of sects have split off because they thought they were reverting to the purer and stricter standards of an earlier age.

In spite of these dangers, however, the behaviour of men must somehow adjust itself to the circumstances of their time. And in fact whenever great changes take place in a country's wealth, or power, or in the nature of its social system, moral values are found to alter with them. Prolonged periods of danger or unaccustomed poverty throw men into a religious mood; they abandon the notion of improving this life and look for consolation to the peace of annihilation or to life beyond the grave. Wealth, bringing with it the possibility of civilisation, alters the whole scale of social values, and leads to an increase in tolerance and kindness in some respects and on the other hand a denial of common humanity. Nor are the virtues of the democrat those which allow of survival under the heel of a tyrant.

When such changes take place large numbers of people will find themselves accepting new duties and casting off old obligations. Somehow or other the churches must fall into line unless they are to lose their hold over the minds of the population as well as their standing in the state. But they are in a dilemma, and it is not surprising that they have on the whole taken the line of adjusting themselves but doing it as slowly as possible.

A few examples of improvements which might perhaps have been embraced more quickly may explain this point.

The growth of the science of medicine and the spread of ideas about hygiene have forced the Christian churches to abandon, or at least to modify that hatred and contempt for the human body which used to form part of the essence of Christian doctrine. Filth was a sign of holiness and this belief held in Russia until it was swept away by the propaganda of the Bolsheviks. Now it lingers only in convents and monasteries, and even there as an opposition to the pleasure of cleanliness rather than as an admiration for dirt. By the bulk of the population of Europe it is largely forgotten. But the changes in moral values which have flowed, and will continue to flow, from the cult for swimming baths and American plumbing, should not on that account be underestimated. If the body must be cared for and becomes a source of pride, it will not be hated and despised and mortified as the source of the sins of the flesh. Further, as we should expect, the tolerance thus engendered has greatly changed the general attitude towards some of those sins themselves. One of the consequences of this is that those who disapprove of semi-nudity are felt to be out of date generally and unreliable as moral guides. Another controversy which divides Christendom and will probably continue to do so is the permissibility of complete divorce. Lay opinion differs widely upon the degree of latitude that is desirable, but it is probably true to say that all who oppose divorce entirely do so on religious grounds.

A third instance is the rejection of the old belief in the divine right of kings. This strikes us now as a political theory, and it was rebelled against for social and political reasons. But it had been taught to the generations who accepted it as part of their religion, and as laying upon them an unescapable moral obligation. No one can read Jacobite literature, and particularly the sermons preached on the subject between 1650 and 1750, without realising how thoroughly it was believed by many to be part of God's teaching and what a strong hold it had upon the consciences of thousands of honest men. Even in our own days the broadcast service of the coronation of our present King and Queen must have altered the attitude of many whose minds were loth to relinquish their allegiance to King Edward VIII.

All these necessary adjustments place the adherents of revealed codes in very uneasy positions. Sometimes it is possible to justify a change which can no longer be deferred as a return to the original doctrine. The criticism of medicine which took the form of saying that God knows what is best for us and sends in His wisdom sickness or health as He pleases, was met, when it became clear that medicine had come to stay, by remembering that Christ healed the sick, and calling Him "The Great Physician." On other occasions texts hitherto ignored can be found and stressed, while the passages used to support superseded doctrines are allowed to fade from mind. "Compel them to come in!" is no longer, for the moment, held to justify religious persecution. A third possibility is to take a different view of the whole spirit of the texts. The teachings of the Old Testament, for instance, must be reinterpreted to fit with the teachings of Christ, even though Christ himself says repeatedly that his message did not differ from those of Moses and the prophets.

The Catholic Church escapes from the naked dilemma by its doctrine of Papal Infallibility. This gives the necessary new revelation. For the rest of Christendom the problem remains. A divine code should require no readjustment. All the codes used by men have required readjustment and the more stress is placed by the guardian of the codes upon errors in the past, the more probable it will seem that errors may still persist.

The reader may think that this is unimportant so long as very few people let themselves see what is happening. It is good that men should feel that their moral codes rest on an unchanging foundation, and if this idea can be retained through and in spite of a process of evolution, so much the better. This is, I think, a superficial view. Inconsistencies in anything so important as moral doctrine do matter, especially when they give rise to self-deception. Morals should not depend upon inability to face the facts.

Other types of difficulty that arise through the attempt to found morality upon revealed codes may be seen if we examine our own Ten Commandments and consider how they appear today to ordinary men and women who think of themselves as Christians.

The Commandments are taught to most of us. We learn them by heart, we see them inscribed in our churches, they are read in the Communion service and explained in the Catechism. Some of their provisions are embodied in our criminal law. Most of us take it for granted that they express God's will and that we have a duty to obey them. Yet, in practice, two different tendencies affect our feelings towards them, both of which are generally accepted as sensible and right. On the one hand some of them have lost their binding force and are tacitly disregarded: secondly, some surprising beliefs have been added to them and come to share their sacred character. These facts are familiar enough, but the deductions that follow are not usually drawn.

An example of the first tendency is, of course, the Second Commandment: "Thou shalt not make to thyself any graven image; thou shalt not bow down to it nor worship it." The two greatest of the Christian churches, the Orthodox Greek and the Catholic, make conscious and deliberate use of graven images, enjoin bowing down to them, and only fall short of worship by distinctions not perceptible to simple minds. Some Christian sects regard this as wicked, and refuse to display in their chapels even the symbol of the Cross. None of them goes so far as to object to statues of famous generals and kings and queens. Moslems, even nowadays, accept the prohibition and obey it literally.

Here we have an injunction which is largely ignored even by those who believe in its divine origin and continue to teach it. The tenth Commandment, on the other hand, would be accepted by most of us in theory, even though it involves a moral condemnation of our existing economic system. " Thou shalt not covet thy neighbour's house, thou shalt not covet thy neighbour's wife, nor his servant nor his maid nor his ox nor his ass, nor anything which is his." We do not like the use of the word " covet " in connection with our endeavours to better our social and economic positions. We prefer to find some question begging epithet, and say that healthy competition is the life blood of commerce, and the desire for another man's place the last infirmity of noble minds. But there the matter ends. To covet Jones's corner site and deprive him of it by any means that lie within the law is considered a legitimate business operation, and sincerely so considered. The commandment has lost its authority in relation to extensive fields of conduct.

It is probably not going too far to say that the majority of church people no longer believe those passages of the sacred texts which do not fit in with existing social arrangements. Although they would not admit it, in fact they judge the Commandments by the current standards of their community whenever it suits them to do so. The excuse generally given is that the injunctions so treated are not the important ones—which is another way of saying the same thing.

The second tendency to which I referred is that beliefs for which the code gives no authority are adopted for extraneous reasons, and then felt as sacred by a process of association. Only a generation ago millions of people believed that the institution of private property was ordained in Heaven, and even today it is widely felt that any process of interference with it is wicked. The Pope in recent pronouncements has seemed to sanction this belief.

Most people are surprised when they first realise that lying is not forbidden by the Decalogue except in the form of giving false witness against thy neighbour. Adultery is prohibited, but nothing is said about monogamy. And a minority of Christians have always held that the command "Thou shalt not kill" forbids taking part in war as well as private murder.

In short, when morality is felt to be the observance of a divine code, then not only accepted traditions, but the dicta of fashion and the private convictions of individuals will tend to be held by those who deeply desire to hold them as though they were sacred. For this gives the necessary excuse for defending them with savagery.

These reactions are serious and inevitable. Another has not, so far as I know, been mentioned by moralists, although its consequences are grave enough. This is, that new precepts made necessary by advances in human knowledge and mastery over nature, or by changes in the structure of society, are regarded lightly in comparison with the traditional injunctions of the code. Many people who would not steal bread if they were starving will be careless about such a matter as spreading a dangerous infection. They "know perfectly well" that they ought not to do it, but they do not feel in their bones that to do it is a sin. The concept of sin, which to them is the important concept, remains attached to a special category of actions forbidden in church, and to extensions of that category which have been made under the stress of powerful personal impulses and feelings. Where these are lacking, the link-up is not achieved. Other instances of the same reaction are dangerous driving, and the host of commercial transactions which fall short of honesty. Men do not recognise that a man who drives carelessly past a group of children has already in his heart risked killing them. They do not feel that to sell shoddy goods at high prices to ignorant people is to steal their money. They do not think of such actions as wicked. In fact when the late Archbishop of Canterbury urged that the Christian virtues generally should be practised in the spheres of business and politics, the press was flooded with abusive and indignant letters signed by believing members of the churches.

These states of mind would not occur if conduct were regarded as evil in the degree to which it harms or is likely to harm, one's fellow-men. As it is, the command to love thy neighbour as thyself is felt as impossible of achievement, and when a child is killed, or dishonesty uncovered, those concerned often excuse themselves as the victims of bad luck. More sensitive people may of course suffer when the conscience which failed to control them at the time turns upon them in the face of disaster. But this does not alter the fact that an important rule of civilised behaviour has not been accepted whole-heartedly as binding.

Even the purely verbal element in these associations is far more important than we should imagine at first sight. We can tell this from the fact that when human beings break a well-known moral law they like to find a new word to describe what they are doing. " Eliminate " is used instead of " kill " or " murder." The stealing which has become so widespread during the war is now described as " winning." This, no doubt gives the act a colour of achievement; to admit that one had stolen would set one's conscience nagging. To champion " Free Love " is easier than to defend seduction and adultery. In the same way " All-In " wrestling and " total " war were useful covers for deliberate brutalisation.

A third corollary of believing in inspired codes—though here again the inference is seldom drawn—is that it involves belief in a personal God of an anthropomorphic type who can notice one's smallest lapses and approve one's obedience. Immanent and universal spirits, idealistic interpretations of the universe, will not serve the purpose. Such entities cannot deliver texts, nor give verbal inspiration to Popes and Prophets, nor carve on tablets of stone. Unless we assume a mystic link between the spirit of the universe and the human conscience, they cannot direct morality in any way whatever. And such an assumption is not only unsupported by evidence, but runs counter to all that we now know about the conscience and its functions.[1]

In short the revealed code carries with it a primitive cosmogony.

This objection is important because the idea of God as " an old gentleman with a long white beard who lives in the sky " is no longer acceptable to most educated people. Their reason rejects the conception even though they may be haunted by it and wish, in the depths of their minds and in moments of stress, that it were true. But they cannot believe it to be true. And as terror and awe of the human father diminish this lack of ability will tend to spread. Therefore if morality be based upon laws said to have been communicated by such a being, doubt will attach itself to the moral system closely linked with him. It is partly for this reason that we find people asking every day : " If there is no supernatural sanction for morality then why should men try to be good ? " " How are we to tell what is really right ? " They

[1] Cf. Chapters 4 and 5.

feel that they have been deceived by the mentors in whom they had trusted; that they are left adrift in life without purpose or guide. This is a real and a most serious grievance.

Before leaving the subject of revealed moral codes one more point must be mentioned. It is often said, as we have seen, that whatever the faults of the ancient scripts, belief in them does at least secure recognition of the concept of duty. Unless morality is firmly based upon the word of God men will not feel themselves under any obligation to act rightly.

There are several reasons why this is not true, and the most important will be found in Chapters 4 and 5. Men do and always must feel themselves under such an obligation. But another reply is, briefly, that basing morality upon religion has not made men moral. On the contrary, some of the attitudes most strictly enjoined upon the religious are formidable impediments to good behaviour. Evidence for this statement must of course be given, and given fully. In the meantime anyone who thinks that the sceptical young people of today are peculiarly immoral, should study the laws passed in mediaeval Europe to deal with the conduct of apprentices, and contemporary denunciations of their idleness, drunkenness, unchastity and riotous behaviour.

To say this is not to say that great moral leaders who have been deified have not improved the prevailing standards of morality. It is merely to assert that the improvement would have been as great without the deification—a statement which is obvious once we admit that in every case but one the deification was an error. The followers of Confucius, moreover, have been some of the most moral men and women who have ever lived.

On the other hand it was a Christian Europe which broke down into the welter of evil which so nearly submerged our world. It is useless to reply that this ought not to have occurred; that if men had taken to heart the precepts of Christianity it would not have occurred. What ought to have taken place is beside the point when the question at issue is whether a supernatural moral code and sanction for morality is an *effective* way of securing good behaviour. It has not been effective, since it has not secured it. To quote: " Water has been in the world for a million years, but look at your neck ! " is not only a jeer, it is an irrelevant jeer.

If we consider the facts in more detail, they bear out this contention. It was not the sceptics and the believers in the unfettered use of reason who tortured, murdered and committed almost incredible cruelties all over Europe. They fled, or were killed, or immured in concentration camps because they refused to abandon their moral standards and to believe that everything the Führer or the Duce said was right. Those who did become converts *en masse* were peoples brought up in " simple faith " like the Italian peasants ; ordinary Germans who had been taught religion in their schools and homes ; the right wing parties in France with their Catholic affiliations. It is in fact one of the principal objections to simple faith, even when it is faith in the good, that it can be switched from one object to another with comparative ease under the pressure of fear or anxiety. It is reason, with its demand for proof, for adequate grounds ; it is the ability to think for oneself in logical fashion, which guard men from the wiles of the spell-binder and his appeals to primitive urges and emotions. Teach men to believe in miracles, and when they are in such a plight that only a miracle, it seems, can save them, they turn to the leader who promises the miracle that they want. And once they have turned to him, his standards become theirs. For to their minds morality is essentially a matter of accepting commands from above.

There have been, of course, exceptions to all these generalisations. The times have produced religious martyrs as well as believers in reason who have ratted from their beliefs. But they were exceptions. The Catholic Centre Party in Germany supported Hitler, after he had published *Mein Kampf*, and ordered their flocks to vote for him. Long after it had been thought politic to complain of the treatment of Catholics in Germany, and to order the German Catholic priesthood to defend the rights of the Church, a crusade against Russia was still being preached in Europe, and the whole weight of the Papacy used to set up and support Fascist régimes in South America. The most fervent belief in Christian principles did not prevent this trafficking with evil.

At this point I should expect a good many readers to protest that the whole of this chapter is mere quibbling and carping and beside the mark. What matter if there be inconsistencies ? The churchmen will say that logical inconsistencies must be met in a spirit of faith. The Church exists to fill in gaps, to interpret texts, to help us when decisions are difficult and moral duties appear to conflict. If the guidance of the Church seems to fail us, then we must fall back upon conscience, the organ implanted in man by God to render just this service. The spirit of Christian doctrine is clear, and the individual under a duty to apply it to the problem in hand. In such a task, sincerely approached, he may count upon the Grace of God.

Those less inclined to theology will often argue that no cultivated man or woman believes in textual revelation nowadays, or in the word-for-word sanctity of ancient writings. What we can all accept is the broad spirit of Christian teaching as we find it in the New Testament. When interpreting it we must not lightly depart from accepted interpretations and the traditions of our race, but so long as we keep within their spirit we are safe.

There is a good deal of truth in this argument. It is through Christianity that what we call the humanitarian values have descended to modern Europe, though they were the commonplaces of Chinese thought centuries before Christ was born. But to adopt this line of thought is to abandon that very advantage of a revealed morality which, oddly enough, blinds men to its imperfections. This is that it is absolute and invariable and able to give us certainty in matters of right and wrong. Once the code may be criticised and judged by conscience there is an end of its absolute quality. We must look instead to the voice of God speaking within our hearts.

CHAPTER 3

THE CONVENTIONAL VIEW OF CONSCIENCE

The official view of conscience is that it is an organ implanted in man by God to guide his conduct and show him what is right. We know now that this description is inaccurate. To begin with, it fails to separate two different things. The first—conscience itself—is the force in our minds which controls, or seeks to control, those elements in our natures which are either abhorrent to us or regarded as sinful. The second is the code of beliefs about good and bad which the individual acquires on his way through life—his moral standards. Whether these are good, bad, or a jumble, conscience will do what it can to get them obeyed. But it does not create them.

These two entities, conscience and the moral standard, are variously related in different people. One man will have a strong, well-organised conscience which makes him live up to most of his beliefs. His moral code, on the other hand, may be confined to a narrow sphere of conduct. It is possible to possess a number of personal virtues without having any sense of civic duty.

Another type is the man with a strong sense of duty whose moral code does not correspond to that of the community in which he lives. If the difference seems to us small, we call him a crank. If it appears to be dangerously large, we punish or kill him. Yet another relation is found in him who makes himself miserable because he cannot achieve impossible ideals. This is sometimes called having a morbid conscience, but often enough most of the blame should be thrown on to an inhuman moral code.

In these cases what causes the trouble is not lack of conscience, but the nature of the beliefs which it is asked to enforce. Sometimes, however, the boot is on the other foot. Millions of human beings have sensible ideas about what they ought to do, but because their consciences are weak or work intermittently, or are otherwise faulty, they fail to live up to them. It is unnecessary to give examples : the reader has only to search his memory.

In the next two chapters I shall discuss what modern knowledge has to say about the origin and development both of our consciences and of our moral codes. But before doing that it may be as well to draw attention to some of the consequences which have flowed from our failure to distinguish between them.

It has generally been felt, even when it was not clearly recognised, that if every man were to follow his own convictions morals would fall into confusion. For there can be few actions possible to a human being which have not been approved at some time by the conscience of their performer. Jack the Ripper believed that God desired him to mutilate and murder prostitutes. Him we think of as mad. Mahomet believed that he was commanded by Allah to root out infidels. Him we dismiss as intolerant because he died a long time ago. If pushed, we might admit that none of the great persecutors was altogether sane. But consider for a moment the different convictions held by normal human beings about wives—one wife, four wives, wives galore up to Solomon with his thousand, and no wife at all. Nowhere do morals vary more than in the province of sex, of all the most disturbing to most moralists.

This instance, by itself, out of the hundreds available, disposes of the belief that conscience is the inner voice through which God enables man to distinguish between good and evil. If it were, why should the Zulu not recognise that to invest one's capital in wives is wrong? Why should the heathen have inferior morals? Surely not to punish them because they are heathen, for that is not their fault.

Everybody knows all this, but few are prepared to change their beliefs about the efficacy of conscience on that account. The Catholic Church, by making itself the sole arbiter of morals, denies it in practice. The conscience that does not enjoin complete obedience to the church is condemned as bad. The rest of western Christendom regards the Catholic claim as intolerable. In most Protestant sects some Council, Synod, Congress or the like attempts to deal from time to time with particular vexed and hurting questions, but in the main they are left, as they must be, to the spasmodic utterances of leaders, or to settle themselves. For not only do opinions differ among Protestants as to the scope which should be allowed to the individual conscience, but there is no practical method of settling its authority in relation to that of the traditional code. It is not possible even to decide who is sincere, and who is insincere.

It may be noted that even the " Groupers," who believe in direct guidance and ask their members to listen each morning to

B

the voice of God with pencil in hand, prefer that the counsel thus received should not be acted upon until it has been endorsed by the group. I gather that this attitude is based upon cogent practical reasons.

Among Protestants, then, the individual conscience is respected and taken seriously, but not accepted as an absolute guide. There are no accepted formulas for solving marginal cases—in the nature of things there cannot be. Even where tradition is enforced by law cases occur in which the churches will allow individuals to break the law, possibly with their approval. One instance is the case of the " passive " resisters " who refused to pay their taxes after the passing of Mr. Balfour's Education Act. Another is the attitude taken by many Irish priests towards murders committed by the I.R.A. The practice of absolving the killers was finally condemned by Rome, but only after a considerable time and many protests.

That conscience is a doubtful guide is not a new discovery. The prestige acquired by individual feelings about right and wrong was due to the fact that freedom of conscience had been the symbol and rallying-cry, the General de Gaulle, so to speak, of the Reformation. A core of solid value was surrounded by a nimbus of claims and pretensions which soon began to trouble earnest men. In Britain especially, the number of sects which appeared, their fantastic doctrines and aptitude for violence, gave rise to speculation on the subject, and as soon as politics ceased to monopolise attention moralists began to discuss the question. With the events of the preceding years in mind they were naturally agreed that conscience of itself is not enough. But they differed as to why this is and what can be done about it.

The most popular doctrine was that before conscience can be an adequate guide, it requires a good education. The disadvantage of this theory is that it leaves us in doubt as to what it implies. Can any education be good which fails to produce a virtuous individual? How is the individual himself to tell whether or not his conscience has been well educated? And how can he be blamed if it leads him into error if it has been educated by people over whom he had no control?

The eighteenth century was not ready for the doctrine that the sins of the individual lie on the shoulders of the community, or of his parents or indeed of any but his own, and they were concerned to retain the right to blame and punish a man for the evil that he does. So that to them these objections should have seemed conclusive. What they did find more convincing is the argument that if the conscience needs training, then something else, which is not the conscience, must provide the principles in accordance with which it is to be trained. It is useless to say that this must be the consensus of opinion, even if opinion be limited as Sidgwick limits it in another connection, to that of educated men with a serious concern for morality. This is to assume that men are agreed as to these principles, and they are not. The training of the conscience of a Catholic has a very different basis from that of a Quaker, and is undertaken by widely different methods. And so the search for an ultimate begins again.

Partly for these reasons other moralists put forward the opposite theory—which is that conscience, as implanted by God (or Nature) does enable us to tell the difference between right and wrong.

And since God is good (or Nature natural) the conscience must be capable of reaching true results. If consciences differ, as it must be admitted that they do, though not, perhaps, so often as their owners would like to pretend, then all but those which do give accurate guidance must have been corrupted or sophisticated. The sophisticating agent is variously described as Satan, or human beings and governments which are themselves corrupt.

Unhappily for this theory, which is attractive in many ways, it destroys precisely what it seeks to establish, which is the practical value of conscience. For who or what is to decide which is the warped conscience and which the uncorrupted? We are sure that the consciences of Hitler's loyal followers were warped : they were equally sure that ours had fallen into decay. And unless a man has some infallible means of deciding whether or not his conscience has been corrupted, it is useless as a guide. This theory too throws us back upon the need for some further authority.

As a rule the thinkers who took either of these lines have been minor figures. The greater moral philosophers have usually held that conscience cannot be trusted in the matter of individual moral judgments. Its proper sphere is not to answer conundrums as they arise, but to decide the fundamental moral principles. From these individual conclusions must be deduced by the exercise of reason. Conscience—or Intuition—can tell us in what the good consists. After that conduct must be worked out by considering the consequences of our behaviour.

Here again it is an unfortunate fact that as soon as we leave the two words " The Good " all the old difficulties meet us once more. Throughout history there have been philosophers whose intuitions told them that the only good is pleasure or happiness, and others who have seen just as clearly that it is nothing of the sort. The Good which all should seek may be the performance of duty—defined in different ways—or the contemplative life, or union with God, or the well-being of one's fellows or one's State, or non-existence. Churchmen, on the whole, discourage the idea that earthly happiness can form even part of the moral goal, though they often maintain that it is wrong to destroy the happiness of others except for a moral reason. If we believe in a future life, it seems just to say that Christians consider that man has a right to consider his total happiness, and so to shape his conduct as to secure it. But even then they would add that a greater good, and a purer source of action, is to glorify God, and to do His will.

This problem of happiness and its relation to duty is discussed in Chapter 9. Here I will only mention Aristotle's formula that men must strive after goodness, truth and beauty. Few will disagree with it, but as a yard-stick it is not of much use. Since it neither defines what is good, nor helps us to decide what is true, its chief adherents were those who felt convinced of the importance of beauty. But upon what subject can there be more bitter disagreement? One man's vision of delight is another man's nightmare. Moreover all beauty but the beauty of goodness or God is felt to be dangerous by the ascetics. " Beauty is the snare of the devil."

Philosophers, then, differ in their fundamental intuitions as widely as they differ in their descriptions of the nature and functions of conscience. We get from them nothing but a welter of suppositions about Regulative Principles, Moral Faculties, and the place of reason, and a general belief that there is an ultimate Good, and a duty upon man to follow that Good. On practical details, as we shall see later, they were more closely agreed. They give almost the same list of subsidiary goods, such as Justice, Benevolence, Veracity, which they either deduced from their Ultimate Good or obtained from a series of final moral judgments. But each of these again becomes the starting point for violent controversy as soon as any real attempt is made to define it and work out its implications. The general impression made upon the mind of an inquirer with any sort of scientific training is, I think, of a hopeless muddle in which lofty ideals, while sometimes inspiring, have become entangled in untenable systems.[1]

It was perhaps in despair of the findings of the philosophers that certain thinkers, whom it is difficult not to consider naïve, turned hopefully to savages, Confused by the double meaning of the word " primitive " they seem to have felt that savages are closer to nature, and therefore simpler, and therefore better, than other people. Since none of these facts is true in the sense that they thought them true, none of the theories based upon them is likely to be valid. Savages are just as complex as anybody else, and so are their ideas about right and wrong. As to their views on conscience, some anthropologists have held that they did not distinguish between sin and error. A man observed the customs of the tribe or he did not observe them. His intentions were irrelevant, and his punishment necessary to appease the spirits who would otherwise have avenged themselves upon the whole of his tribe. Whether this be true or not, I doubt whether the very various attitudes of savages, when closely examined, will be found helpful by the average civilised man when he finds himself in a moral dilemma.

In the meantime, what of this " average civilised man " and his opinions on the subject ? In this country men and women do try on the whole to obey the promptings of conscience in their own lives, and hesitate before ignoring them in others. Roughly speaking, we feel that something is wrong if a man cannot do what he honestly feels to be right, but we feel, too, that he ought not to be too obstinate in exercising this freedom. Those who carry out the injunction " Do right though the Heavens fall " have seldom been popular for long.

In practice, this attitude seems as a rule to rest upon four suppositions. (*a*) The consciences of ordinary men will tend to agree, or at any rate ought to agree whether they do or not. (*b*) Disagreements between individual consciences are unimportant compared with the fact that people who obey conscience are trying to do right. (*c*) One has no moral right to blame a man for following his conscience and only doubtfully and in extreme instances a right to punish him. (*d*) The consequences of disobeying one's conscience are subjectively serious, and such a behaviour sets a bad example to others.

[1] Readers who wish to test this statement, and, indeed, everything else that I have said on the subject without wading through the works of the greater moralists may find the following books useful. *The Methods of Ethics* by Henry Sidgwick. *The Theory of Good and Evil* by Hastings Rashdall, and *Five Types of Ethical Theory* by C. D. Broad.

Perhaps it would be convenient to take these points in order.

(a) The consciences of normal men will tend to agree, and ought to agree whether they do or not.

In one sense the consciences of normal men are in complete agreement. They are the instruments by which moral behaviour is controlled, and where human beings have been taught to think in terms of right and wrong, they control human behaviour by bidding us do right and avoid wrong. On the other hand as we have seen it is not true that moral codes agree. In the past they have been more or less uniform within communities, once allowance has been made for group moralities, sex difference, and the latitude allowed to powerful individuals and privileged classes. But these differences were long established and accepted as natural. They shocked nobody but reformers, of whom there were fewer in the past than there are nowadays. The soldiery were dreaded, but nobody expected them to show the self-control which was demanded of peaceful citizens. " Business is business " is not a modern axiom, in fact we may say that a certain latitude has always been shown towards occupational sins. Women like priests have always been required, for obvious reasons, not only to observe the moral code more rigidly than men but to believe in a stricter code and set a good example. To deprive them of any particular merit in so acting, it has generally been held that they have fewer temptations and are more conscientious than men.

As for the powerful and the privileged, they have always, except for short periods of social revolution, had not only custom but law upon their side. The baron was entitled to treat his retainers in a way that meant death if the retainers attempted to try it on the baron, and up to quite recently in this country the squire's foxes stealing chicken were regarded far more leniently by most magistrates than the cottager's children stealing apples.

All these modes of ill-behaviour were of course condemned in theory but they sat easily upon the conscience and groups concerned, and were accepted by the community as long as the customary limits were not overpassed.

This was a very different thing from the questioning of moral standards which is going on today. For all the reasons given in Chapter 1, only ardent churchmen and people who have never considered the subject believe that they possess a perfect code, and even they, even if we may take the Church of England as an example, find themselves deeply divided on important subjects.

On this point it is necessary to realise how fundamental these divisions are. On the one side we have schools who agree with the following statement, taken from a book called *The Screwtape Letters* by Mr. C. S. Lewis. " The majority of the human race dies in infancy ; of the survivors, a good many die in youth. It is obvious that to Him human birth is important chiefly as the qualification for human death, and death solely as the gate to that other kind of life." This point is stated repeatedly. Nothing really matters but being in a state of mystical union with God at the precise moment of death. Wars, disease, madness, the extremity of suffering and even sin, must all be judged by this and by this alone. Sin—or so one gathers from other passages—may be the means of bringing sinners to repentance, which is apparently so pleasing in the sight of God that he prefers it to unrepentant virtue.

The main flaw in this argument seems to be that the moment of death depends upon God alone—for we may take it, I think, that suicide at what looks like a hopeful juncture is ruled out. Therefore the whole business passes beyond the control of man and his weak understanding. All human values disappear behind a veil of divine mystery, and life and conduct become a gamble.

This is a theory which suits and comforts people whose sense of guilt is so strong that they cannot hope for salvation on any rational basis. But there can be no common ground between it and the opposite belief that cruelty and suffering are not only bad in themselves, but often the cause of human degradation. Like the controversy on salvation by faith and salvation by works, it is a cleavage on a final issue.

As for marriage, the same writer says : " Mere copulation, for him [St. Paul] makes one flesh . . . the truth is that whenever a man lies with a woman, there, whether they like it or not, a transcendental relation is set up between them which must be eternally enjoyed or eternally endured." No compromise is possible between believers in this dogma and those who consider it nonsense.[1]

To return to the main argument—the feeling that consciences ought to agree in their findings, even if we restate it in the form that there should be one moral code for the whole human race, may have seemed true in limited areas, for limited periods,

[1] I quote this particular thinker because he is a contemporary, and one whose writings are said to exert great influence over young men of the present generation. They are no more irrational than hundreds of other attempts to explain that evil can proceed from perfect good.

but nowadays it can only be a prelude to disagreement as to what that code shall be.[1]

(*b*) Disagreements between individual consciences are unimportant compared with the fact that those who obey conscience are trying to do right.

It seems to me true that the fact that a man tries to do right is as a rule the most important thing about him. Failure to make this attempt marks him as morally worthless. There are people who are thought so valuable that man will admire them even though—and in part because—they are bad. Great artists and successful generals are usually allowed to be above the restraints imposed upon common men. Generation after generation enjoys reading about their love affairs, their recklessness and their general goings-on. It is a pleasure to feel that there are people who have kicked over the traces and got away with it. And nobody bothers about whether they thought that they were doing their duty.

These however, are exceptional men, and no fit example for John Jones and Mary Smith, who must toe the line like the rest of us, and plod along doing their duty.

So far so good. But to add that the attempt to do right is more important than what is thought to be right, is another matter. For this is to say that a powerful conscience is more important than a sound moral code.

So long as conscience was thought to lay down the moral code it was natural to minimise the discrepancies between moral opinions and, when they appeared, to adopt such devices as impugning the sincerity of one's opponents. It was easier to think of conscientious objectors as cowards and divorced women as harlots than to admit what seemed like moral chaos. The events of the last half-century, however, have undermined this convenient defence. The havoc that can be wrought by sincere fanaticism is fresh in all our minds. We may continue to feel that those who disagree with us " ought " to have known better, but we are faced with the fact that they did not. The real question here is whether it is better that men should strive after evil, believing it to be good, or that they should know what is good even if they make little attempt to do it. Once stated in this form, the problem will be found to solve itself. For as we shall see in the next chapter,

---

[1] How deep is the conviction that there is one universal moral code, appears from the fact that most dog-owners apply the principle to their animals and consider it " wrong " of them to steal, fight—if their master dislikes fighting—lie on the sofa, fail to come when called, and so on. The " moral " criterion here is, of course, the convenience of the owner.

every man, in part at least, not only desires but struggles to be good even if not always successfully. Therefore, as Confucius said, knowledge of good and evil is the first prerequisite of virtue.

(c) One has no moral right to blame a man for following his conscience, and only doubtfully a right to punish him for it.

This is a lesser problem arising out of the last. The honest fanatic need not be blamed, but at the same time it may be necessary to prevent him from continuing his behaviour. The community is always in the position of having to balance the rights of various groups of its citizens, and the subject that confronts us here is the purpose and usefulness of punishment. Most of us have rejected the old idea that we are entitled to revenge ourselves on people who have frightened or even injured us. Either we do not believe in revenge at all, or we accept the warning " Revenge is Mine " saith the Lord. But I think it true to say that the majority still hold that punishment is a very powerful deterrent. Even if it fails to prevent the original extremist from repeating his offence, it will prevent a good many other people from joining him in it. It can therefore be justified where there is any real danger of this happening. Unless, of course, the sinner can be regarded as a martyr, when it will encourage others to follow his example.

There is a third school of thought—those who regard punishment as a method of producing actual moral reform. Many parents, for instance, when they feel goaded beyond endurance, believe that a good hard slap will improve a child's character. If true, this would be an excellent reason for punishing most of us for nearly everything we do.

In order to show the extremes between which opinion seems to range, I will give two instances. From time to time a father is brought before the Bench for burning his little son with a red-hot poker or other handy instrument. In the cases that I have followed the prisoner has invariably given one of the following excuses : " The child is bad. He is a thief and a liar", or " He cries all night and keeps his mother awake." " What I did I did for his own good." Magistrates, without reflecting that this sort of thing, after all, is only what Mr. Lewis's God, according to Mr. Lewis, is doing all day long, either disbelieve the man and sentence him for a scoundrel, or order an inquiry into the state of his mind.

To give the other extreme : A short time ago a number of young men in Northern Ireland murdered a policeman who was doing his duty. They were tried, found guilty, and sentenced to death. Letters immediately appeared in more than one English newspaper begging for mercy for them on the ground that they did not believe that what they had done was wrong because they had acted from political motives.

In fact as soon as we begin to make allowances for the conscience of individuals we find that it becomes almost impossible to draw lines, or to compare one action with another. But most men seem to agree that the man who disobeys his conscience is more wicked than he who follows its orders, even when they lead to what is usually considered wrong behaviour. This in itself is a tacit admission that conscience is thoroughly unreliable.

(d) The consequences of disobeying one's conscience are subjectively serious, and such behaviour sets a bad example to others.

This is true. Happiness, self-respect and health of mind depend very largely upon our keeping on terms with our conscience such as it is. The man who fails to do this will be weighed down with guilt, haunted by bogys and torn by inner conflicts, even though he remains unaware that anything of the sort is going on. It is, I think, because we realise this that we are so slow to condemn even what we regard as excessive and unreasonable displays of conscience. That it has authority we are sure; what we do not understand is why that authority should be exercised in such an uncertain way.

The common man, then, has not succeeded in drawing for himself a picture less confused than that of the moral philosophers. He may be happier than they in that he does not realise just how confused it is, but that, though fortunate for him, does not assist anyone else who is trying to achieve a greater clarity. This can only be done by taking a scientific view of the matter. By this I mean that one must find out the part that conscience really plays in our minds, acquaint oneself with the elements of the work that has been done on this subject, learn how conscience develops, what its functions are, and how it is related to our moral ideas about right and wrong, and to the impulses which we want it to control. This information is not easily available for anyone but serious students of psychology.[1] I shall attempt therefore to sum it up in outline in the next two chapters.

---

[1] Since this book was written Professor Flieger has published *Man, Morals and Society* which gives an excellent account of the present state of our knowledge of the Super-Ego.

CHAPTER 4

THE ORIGIN OF CONSCIENCE

Since the foundations of personality, including the moral character, are laid in early youth, it is to the child that we must go if we wish to discover the nature of conscience. This important part of the mind has the business of controlling impulses and desires which are felt by human beings to be dangerous, wrong or shameful. Psychologists use a somewhat wider concept which they term the super-ego because they find that other than merely moral aversions are included in the same mechanism. Some men and women regulate their conduct by such emotions as hatred of ugliness, or vulgarity, or by what we call snobbishness. " The one thing I really dread is being killed by a bomb in one of these cheap shops " is not a moral point of view but can be—and in this case was—a powerful determinant of behaviour.

The conscience or super-ego is not present at birth. On the contrary its final form is the result of a slow and complicated growth which starts in infancy and is not completed until about the age of five or six. It is born of fear—a fear which is due to helplessness. This helplessness is of two kinds, for a small child can neither cope with the outer world nor control certain aspects of his own behaviour.

The first of these situations needs neither explanation nor description. We all know that very small children, unlike insects, depend for their survival upon the care of those around them. They cannot recognise danger, nor run away from it, nor do anything effective to defend themselves against it. What is not so often realised is that this situation often gives rise to acute anxiety and fear. Take, for example, the experience of hunger. If no food comes when an adult wants a meal he can as a rule do something towards obtaining one. If his first attempts are unavailing he may be spurred to greater effort or lose his temper, but it will be some time, most probably, before he begins to feel frightened. He will grow frightened only when repeated endeavours have failed, and with them all his hopes of outside aid. The more regularly he has fed in the past the less soon he will feel that there is any real danger of starvation. " Men have held out for weeks with only a little water . . . they will have missed me long ago. . . ." Both experience and imagination will help him out.

But a baby has none of these resources. When he is hungry he can only suck his thumb, and when that ceases to comfort, cry and struggle. He has no experience, and he cannot reason. He does not know that he is loved and valued and that people are near who would rather die than let him starve.

It may be objected here that for this very reason he will not be frightened, since he cannot have any idea that he will starve But it is a matter of common experience that hungry children do grow frightened, and that their fears may increase into a state of panic, as might those of a solitary prisoner in the hands of a race of unknown savages.

Fear of hunger is a rational fear and, in the case of most children, its extremes will be averted by food appearing in good time. From strains of this sort a child can be shielded, but no one can guard him altogether from every alarming stimulus. Loud noises, flashes of light, sudden dark objects looming near, contact with strangers and internal pains may all be felt as terrifying or call for some defence against fear. Matters are not improved by the fact that he does not realise what has made him afraid. Nothing is more alarming than terror which cannot be explained.

If a child is well cared for he will learn to tolerate many of these stimuli. But even while he is doing this a fresh set of dangers are presenting themselves. For from the beginnings of his life a human being is between two fires. The outer world impinges on him with an uncompromising demand that he shall adapt himself to its requirements And at the same time his primitive impulses, his racial and family inheritance of feeling and desires, are urging him to behaviour which may conflict with these demands. He is born a creature who longs for immediate pleasure and tries to avoid present pains: he is greedy, egoistic, sensual, and completely unable to control these impulses. In short he is helpless not only in regard to the world, but to himself. It is this which exposes him to further dangers.

For after the first year or so—or even earlier—he is expected to conform in many ways to the wishes of the people round him. This is thought of by them as being " good." He must make less noise than he would like, soil as few napkins as possible and refrain from throwing breakable objects on the floor, crying when he hurts himself, whimpering for what he wants, or otherwise offending the canons of those who control him. These demands are often enforced by real or pretended displeasure, by ill-temper and even slapping, all of which increase the distress produced by the frustration of his desires.

Reactions of this sort on the part of adults are alarming in themselves. A face made hideous by rage or the pain of " a good hard smack " have been known to haunt nervous people for the whole of their lives. But these childish miseries do not end with fear. All deprivations, all pain, all thwarting of instinctual urges, evoke resentment. If they continue for any length of time resentment will be accompanied by rage, and rage will arouse passionate wishes to hurt and destroy the cause of one's sufferings, or what is taken to be their cause. The baby kicks, screams, bites, hits out at the person who picks him up. An older child will attack his nurse or mother in all these ways and call her names as well. In so far as he can he " goes berserk," " runs amok "—his whole being explodes into hatred and violence.

If he were a grown-up man we should all realise that this is a serious condition of affairs. But few adults take it seriously in children. " Martin is in one of his tantrums ". " I expect there is a tooth coming, Madam—isn't he strong for his age ? " All adults in charge of children tend to minimise these disturbances. Because the child is small and weak and can do no real harm, they fail to realise that to scream until one is red in the face, kick with all one's might, to bite and almost choke with fury, are expressions of extreme states of feeling. If an adult were so transported with rage that he started knocking his head against a brick wall, the fact that he could not hurt the wall would be no measure of his fury. The same principle holds with children. Moreover the child does not know that he has done no harm, and where the adults whom he attacks are silly or irritable or, say, afraid that someone will hear, their behaviour may lead him to feel that he is a wicked and abandoned child.

When they are able to speak children will often express these destructive wishes in unmistakable form. A little boy known to me will sit watching his grandmother as she works in the kitchen and say : " Grandma, I wish that kettle would boil over and scald you to death ! " " Grandma, I wish that hot iron would fall on your foot and burn it off ! " " I wish the broom would trip you up so that you fell and broke your leg." His grandma repeats these things proudly. " You should see him looking at me,

Madam, with real hatred shining out of his little eyes! He stood there looking at me with a knife the other day and said, 'Some day I shall kill you with this knife!' And would you believe it he is just the same with his mother! She came up to see him on Sunday and brought him some chocolates. 'I will take the chocolates,' he said, 'but I wish you would fall dead at my feet just the same!'"

In this particular case one of the reasons for these outbursts is that his mother and his grandma are for ever telling him that God, or the devil, between whose behaviour they do not seem to differentiate, will carry him off to hell, or be after him and punish him properly, if he does not clean his teeth, or dust the stairs, or take round those pretty flowers to Mrs. White. And if Mummy and Grandma think it all right for God to be so savage, why should Edgar not be savage too? No one who heard him could doubt that the wishes so freely expressed are there. There are unreal in the sense that he does not mean to carry them out, but they exist.

This little boy is an exception in that he says what he thinks. But all children have wishes of the same sort lurking in the depths of their minds, and whether they utter them even to themselves depends upon circumstance.

Little children, in short, when they are frustrated and alarmed, feel and behave in a thoroughly hostile manner. And for the first years of their lives this hostility must be directed against the people whom they also love, and upon whom they depend for their safety. They do not, of course realise this clearly, and certainly could not put it into words. Indeed the situation comes into being before speech is possible. But even at this early age the wish to injure those whom they love is felt by them in some dim way to be dangerous.

This is a very important fact, for from this embryonic feeling, this sense of guilt or state of tension—we have no exact nomenclature for describing the minds of tiny children—there develops the whole range of moral emotions which end in the establishment of a sense of right and wrong.

Biologically speaking it is not absurd that children should fear their own hostile behaviour in this way. Such conduct can be really dangerous. Millions of infants have died through parental neglect and harshness, No doubt the parents concerned were lacking in natural affection, but to be an ill-tempered, screaming child would not increase one's chances with them.

To repeat, a small child who is thoroughly frightened and

thwarted is the victim not only of uncontrollable fury and hate, but of a feeling that to display such feelings is in some way evil. And this feeling produces in its turn a fresh wave of fear, known as secondary anxiety. He becomes still more terrified by his own behaviour. As nurses say: "He is only frightening himself by his own noise." This fear, since it is painful, produces fresh resentment, and so the vicious circle goes on. It is ended by exhaustion, or more often by some change in the environment which calls out a different instinctual response. Food is brought, and as soon as the smell and touch stimuli connected with feeding catch his attention he reacts to them, and the preceding misery seems to vanish like a dream. But it has vanished only from the conscious mind, and the anxiety, guilt and hostility called into being will continue to play a part in his life however thoroughly they may have been forgotten.

The amount of harm done by these wants depends upon a good many things: their number and intensity, the inherited stability of the child, and the treatment he gets from his parents. All children go through such experiences; many are unscathed by them. But in every case the emotions accumulate beneath the surface of the mind and become more and more difficult to deal with as their amount increases. For whenever a human being is confronted by a situation resembling one which produced some early buried fear, that fear, and its attendant feelings of guilt and resentment, will rise to the surface of the mind and be felt again as though they had been caused by the present danger. This is one of the reasons why people vary so much in their reactions to similar difficulties. One woman will break down over what another takes calmly. Or the man who has physical courage will dither when his employer is in a rage. What we have to face is not only the real present, but an accumulation of misery from the past.

For this reason even small children, if badly frightened, will feel a disproportionate and irrational amount of guilt on account of their natural and uncontrollable reactions. And most unfortunately another tendency then asserts itself. This is the need to feel: "Because I wanted to hurt them I deserve that they should want to hurt me, and so they do."

This too is an important bit of mental machinery. Most of us have experienced a similar feeling—say in the form: "If he knew what I said about him the other day he could not like me, therefore he doesn't." Put into words it is recognised as illogical, but the suspicion remains. Those who felt, during the war, that German aeroplanes were looking for their particular houses in order to wipe them out, were governed by a similar mental mechanism.

To return to children : the more guilty feeling a child has stored up in the depths of his mind the stronger will be this tendency to fear that his parents want to revenge themselves on him. And this is why young people whose parents are, to one's knowledge, ordinary, kindly men and women, may be heard describing them as though they had been totally devoid of sympathy, understanding, or tolerance. It is the child's own mind which has projected its destructive wishes upon them and turned them into oppressors.

These injurious forces are not, of course, the only factors which govern moral growth. They should not be the predominating factors. I have dealt with them first because that seemed the best way of stressing the importance of their antidote, the love impulses. Healthy children are not overburdened by guilt and hostility, nor are they seriously afraid of reprisals. They are saved from this fate by two things. The first is the love which they feel for their parents, whose effect may be summed up as : " But I do not hate father, I love him. I am not bad, but good." To love restores happiness, and it also reassures. Unfortunately for infants, they do not mix their hatred and their love. At one moment they are all hostility ; a second later all smiles. The force of each emotion has to be experienced and dealt with separately. But as the child grows the two feelings are, so to speak, compounded, so that if love is the stronger any resentment that may exist is neutralised. A happy child will rarely feel that he really hates his parents.

The second saving factor is the knowledge that one is loved ; proof given by the parents' behaviour that they are not revengeful, but merciful, loving and just. A child who is wisely treated and fairly reasonable feels able to rely upon his parents' real conduct and can disregard the irrational promptings of his primitive fears. If he can feel, as well, that the love he offers his parents is welcome to them and that they value it, this good influence will be reinforced. Steady, sensible, affectionate behaviour on the part of those entrusted with a child's education is therefore essential to his healthy moral growth. The baby sleeps peacefully, gurgles happily, when he feels safe. The older child, too, needs moral and emotional security before his social, unselfish impulses can develop normally. And it is not too much to say that his whole happiness, to say nothing of his value as a citizen, will depend upon feelings of love attaining greater strength than feelings of guilt and hostility. For friendly, sympathetic attitudes in human beings, whatever their objects, all spring from the same stem, the child's capacity to love his parents or their substitutes.

Here, then, we have the raw material of moral sentiments in human beings—on the one hand love, on the other fear of one's own aggressive impulse, and the feelings of guilt which accompany that fear. These last are at first dim, unidentified and irrational, but without them the child could not develop into what we mean by a moral being. They are the basis of conscience, but not the thing itself : a state of mind which can only be expressed in words as : " This is dangerous, I am disturbed and frightened," or even as : " I am bad ! " implies in itself neither obligation nor ability to control the conduct in question. Conscience disciplines distasteful impulses by an authority which springs from within the mind itself, and which assumes that we possess not only the duty but also the power to overcome them. A little child is still largely at the mercy of circumstance.

By this is meant that if a strong external stimulus wakens a natural impulse he will react automatically unless prevented. His mind cannot entertain more than one major impulse at a time. If frightened or hungry, for instance, he will find comfort in sucking his thumb. If his mother does not like this she may say : " You are not a tiny baby any longer—I have told you again and again that you must not suck your thumb." If he fails to obey she will pull the thumb out of his mouth. But the instant she leaves go of it, back it goes.

This is not defiance or " deliberate disobedience " but, so to speak, a form of mental deafness. He cannot attend to his mother's wishes because his whole mind is set on obtaining comfort in one particular way. Even if she shakes or slaps him the impulse may hold its ground for it is irrational, and while it lasts he cannot balance one danger or misery against another. In the case of weaker feelings he may be able to remember what his mother said, or attend to what she is saying now, and try to please her by doing what she wants, but many of his impulses sweep the board and give him no chance of displaying wisdom.

The real wish to please one's mother because one loves her, added to feelings of guilt over conduct which displeases, can look like the operation of conscience to observers. The child may call himself bad, especially if experience has shown him that this will mitigate wrath. Some parents like it. He may say that he is sorry, and promise not to do it again. But all this is more or less in the nature of a ritual. He is learning how best to get on with his parents, and the easiest way out of the difficulties in which their requirements involve him. If the requirements are sensible, this is a valuable part of his education. But so long as the authority to which wishes and fears are referred is an external being, conscience proper is not yet completed. " Mummy will be pleased " or angry : even, " I want to be a good boy to please Daddy," are still not the same as, " I want to be a good boy", " I ought not to do this " whether the parents know what is happening or not.

While this is going on the growth of conscience proper is beginning. That sense of unease which is so difficult to define in tiny children becomes something which can be recognised as a sense of guilt, and the sphere within which it functions widens. It is no longer roused merely by destructive impulses, but attaches itself to most of the actions and feelings of which parents disapprove or are felt to disapprove. In addition, children invent sins of their own, such as stepping on the cracks between paving-stones, which occupy their minds for a time and are then divested of evil significance, as they were invested, without apparent rhyme or reason.

Neither the development of guilt, however, nor the expansion of one's moral field is enough to provide us with what is meant by a conscience. This is completed only when we have taken into ourselves a warning, guiding, admonishing principle which exercises from within the mind the same sort of authority as is exercised by the parents from without. That such a process exists is one of the fundamental discoveries of modern psychology. It is a mechanism known as " introjection" and it means that the child absorbs into himself and makes part of his mind something which possesses the authority of the parents and represents what he assumes to be their attitudes and beliefs about right and wrong. More will be said in a page or two as to the nature of this event. For the moment what must be stressed is that the " still, small voice " of conscience is the moral authority of his parents as the child conceives it. This conception is always inaccurate and confused and nearly always harsher than it should be, but such as it is he will from henceforth be urged, restrained, punished and approved by this force in his mind as well as by real people in the outer world.

Conscience, in fact, is not introduced into the "soul" at birth as a steering gear is fitted into a car. It is grown by the human mind in something the same way as hands are grown by the human body. Unfortunately it runs far more risks than any bodily organ of becoming stunted, warped or diseased during the long and complex process of its growth.

It is because these developments take place in us all that I wrote, in the last chapter, that everyone wants and struggles to be good. The primitive fear of one's own destructive impulses is universal and common to the species. By education and training similar fears are attached to other tendencies disapproved of by parents and society. Under some dispensations they may cover, in the end, almost everything that a human being could possibly want to do. To free oneself from all earthly desire has been the moral goal of millions.

The primary function of conscience, then, is to inhibit primitive urges in order to avoid the dangers to which they are felt to give rise. In addition it incites us to conduct which will gain the approval of the ghostly, introjected figures of our parents. This we feel as striving after a moral ideal. In so acting conscience functions as part of our inmost nature and makes us, as Freud put it, irretrievably moral.

The whole of this description of the origin of conscience will probably seem far-fetched to readers who have not studied the evidence for the statements made, or the sequence of mental events to which they refer. Introjection, in particular, is a novel conception, if only because it is an automatic and unconscious act of which we are necessarily unaware. Even its results, in the case of children, are obvious only to those who are able to look at their behaviour from a scientific standpoint. Others merely feel: "Really, John is improving wonderfully!" or "Mary is getting so difficult that I don't know what to do with her!" In the first place this change is put down to one's own wise handling; in the second, as a rule, to the innate wickedness of Mary. In fact John has developed a good and Mary an unsatisfactory conscience.

Fortunately for those who try to explain the nature of introjection, other acts of the kind occur later in life which are open to observation and familiar to us all. We see introjections taking place whenever a human being becomes the devotee of a hero or a cause. Everyone must have noticed how the new disciple not only admires the leader and copies him in many ways, but how what are understood to be his beliefs are adopted wholesale and with them his attitude towards right and wrong. The revivalist preacher sends the darkies home groaning under their sense of sin. The candidate for confirmation begins to search her conscience, examine her life, discipline her thoughts and blame herself severely for what never troubled her before. On the other hand the youth who falls under the influence of some tough guy relaxes his control over much of his own behaviour and starts bullying others instead. For the moment, at any rate, the enthusiastic convert is guided by what he supposes to be the conscience of his leader instead of by his own. He does not put it like this to himself, but merely states—if he thinks of the matter at all—that he is " changed", " become a new man", " reborn".

It is so much easier to make clear the nature of introjections on the level of beliefs than when we are dealing with the obscure and frequently masked operations of conscience, that further descriptions and examples will be postponed until the sixth chapter, which is concerned with the acquisition of our ideas of right and wrong. Here I will only add that none of these later adaptations have either the force or the staying power of the earlier series by which the conscience itself is formed.

CHAPTER 5

THE NATURE OF CONSCIENCE

We have seen that the Super-Ego is built up as part of our normal mental growth through a series of reactions by which a child seeks to cope with his inner fears on the one hand, and the demands of the environment on the other. This is why the consciences of human beings vary so greatly in their efficiency and are so often unsuited to the demands of daily life. They do not represent any external standard : still less do they derive from any absolute authority. What they are will depend first upon hereditary factors, and then upon the child's relations to his parents and the ideas which he forms about them.

A child who is born with what Dr. Burt calls low mental stability will be unable to stand the strain of normal fears and frustrations. Then he will be governed by fear all his life and develop a corresponding amount of hatred. Whether he turns this hatred against himself or the world at large will depend on the sort of conscience he develops, and that in turn will depend upon the ideas which he forms about his parents' feelings for him. Unfortunately, even in the case of healthy child, these are almost certain to be incorrect, and are often fantastically wrong. The reason for this error was given in the last chapter—it springs from an irrational sense of guilt. It is unfortunate that parents should often encourage this mistake by setting too high a standard for their children and demanding more from them in the way of virtue than they would dream of expecting from another grown-up person. They do this partly for reasons of convenience, partly because their children carry much of their pride and even their self-respect ; they cannot bear to think that they may have moral imperfections.

The harsher and more revengeful the parent is thought to be, the worse for the child, since the authority set up in his mind will be correspondingly cruel, intolerant and therefore irrational. These are not the attributes which a good conscience should possess ; on the contrary, they are extremely dangerous qualities. Most of us believe that the essence of a good conscience is strength : above all, it must be firm enough to hold in check wrongful desires and tendencies to bad behaviour. This function it must be able to perform. But it is just as important to the child, and even to society, that the necessary control should be exercised in a reasonable way. The man or woman who has clothed his parents with spite and hatred may have a conscience which rages at him all his life, making him miserable for the slightest fault, driving him into penance and self-punishment, or into mental or physical illness. People of this sort blame themselves not only for the actions they commit, but for feelings and wishes which are part of man's inheritance, for which he is no more responsible than for being born with two arms and a head. " If I were really virtuous," they feel, " I should not be tempted," and hate themselves as though they had been guilty of the offence itself. Only too often this attitude has been encouraged by moral leaders, with doubtful benefits but a certain rise in the sum of human suffering.

To punish and torment oneself is not the only device open to the owner of a morbid conscience. One can also ease one's guilt by transferring the blame for it to other people. This is the path of the Attilas and the Hitlers—not men with reasonable and kindly consciences. On the contrary, they were the owners of consciences which lashed them with scorpions. " You are so wicked that you deserve to be destroyed ! " To most human beings such a state of mind, if prolonged, is intolerable. And one of the ways in which it can be altered is to project the bitter resentment which it causes upon someone else. " It is not I who hate and wish to cause pain ; I, blameless, am surrounded by enemies waiting in ambush for me." This, for the moment, brings relief, for one can now unleash one's destructive impulse in what seems like the rational cause of self-preservation. " It is prudent—sensible—necessary—to destroy them first."

If this can be done the killer is filled with a temporary elation which sets his mind at rest. " I should not have been able to do this if I were not a remarkable man, above the law, who is able to take his fate into his own hands." Or he may feel : " God must approve my actions, or He would not have crowned them with success."[1]

But since these devices do not remove the source of the trouble, which is an excess of inner guilt and hatred, they do not work for long. The killer has still to face the same scorpions, with the added guilt of having killed needlessly, and the additional anxiety which springs from actual proof of one's destructive power. The whole

[1] For example of this state of mind in murderers, see Bjere, *The Psychology of Murder*.

business begins again with greater momentum. Such men can be turned from their killing only by physical force.

The ordinary bully does not work upon this scale, though he may in the main, belong to the same type. The mechanism, in milder forms, is common enough. Indeed all of us use it on occasions.

There is another way of dealing with an inflamed conscience, which must be mentioned here. This is to repress with all one's might the whole tangle of unendurable emotions, and admit to the conscious mind only loving and kindly impulses. In the result the sufferer appears on the surface a particularly humane and perhaps even serene human being. Where the amount of unwelcome feeling which has to be repressed is small, this is a successful solution. There are saints of this sort.

But two points must be noted. The first is that where the amount of feeling to be repressed is large, so much energy is needed to keep it in a state of repression, that its owner has none to spare for the difficulties of normal life. He must either get into some rut which requires the minimum of effort, or place barriers between himself and the dangerous world. He may fly to a monastery, or to the wilderness, shed all social and family responsibilities and cease to be useful to society except on the theory that prayer has a magical efficacy. The world cannot afford to maintain more than a certain number of such persons. The yellow robe and the begging bowl of the holy man pre-suppose a population who will work to keep the begging bowls filled.

The second point is that ability to make such repressions does not exist in the ordinary human being. It is useless to tell us that we " ought " to behave in this way ; we are not so built that we can carry out the injunction.

A healthy conscience is, then, a pre-requisite of human happiness, as well as of most human goodness.

But whatever form or degree of hostility and guilt he develops and however he deals with it, in his heart the owner of a morbid conscience will hate his fellow-men. This is the mark of the neurotic. What he calls love will be jealous, possessive, possibly sadistic, and however much he may punish himself he will still ooze spite. To sit on the top of a pillar for twenty years, to retreat to the wilderness and live upon grass and herbs are not only methods of escape from the responsibilities of life, and penances for sin, they are also a means of isolating oneself from those whom one longs to harm. It is because such conduct performs all these services for him that the " saint " persists in it. And, unlike the behaviour of those who make themselves ill and take to their beds for the first two of these purposes, it causes little trouble to other people.

In every day life we are often reluctant to admit the same leakage of spleen from the self-sacrificing. They give way so often, they give up so much, they work so hard for others, that it seems ungrateful to realise that much of the help they give is irritating, that one had rather they took their proper share and that their labours are often as much of a burden to others as to themselves. Spiteful emanations which proceed from the determinedly good may do far less harm, from a social point of view, than the naked hostility of those who lay the blame on others, but they are equally destructive of domestic happiness.

In contrast to the raging, savage, neurotic consciences which reflect the unhappy child's belief that his parents long to be revenged upon him, a healthy conscience behaves like a good parent. It is efficient—that is, firm enough to preserve its owner from even wanting to commit heinous sins, as well as from yielding to major temptations. It is sensible : it does not rage at him on account of trifles, and allows him to retain that reasonable degree of self-respect which is the basis of real good character. It encourages his efforts to improve instead of damning him with, " You miserable sinner—what good can come out of you ? " This point must be stressed, since it contradicts the general idea of how conscience should behave. A good conscience should in fact behave towards its owner with the same wisdom and tolerance that a good man will show towards his neighbour. If we wish to produce healthy minds, then the notion that there is virtue in special severity directed against oneself must be discarded as erroneous.

To continue the description—the good conscience is above all reasonable, and does not torture a man for imaginary sins, nor for falling short of unattainable ambitions. It does not expect him to be more than human. And because of this it is able to tolerate the existence of primitive " animal " impulses, demanding only that they shall not have too great an influence over actual conduct.

Whether any particular child is able to introject a super-ego of this type will depend very much upon the behaviour of his parents. If they reassure him when he is anxious, and make him feel that his love for them not only counts for more than his bursts of resentment, but makes amends for these when they occur—and if, of course, they show common sense in their general treatment of him—then with any luck at all he will be guided throughout his life in a way that allows him to be happy, healthy, as reasonable as most men, and a good citizen. It cannot of course ensure these things. That is not the function of a conscience.

Before returning to the more strictly ethical aspects of the subject, one more point should perhaps be made. This concerns punishment. It would not be true to say that punishment never achieves its immediate object. If a child is found stealing jam and severely punished, the memory of his pain may intervene when next he wants to steal and stop him from doing so. Since stealing jam is a bad habit, this is something gained. But along with the memory of pain there will well up the resentment and fright which were felt with the pain, and they will add themselves to the frustration caused by not having jam when one wants it badly. The would-be thief may be left sore and sulky and prepared to turn on anyone smaller who happens to come along. Moreover, even cruel punishment may fail to attain its object. The child who steals and has been savagely thrashed for it will often steal again. In some cases the lesson learned has not been: " Thou shalt not steal " but, " Thou shalt not be found out." This is the attitude of the habitual criminal.

The reason for this is that the punishment, when given, roused resentment and hatred against the person who inflicted it. This gave rise to a fresh flood of anxiety. Now when a child steals and misbehaves it is for gratification. The jam, or sliding head-first down the banisters, brings him pleasure. And pleasure is one of the most powerful remedies against anxiety.[1] It soothes, alleviates, prevents one from giving way and falling into despair.

The more loaded a child is with anxiety and guilt, the greater his need for immediate pleasure. And when he sees the object of desire within reach either he will forget the thrashing, or its memory will rouse such a turmoil of discomfort that the need for alleviation is sharply increased. In either case, the act is performed once more. As one mother said to me in a bus : " There, you see ! Every time I hit her she does it again ! " I said : " Then it does not seem much use hitting her." To which she replied, " Well, no—but you feel you must do something, 'specially in a bus ! "

This is why parents who have acted on the principle : " I

[1] Cf. the enormous increase in the consumption of tea and tobacco during air-raids. More will be said on this subject in Chapter 9.

will thrash this out of you if I break every bone in your body " so often fail to produce virtuous children. Their brutal behaviour has increased the tendency which they set out to cure.

Any adult who is in the habit of smoking more than he, or his doctor, thinks good for him can check part of this argument for himself. Here the painful memory will be of indigestion, insomnia, heart disturbances and the like. As a rule it will pull him up before he takes his twentieth cigarette. But in moments of real anxiety either he forgets all this and helps himself automatically, or it flits through his mind but does not seem to matter. The immediate need for solace wins the day. So it is with the naughty child.

I said that the failure of punishment to achieve reform is important. It is important because it explains why centuries of effort to improve human beings by the use of fear has failed so badly. To threaten them with worms and undying fire, to tell them that they will lose their father's—or God's—love if they do not obey, in short to create as much remorse, anxiety and sense of sin as possible, does not make men good. It may deter from certain sorts of behaviour, but it creates a well-spring of blind hatred which may be compared to the seven other devils.

It may be as well to add that this does not mean that a child should never be allowed to suffer when he has done wrong. Everyone must learn that acts have their consequences ; that if you behave badly to other children they will not want to play with you ; that you cannot eat your cake and have it. It is a mistake to encourage unnatural expectations about life. But this is a very different matter from cold-blooded executions, hurting children deliberately, long periods of disgrace or of keen anxiety while father or the headmaster turns one's sins over in his mind. All these things strengthen his tendency to regard those in authority as harsh, avenging figures, besides setting up on their own account vicious circles of anxiety, guilt and hostility. In the long run the states of mind of a child are far more important than most of his actions.

Conscience, then is the voice of our fathers speaking in us with all the authority which parents exercise over little children. It is natural that we should regard it as all-wise, because to a little child his parents are the repository of wisdom. It tells us, just as they did, that we must be good, do right, and resist temptation. It exercises these functions, more rather than less successfully, in all but idiots and certain types of lunatic. But in different individuals it exercises them in a considerable variety of ways and, as we shall see in the next chapter, the directions in which it will make its pressure felt are even less uniform than its methods.

It is because these facts have only recently been discovered that thinkers in the past have asked of the human conscience more than it can perform, and held it responsible for functions which it is incapable of exercising.

What the existence of conscience does ensure is that man, whether he likes it or not, is a moral creature. And when we ask—as all of us are entitled to ask—" Why should I do right? Why should I not do as I please in so far as I am able?" the answer is, " Because you cannot help yourself. You are a moral being in virtue of your membership of the human race. You possess a conscience—imperfect perhaps, but still a conscience. And for most of your time you obey it without question."

Sometimes the questioner then explains that he obeys his conscience only because it pays him to do so, and not because he feels that he should, a contention which will not bear close scrutiny.[1] On the other hand he may reply : " Of course I do not propose to burgle the Bank of England or ravish all the pretty young women at this party. But what I want to know is why I should not conceal some shares from the Income Tax people, or persuade young Phoebe that she is not as good as she thinks?" Then the problem to be dealt with becomes the entirely different question of why honesty in regard to taxation, or virtue in the matter of Phoebe, should form part of the individual's moral code.

It is the common confusion between conscience itself and the ideas about good and bad with which it works that make men ask themselves why they should do right. The most depraved human being—unless, again, he is a madman or an idiot—is controlling most of his primitive impulses all day long. To give only one example, his personal habits are cleaner than those of an untrained infant. He does not regard this as a moral victory because he is governed by feelings of disgust and shame which, in sane adults, function automatically. But he did not reach this stage until he had passed through a long struggle to control his sphincter muscles in order to please, or because he was afraid of, his parents. The gaining of such control is to a tiny child a very important issue of right and wrong.

In the same way most of us are automatically honest in all but a small proportion of our dealings. We do not look with a

[1] Cf. Chapter 9.

covetous eye on the pennies in a beggar's tin. We do not walk through shops in the hope of pinching something useful. Nor do we poison our wealthy aunts, nor trip up passers-by in the streets for the fun of seeing them fall. In short, we obey our consciences very nearly all the time. When we fail it is because some special temptation, or class of temptations, is too strong for us. This is a different matter entirely from failing to carry out what are commonly regarded as duties because we do not see them in this light.

Where moral training has achieved its object impulse is checked automatically and without our knowing that any conflict has occurred. This is the second factor which prevents us from realising how moral we all are. For it seems to us then that we do not want to sin in this way, just as we say that So-and-So has good habits. We know—or think we know—that in these cases we run no risk of failure. In normal circumstances we are right. But it is one of the most important discoveries of modern psychology that even the most successful moral training neither destroys our primitive impulses nor stops their activity. In the depths of our minds they continue to demand gratification, and continual effort is needed to control them, though we have become so used to making it that we no longer notice the need. In the same way we learn to walk without making conscious efforts to keep our balance. To use another analogy : the animal impulses resemble a population which has been conquered but not won over. The occupying troops must still retain their ceaseless vigilance because an underground movement is always watching for a chance to rear its head.

Like the waiting rebels our most primitive impulses will break their bounds as soon as conditions allow them. Sick people sometimes display a greed and selfishness which seems foreign to their natures : the starving may eat their fellows : terror may reduce a man to the level of a wounded beast. Therefore even the duty which is performed without an instant's hesitation is still a renewed conquest. When this is realised it is possible to see that man is a race of highly moral beings—that conscious temptations are marginal cases, and that to yield to them, even to yield frequently, makes a man immoral only in a limited sense of the word—that of falling below the customary standards.

To repeat : We all have consciences which urge us to do right. We all admit their authority since we all obey them in countless ways, though it costs us, whether we know it or not, expenditure of energy to do so. When we feel inclined to challenge the dicta of conscience it means that the balance of power in the mind is more even. Conscious struggle is necessary before a decision can be taken. It may be, in a particular instance, that conscience is demanding compliance with mistaken standards. We may do well to resist its claim on this account. Or it may be too harsh; when we are entitled, if we can, to appeal to the higher court of reason. But of its nature it commands us to do " good " and avoid " evil," and of our natures we respond to this command, even if we are not always capable of translating our response into virtuous action. Man is a creature who wants to do right just as often as he wants to do wrong. We doubt this because in very many cases we can judge ourselves only by results, and are not aware of the unconscious struggles which have preceded them.

Many people will deny these statements. They believe that man is fundamentally evil; that virtue sits awkwardly upon him and is foreign to his nature. Some would add that he achieves the most trifling goodness only by external aid from the grace of God. And before going on to consider why the judgments of conscience vary as they do it may be as well to say something about this opinion.

That it is wrong goes without saying if the account given here of the nature of conscience is even roughly accurate. But the feelings of guilt which make us think ourselves innately wicked are strong, and facts can be quoted which seem to bear them out.

The first is the effort which it costs us to live up to our moral standards. We find it hard to be as good as we should like to be, and often we fail.

The second is the existence of people who " seem to have no moral sense at all " the spectacle which the times afford of human beings acting vilely.

The third is the illusion from which many good men suffer that if some particular safeguard were removed, or some chain of argument shown to be invalid, they themselves would cease even to try to act rightly and be left abandoned to their most dreaded passions.

None of these criticisms is incompatible with the statement that man is essentially a moral being. To be moral does not mean that one is perfect. It means that there are actions and states of mind from which one recoils because they are thought to be wrong, and standards one would like to reach because they are held to be good. The word " like " is indeed an understatement.

Most people know what it means, at moments, to " hunger and thirst after righteousness."

All of the objections mentioned are based on a confusion of thought. To possess primitive impulses which must be curbed in a given environment does not imply that man is not moral. He is moral because he possesses not only these impulses—without which there would be no need for morality—but also an apparatus which compels him to control them. The sneak thief will never commit robbery with violence : the fraudulent business man is good to his wife and family.

" But," it may be said, " look at the appalling crimes that have been committed during the last few years—the mass murders, the sickening, indescribable cruelty ! The men and women who did these things are totally immoral. In them we see what happens when human beings throw off the restraints of religion and revert to their natural state."

The answer to this is that beings who behave like this are not in a natural state. If our ape-like ancestors had all behaved like the Gestapo they would not have survived to father the human race. The torturers and mass murderers of Nazi Germany were carefully chosen on account of their strong sadistic tendencies, and these trends in their characters were encouraged and intensified by deliberate schooling in vicious cruelty. Every sort of propaganda and pressure was used to attain this end, and even so it is known that many of the Gestapo killed themselves because they could no longer endure the burden of their own behaviour. Others went mad ; others still, no longer able to continue their crimes, will certainly go mad. These were not natural men— indeed the first adjective that comes to mind when we think of them is "inhuman." Yet even they must have obeyed what consciences they had in countless matters.

When the existence of evil makes us deny that man is naturally moral, the deepest reason lies in our inner fears : " I too have impulses of this sort. Without protection I too might behave in such a manner." We have all failed in early life to restrain our destructive impulses, and we must all look forward to many of the minor failures which disfigure the conduct of responsible adults, even if they are only failures in kindness, tact and courtesy. But these deficiences are only felt as wrong because we are moral, and therefore believe that we are under an obligation to succeed. To doubt the tenacity of one's desire to act rightly is to yield to illusory fears which are the product of irrational guilt.

Experience shows that those who abandon supernatural sanctions for morality do not plunge into general depravity. Indeed they are just as likely to tighten up their moral standards : " I have now assumed the responsibility for my own behaviour. The familiar guides are gone. I must take care."

In the same way those who have based their belief in morality upon systems which are now considered invalid, have not lived wickedly on that account. Nobody but Bentham can have thought that it was possible to work out his Hedonistic Calculus. But the followers of Bentham seem to have been a particularly moral set of men.

The truth seems rather to be that if good behaviour by itself be our object, it can be achieved without any other system or sanction than the example and authority of elders who were both loved and good. It is because they put the cart before the horse that many people cling to religion as the guarantor of goodness. In order that they may retain what seems to them an essential safeguard, they are prepared to accept dogmas which they would otherwise reject as ridiculous and inconsistent. In these cases it is not morality which depends upon religion, but religion which maintains its footing by clinging to the skirts of morality.

To this it might be objected by many men that they have had actual experience of the efficacy of religion in guarding the soul from temptation. They prayed for help and guidance and these were given. Had it not been for the Grace of God, they would have fallen into grievous sin.

Such experiences do occur. But there is nothing supernatural about them. When a severe moral struggle takes place, conscience does in fact call up memories and associations connected with the idea of goodness in order to strengthen the forces at its disposal. One man in these straits will think of his mother, another of his duty to his children, a third of his ambitions, and a fourth of some cause or ideal which he wishes to serve. If the upbringing of a particular man has been religious, many of these memories will wear a religious dress. All are invested with a certain amount of mental energy which is made available as they come into mind. The belief that God will grant his aid—if it has been useful in earlier conflicts—is one of these sources of energy. But there is no proof whatever that those who make use of it are better human beings than those whose memories take a different form.

Man is moral, therefore, because he possesses a conscience,

a mechanism which is common to the species, and which together with reason distinguishes him from the lower animals. It is the business of his conscience to make him carry out his ideas of right and wrong. Whatever these are, his conscience will enforce them. It is because they differ so greatly that we say that the findings of conscience are unreliable. In fact the blame for this state of affairs should be placed not upon conscience, but on the ideas and beliefs which it is obliged to administer. Therefore in the next chapter something must be said about this subject—how man acquires his particular standards, his lists of sins and virtues and his notions of right and wrong.

CHAPTER 6

THE MORAL CODE OF THE INDIVIDUAL

In order to understand the origin and nature of conscience it was necessary to look deep into the human mind and to uncover mental processes which are hidden from ordinary observation. This entailed a description which was long and far from simple. There is less to be said about the origin of our moral ideas, as they are acquired, for the most part, through ordinary experience, and where unconscious mechanisms are involved these have already been explained.

Children begin to collect their notions of right and wrong as soon as they are old enough to realise that one course of conduct results in approval and another in disapproval. Approval brings pleasure of various kinds and disapproval pain, and these are forces to which infants react from the start of their lives. Moreover what brings approval is right, and what brings disapproval is wrong—to put it with greater accuracy, it is the attitude of the parents which gives meaning to the idea of right and wrong.

Each child makes his own collection of ideas, and the contents of his collection will depend upon his environment, and in particular, as I have just said, upon his parents' attempts to train him. This they do both consciously and unconsciously, and by two methods—precept and example.

Unless he is extremely fortunate the lessons he learns will conflict. No grown-up person can be aware, at all points, of the effect which his conduct is having on a little child. Children notice both more and less than they are thought to do, and the meaning they attach to adult behaviour is often unpredictable and sometimes fantastic. Apart from this, parents do not always practise what they teach. Tommy may be told that it is greedy and naughty to beg for sweets. If, nevertheless, when he coaxes her, his mother gives him sweets, he will not stop short at the simple view that begging for sweets is bad. If she yields in a bad-tempered way he may or may not feel " it was worth it ! " If she gives way fondly he is likely to imbibe the idea that grown-up people, or perhaps only women, do not always mean what they say, and that coaxing works.

Again most mothers teach their children that it is wicked to lie and to deceive. Those who think the father too harsh and those who are engaged in a perpetual struggle with him for the children's love, sometimes then proceed to spoil the boys behind their father's back. They allow pleasures which he has forbidden, conceal actions which he is likely to punish, and even lie in set terms to defend their sons from his anger. Where this happens the boys will often take it for granted that wives are disloyal and illicit pleasures permissible, that deceit is a normal factor in family life and hiding behind a woman's petticoats a suitable method of avoiding danger. When they find later on that other people take a different view they may change their ideas or feel that they know better. In practice, the over-strict father and the pampering mother taken together fill our police courts with their sons.

Another reason why example has more force than precept is that children tend to imitate their parents. They may copy them deliberately, or adopt without knowing it not only such things as tricks of speech and gesture, but attitudes towards life. Parents who " keep themselves to themselves " may produce children whose natural sociability is stifled—a result which will have important effects upon their moral outlook. Friendly and hospitable parents may have children like themselves. The verb, however, must always be " may " and not " will " for none of these reactions is simple. The child of " good mixers " may be jealous and come to hate " the crowd " because he longs to have more of his parents' company. Or he may be frightened by the noise and confusion that to his elders mean good comradeship, and develop a passion for solitude under the stairs.

In the same way a hunting family may be perplexed by a son whose spiritual home is their neglected library ; and cultivated parents by a daughter who pines for " life in the raw." Where these reactions are strong and seem inexplicable, the non-conformists will either spend their lives in states of bewilderment or resentment wondering what is the matter with them, or swallow voraciously any ideas they may meet which seem to excuse and justify their feelings and behaviour.

The fact that example is a powerful force does not imply that preaching is unimportant. General ideas may be implicit in particular instances, but they are not always perceived. Virtue may be despised or overlooked unless accompanied by propaganda. The devoted, toiling mother who makes it clear that she is inspired by ideals and a sense of duty and asks for these from the children, in set terms, will probably obtain them so long as she is also loving and just. To drudge without explanation may give the idea : " There is nothing mother enjoys so much as fussing after us " or " pottering round the house." Or its effect may be : " She may have the mind of a slave, but thank God I haven't."

In short if actions are to bear the special mark of " moral " it is better that this should be clearly stamped upon them. Small children, as we all know, are apt to transfer the notion of " good and bad " to the whole sphere of " this pleases or displeases me." The corner of a chair is naughty if it hurts one ; and a brick is good if it stays on top of another. The classification is natural, and all of us fall into it at times. Our enemies are wicked and our friends are virtuous : those social arrangements are right which preserve our comfort and further our ambitions. To neutralise this tendency and prevent this overlap is an essential part of moral education.

It is experience of life, and not any inborn faculty for knowing what is right to wrong, which provides us with our first stock of moral ideas. When conscience begins to function it is with these ideas that it will have to work. This fact explains in part why the " findings " of human consciences vary as widely as they do. For though in a given community most parents will agree to some extent and teach, in words, that lies are wicked and tidiness and obedience good, their behaviour will be of every possible kind. The child who is taught, for example, that he must not swear or lose his temper may observe that his father frequently does both. This in itself is bewildering since he is often encouraged, in words, to copy his father—to grow big like father, and be brave like him and wash his hands before meals as father does. But in addition, since it does not occur to him at this stage to doubt that his parents' goodness is complete, he will tend to conclude that children must behave themselves but that adults can do as they please—an uncertain foundation for civilised behaviour.

It is sometimes objected that the lessons a child learns in the nursery are of small importance since they will be supplemented and corrected when he goes to school. Whether this is true depends partly upon the school, and partly upon whether he is happy there. Some boys in some schools learn chiefly to dodge, to feel outlawed, to hate or resist authority, to feed upon the bitterness of their hearts. But however good the school and happy the child, his early ideas are very much more important that they seem. They are important because they are absorbed innocently, and unreservedly, and because they are accepted as absolutely valid. Further, they are important because they are the first, never to be completely evicted from the mind. No later notions which conflict with them will be regarded in quite the same way as " natural " or have quite the same binding force.

Little children conceive of their parents as the embodiment of power and wisdom. The most ramshackle little nit-wit, the meanest criminal, the lunatic, all get the benefit of this attribution. What flows from them is taken implicitly for granted and invested with a quality of certainty. Where what is learnt is confusing, or even self-contradictory, the result is far more likely to be that the child is left with a set of conflicting " certainties " than that he will find himself forced to set his ideas in order and sort out what is true from what is false. It takes a highly trained mind to do this well, and the children of bad or muddle-headed parents will in all probability belong to the very large class of those whose minds are divided into water-tight compartments from which they draw out whatever maxims happen to be convenient at the time.

Sensible or silly, clear or chaotic, these early ideas will be enforced by the child's conscience, and the values which he imbibes in this way will haunt him for the rest of his life. However, thoroughly he may believe that he has discarded them, he will never be freed entirely from their influence.

This is a statement which, taken by itself, is not convincing. Nowadays almost all of us know people who have changed, with apparent ease, many of their basic beliefs, and with them have shed large portions of their systems of moral values. During the last quarter of a century conversions have taken place on a very large scale from almost every current creed to almost every other. Atheists have become Christians and Christians Communists; Pacifists have joined the Fascists in some countries and taken up arms in others. Never, probably, have established creeds seemed less secure, or a greater number of ideologies come into conflict.

As for the conversions involved by all this movement of opinion, sometimes the change was the result of a prolonged and difficult mental struggle, sometimes one speech by Hitler or President Roosevelt did the trick. But by whichever process they were achieved these changes in attitude have as a rule been very thorough. In many cases no trace seems to be left of former opinions or scruples or ideals. The man who believed in reason now talks about fairies or Yoga or miracles and faith. Marx and Lenin and Darwin take the place of God and the Tzar. The

Pacifist throws himself eagerly into the life of his Commando unit. The metamorphosis appears complete.

Nevertheless, behind all these appearances, it is neither as complete nor as final as it seems. And in saying this the modern psychologist is only restating facts long familiar to workers among converts. Students of religious revivals have pointed out again and again that the wave of passionate repentance which sweeps the whole community is generally only the prelude to a period of back-sliding. The British Union of Fascists contained few long-standing members who were not on its pay-roll. Those who joined it in a state of fervour as a rule drifted out again after about eighteen months.

The Catholic Church with its world-wide experience regards converts with a tinge of scepticism. One Jesuit Father went so far as to say that it takes three generations to make a good Catholic. He may well have been right.

Psychologists, then, did not discover this perseverance of discarded doctrines, but only the processes which caused it and account for it. The facts seem to be that nothing experienced by the human mind is ever finally lost. This is apparently true even of trifles. Patients under hypnotism, or in delirium, will recollect details of their past lives which they can hardly have noticed at the time.[1]

Though not lost, many trivial memories sink so far below the threshold of consciousness that they cannot be recalled by any conscious effort. But ideas and feelings which were once of sufficient importance to influence our behaviour not only survive, they retain some at least of the energy which they possessed at the time of their influence. And this energy is continuously, though unconsciously, employed to defeat the ideas which have taken their place and driven them from control of the mind.

The new ideas, in their turn, can only retain their supremacy by resisting this effort, so that the mind becomes the scene of a mental conflict which may absorb a good deal of its energy, and affects its working in various ways. It is for this reason that converts to a doctrine, however filled with enthusiasm, are considered less reliable than those bred up in it. Their original feelings persist, and can be roused again by a suitable stimulus.

One sign that this process is going on is the presence of blind

---

[1] Cf. the famous case of an illiterate German servant girl in the service of a Rabbi who unconsciously learned by heart, and repeated when she was in a fever, the passage of Hebrew which her master used to read aloud. *Outline of Morbid Psychology*, MacDougall.

and excessive fervour. It is because of the conflict raging below the surface that it is necessary to throw all one's energy into acting out the new beliefs, to defend them with all one's strength, to allow no exceptions and no compromise. And even when all this has been done, their victory, overwhelming though it may seem, is and always will be precarious.[1]

We may see, for example, a boy with high standards taking a job in a dishonest firm. After a time he adopts the attitude that business is business and all idealism soft and silly. No one will attack more bitterly than he any idea of raising business standards.

Again, a girl who was taught both at home and in school that lipstick is vulgar and that nice girls look upon nice men merely as brothers and should not look upon not-nice men at all, will be found arguing that she has a perfect right to live with a married man whose wife and children have been evacuated. Both stick to their point of view : the change of ideas in both seems absolute. But in reality it is only superficial. If they believed what they were taught at first they will be loaded with unconscious guilt, and neither is likely to be happy.

In short we are dogged all our lives, for good or ill, by what we accepted as right or wrong when we were young, and by the authority of our parents and those who represented them. This makes it of extreme importance that the moral codes taught to children should be sensible and consistent.

Another unpalatable fact that must be faced when we consider the building of our moral codes is that when we repudiate basic beliefs we do so far more often under the influence of feeling than through the use of reason.

The majority of these changes occur not as the result of careful research and accurate reflection, but as part and parcel of one of the introjections described in the last chapter. What happens with regard to the conscience happens even more readily in the field of ideas. A book, a man, a sermon, rouses enthusiasm, and everything that the book maintains, the hero says or the sermon is held to imply, is first felt as fascinating and later, if the attachment strengthens, taken as true. Qualifications made at first tend to disappear. Gradually all that conflicts with the new system of ideas loses its interest and becomes of no importance. The " thorough study " of the subject which is sometimes undertaken will be found to consist of devouring and absorbing every-

---

[1] Other factors count here—the amount of satisfaction brought by the new beliefs, the number of adherents they gain and above all their success or failure in dealing with unconscious anxiety and guilt.

thing which supports the new interest and rejecting impatiently whatever tells against it. On many subjects it is often possible to guess a man's opinions when he tells you the name of a book on it which he has read.

If this is true of beliefs in general, it is particularly true in the field of morals. The followers of Joseph Smith lost their faith in monogamy ; many who adored Russian ballet adopted or lauded homo-sexuality ; the disciples of Savonarola felt that all that is beautiful is also wicked and ought to be destroyed. The admirers of the genius who has taken to drink do more than get drunk themselves. Drinking is illuminated with the halo of the master, it becomes part of the new faith, and to be half-seas-over is thought to be a noble state and productive of mysterious insight.

For these reasons it is of great importance to the community that rulers, teachers and outstanding persons generally should set an example of goodness, and equally true that the more widely this is set the greater its cumulative results will be. Nevertheless the presence of good examples is not enough to secure high moral standards. Numbers will remain impervious to them, despise and mock at them, either because they represent authority, against which some men will always rebel, or because a show of goodness, and much talk about it, have become associated in the mind of a child with harshness and hypocrisy, or because the virtue displayed is felt to be unattainable, and on this account creates both resentment and despair. Gangs of criminals do not spend their lives in wistful admiration of the honest ; they dislike them and jeer at them for fools who are the natural prey of those more astute than themselves.

Simple goodness, the lovely virtue of Christ, the sweetness and loving kindness of St. Francis, the moral grandeur of Confucius, the wisdom of Aristotle, attracted and having attracted transformed, groups and even multitudes of followers. But all men are not attracted by them, or even by virtues at all. Hitler, who was vicious as only a neurotic can be vicious, who murdered and tortured more human beings than any other man who has ever lived, was adored by millions not only when he promised them all the kingdoms of the earth but when he taught them to believe that they were born to die for Germany. Even the Devil has had his worshippers.

Important introjections, then, not only change men's characters but influence their views and beliefs. And these introjections are governed very largely by the child's attitude towards his parents. If he resents them and their attempts to discipline him he will tend to break away from their beliefs. If he hates them, even unconsciously, he will espouse just the doctrines, out of those which he comes across, which would distress his family most and thus enable him to repay old scores.

The Hungarians say—or said before the war—that the child of a Fascist becomes a Communist and the child of a Communist a Fascist. This does not suggest harmonious family life.

If on the other hand the predominant feeling of the child is love, the youth will choose leaders who remind him in some way of his parents as he believes them to be. Both these processes can be traced exactly in the mind of an individual by the use of the appropriate technique—indeed many of us can see them working out among our friends and neighbours. It is more difficult to discover such things in oneself, since pride intervenes.

It may be objected here that the standards we pick up from our school-fellows often seem more important, and are more easily and closely obeyed, than the moral doctrines preached by our parents. " Good form " can be just as exacting as the demands of virtue, and rules its followers with an iron hand. And it will be obeyed where the moral ideal is disregarded.

It is true that this often happens, because good form is the badge of some class division, and large numbers of people in all ranks of life depend for much of their self-esteem upon their membership of some particular class or group. It pays those who consort with the English gentry to wear collars at their evening meal, however hot the day, and to refrain from obvious forms of boasting in public. It pays many Americans to be " good mixers " and possess the art of " selling themselves " efficiently. But apart from all the social and economic advantages which accrue from observing shibboleths, it must be remembered that most men who are governed by " good form " have parents who approve of it, and have been sent to schools where their heroes approve of it also. When the headmaster lays stress upon the atmosphere of the school he does not always realise the extent to which this is absorbed through emotional relations formed between individuals.

The same thing holds true of the groupings which have strong effects upon adult opinion. Such important moral feelings as loyalty to the regiment, or between shipmates, are felt as a bond between members of the group. According to Freud this bond will depend for its force, in the long run, upon shared loyalty to the group leader. The ship with an unpopular captain in whom the men feel no confidence is not a happy ship, and the bonds between members of the crew will crumble, if they have ever formed. It is at bottom shared love for the common leader which colours the horizontal relations in a group and charges them with their special significance. This explains in part why except in disciplined units the very strong bond forged by common danger tends to disappear as soon as the danger passes. " We went through the Blitz together " may still be felt as a tie, but you would no longer risk your life for the man, instantly and automatically, as you would have done at the time.[1]

It is because moral ideas tend to be acquired by way of personal feelings that many people are unable to extend their sympathies beyond the small groups and sets with which they come into immediate contact. During a war almost all of us can realise sharply that we are members of a national group, feel allegiance to a national leader and govern much of our conduct by these broad conceptions. In ordinary times we fall apart into smaller groups united by special ties and our moral outlook shrinks accordingly. We no longer place our lives and our fortunes at the service of our country, though we stick to the rules of—and work hard for—the Village Institute or the cricket club. Or the good of seaside boarding-house keepers may become our most important good. It is these who now are felt to be brethren, the righteous, those to whom one owes loyalty, threatened as they are by promotors of holiday camps, local authorities who refuse priorities, and charabancs which ruin the place by flooding it with day-trippers. And it is Joe Biggs, who told the Inspector what he thought of him, who now wears the halo of a champion.

Wide philosophic outlooks are extremely desirable, but in the absence of suitable leadership they are difficult to maintain.

The earliest moral ideas which a child absorbs are, then, of especial importance. If his parents are kind and sensible and take pains with his moral training, so that the ideas with which he starts his life are rational and workable, and not too different from those of the people among whom he will have to live, he will, with luck, grow up a virtuous human being. He will be incapable of many sorts of behaviour prohibited by his group ; he will be reasonably successful in living up to his ideals, and these in their turn will be sound.

If, on the contrary, the moral ideas imparted by his parents

---

[1] The link between old shipmates remains. Cf. Freud's *Group Psychology and the Analysis of the Ego.*

are silly, or fail to cover important fields of conduct, or conflict seriously with the moral code of the community, he will have a much more difficult time. Sensitive and overmodest parents often feel, for instance, that the world is a forbidding place, and seek to shelter their children from it during the years of youth. They inculcate numbers of absolute ideals, which they treat as though they were normally attainable, and send their families to schools where the same attitude is maintained even at the cost of isolation from the life of the community in general. They do this for various reasons. In the first place, as Freud has pointed out, there is a strong tendency among adults who were happiest themselves as children to hand on the precepts and attitudes to life which they themselves were taught when they were young. " I was good and happy then, before I had lost my illusions and came to grips with the sordid realities of life. The world will never again be as bright or as lovely as it was in those lost years. Let the poor little beggars have at least that period of happiness on which to look back ! " Or they may think : " We are a degenerate lot. Our fathers lived in a simpler age—they had a stronger sense of duty and were not tormented as we are tormented by doubts." And they try to resurrect for their children a fragment of this vanished and largely imaginary world.

It does not occur to them that life might not seem so sordid and dangerous, nor their own behaviour so dubious, if they themselves had not been nourished upon illusions. What really kept them free from sin was the fact that when they possessed a simple faith they were children, leading protected lives. The longing they now feel is a longing for freedom from responsibility, from knowledge of good and evil. It is what we call escapism. And they do not realise that if they bring up their children as they were brought up themselves, ignorant of the real nature of the world in which they will have to live, and of the codes which obtain in that world, they are making sure that these children too will have to cope with a mood of disillusioned misery. That this mood is common, and much aggravated by the fact that one's parents are thought to have deceived one, most workers among young people will agree.

For all this, the question of how far children's ideas should be adjusted to those of the world about them is by no means simple. It is a matter of finding a middle way which is not easy to trace. Unless a man can tolerate to some degree the faults of his society he will lead a solitary, possibly a quarrelsome, and almost certainly a self-righteous life. On the other hand no good citizen should feel content to profit by those faults, or fail, if they are serious, to take his stand against them. What is needed here is firm ground under one's own feet, together with a sense of what is possible, and sympathy for the points of view and dilemmas of other people. The correct mixture of these ingredients is not easy to achieve, and only with great good fortune can it be handed on to others.

With another type of parent the ideals taught, instead of being impossible, will be defective. Parents who are ambitious for their children—as well as others—will often fail to inculcate a proper respect for the rights of other people. This should be a fundamental part of the moral code of all but anchorites, and it is one which is difficult to instil if the necessary foundation has not been laid at home. Wary and selfish young people who have been taught that the big thing is to look out for Number One seldom adopt as heroes, or allow themselves to be influenced by, just and altruistic persons. They are much more likely to drift into the arid and rootless groupings of those who are also on the make.

Again, such instruction as is given may be sound but scrappy, so that the child has no coherent system of principles to which he can turn when confronted by novel problems. " You're on your own now and you won't have me to turn to. So keep out of the way of skirts and mind you put something by every week ! " drew attention to important fields of conduct. But I have often wondered how far it served the rather stolid young man to whom the advice was given.

To put it shortly the child whose moral code is either defective in important particulars, or differs too widely from that of his community, will tend to develop into a bad man by the standards of that community, or find himself involved in exhausting moral conflicts from which he may never be able to free himself.

At first sight the whole of this argument seems to show that there is a very great advantage to be gained from a hook-up between religion and morality. Principles taught by the parents rest merely upon the parents' authority, knowledge and sense. The first may be impugned, the two latter may be lacking or totally inadequate. But if morality can be taught as resting not upon the authority of an erring, earthly father but upon the will of an Almighty God, these strong disadvantages will be avoided— or so it seems safe to assume.

In support of this argument the adherent of any of the great world religions can point to innumerable cases where the result of accepting his religion has been both the adoption of higher standards of conduct and a marked increase in good behaviour. Sinners are saved, and are the happier as well as the better for it. Anyone who knows much about witchcraft and witch doctors, or really bad homes in the slums of great cities, is likely to feel a great deal of sympathy for the missionaries of almost any respectable system of beliefs.

But this does not dispose of the matter. The argument just quoted depends for its validity upon two things—that the moral code of the religion in question is an improvement upon the convert's original beliefs, and that it is an advantage to base it upon the will of a divine being.

As for the first of these, not all religious codes are good, especially when we consider what is actually taught at a given place and time. The Irish priests who encouraged the I.R.A. to plant time bombs in English streets can be paralleled in most ages and all the world over. They afforded comfort to the murderers concerned, but that is another matter.

A good deal has already been said about supernatural sanctions, but something more may now be added which could not have been understood without the information given in the last chapter. Whether a religious sanction works well or badly will be decided largely by the qualities actually attributed to the god who constitutes that sanction. If the god is felt to be a revengeful deity bent on punishment and demanding an eye for an eye and a tooth for a tooth, morbid tendencies in the believer will be strengthened, with results which have already been described.[1]

What nature the individual will ascribe to his god depends as much upon his own disposition and mental history as upon the teachings of his church. For to each of us our personal god is very largely formed in the image of our earthly father.[2] He is the

[1] One of my grandfathers used to tell us that the Minister under whom he sat as a boy concluded a sermon on the Last Judgment with the following sentences :—" And on that Day, my brethren, there will be ' weeping and wailing and gnashing of teeth.' And then ye will call upon the Laird and cry out unto Him : " Laird ! Laird ! We didna ken! We didna ken!.' And the Laird in His eenfinite maircy will say unto you : ' Aweel, ye'll ken the noo ! ' "

Whether the story is true or not, it shows clearly the causes which made an agnostic of my grandfather. That the basic conception is not unusual may be inferred from the fact that whereas " god-fearing " is an adjective which expresses strong approval, the term " god-loving " has never been brought into use.

[2] Cf. *The Future of an Illusion* by Sigmund Freud.

father as seen by a little child with his power and his glory and his all-seeing eye. To one of his children he may be in the main an avenging terror, to another a loving shepherd. The attributes which a child allots unconsciously to his father he will project upon his god. And this is one reason why people who worship side by side in the same church or temple will have such very different ideas of the same god. To one he will be, behind the screen of orthodox tradition, a spirit of wrath ; to a second a being whose mercy and love are infinite. That elements of the first conception are nearly always present to cloud the second, is due to the tendency already mentioned whereby children see their father as more savage and revengeful than he is. Should an objective deity exist, he is hidden from us by our own phantasies.[1]

Later in life this identification of the two fathers may be modified by the character of the congregation among whom one finds oneself, and especially by the behaviour of its priests. Where churches are found to give shelter and comfort, and priests are merciful and help one to achieve goodness as well as rebuking one for ones' sins, harsh conceptions of the deity may be eased especially in the conscious mind. As a kindly old nun once said to me, *à propos* the enthronement of the present Pope : " Surely it must bring comfort to you, even though you are a heretic, to know that our new Pope is a man of peace ? I am not speaking of politics, of which I know nothing, but of spiritual values." It was clearly a relief to her, since the Pope, half-way between man and God, was yet another father.

What is found to give shelter and comfort will vary of course with the needs and fears of the individual. One will crave penance and austerity, another a busy life of service, and a third the stillness of contemplation. Where punishment is felt to be deserved a revengeful god may be more acceptable than the god who forgives us our sins.

When on the other hand young people consider that the atmosphere of the church is less kindly and sensible than that of other groups which are open to them, either their conception of its god becomes vague or they lose faith in his existence. Rebels against the human father will tend to rebel in some form against the discipline or doctrine of his church. It may be as well

---

[1] Cf. the views concerning the nature of Jehovah held by Jeremiah, St. Theresa, St. Francis, St. John the Evangelist and St. Ignatius Loyola.

to add that such identifications are usually complex, and those just given merely simplified illustrations.

Without going into the question of whether, in fact, our conception of infinity is not derived from ideas of inflating the finite, it need only be pointed out that to the little child his father is all-wise, all-powerful and the arbiter of right and wrong. He is an almost entirely different being from the father as seen by a normal adult, though we do find dependent types, especially among women, who continue to look upon their fathers as patterns of all the virtues. It is these early states of mind which are used to build up the idea of an external deity, and the absolute character of the qualities attributed to the god is due to the totally uncritical attitude of the child.

So close, indeed, is the connection between the father, the ruler and the god, that kings and leading moralists, or even men who are regarded in the light of protectors are not uncommonly deified. Instances are some of the Roman Emperors—not always the most deserving—the Emperor of Japan, the Buddha, and a host of king-gods worshipped by primitive peoples. Where there is already a deity whom the priests are not prepared to discard and who will not share his throne, the human leader is regarded either as the Son of Heaven, as were the Chinese Emperors, or a particularly holy prophet, as was Mahommed. Short of this we find every kind of link forged between those who are felt to exercise the authority of a father and the concept of divinity. Kings are kings by divine right and exercise magic powers of healing. The man who starts a new sect is held to be the mouthpiece of the Lord. Miracles were attributed to Mussolini, and prayers were said to Hitler. " Wretched boy ! Do you dare to go through life under the burden of a father's curse ? " was once a threat of awful potency.

Again, the death of a man upon whom many hopes are pinned is often too painful to be accepted as a fact. Generations waited for the return of King Arthur and Barbarossa : thousands of Englishmen refused to believe in the death of Lord Kitchener until the war was won and they had no more need of him.

In fact there is a widespread tendency among those who have taken a man as an idol to regard him either as a new god or the agent or reincarnation of an old one. For the same reason almost every creed has produced a mother-figure whose predominating quality is mercy. The trinities which succeed primitive polytheism are reflections of the family, or rather of its all-important kernel,

Father-Mother-and-I. Subsidiary Buddhas, Arhats, saints, angels, cherubim and similar figures take the place of brothers and sisters, uncles, aunts and other relations. That these additions should occur even when the founder of a particular creed gave no sanction of any kind for them, as in the cases of Buddhism and Christianity, only shows how close is the identification of earthly and heavenly families. There is even a numerical correlation, for the larger and more closely-knit the customary family group the more crowded will be as a rule the pantheon of its religion. Were it not for this mechanism in the mind of man it would be difficult indeed to account for the similar organisation of so many heavens.

To sum up what I have tried to say in this chapter :—The moral code of the individual is not derived from his conscience, whose function is merely to enforce that code, whatever its source and its nature. Its source is in the main the child's impressions of what is taught him by parents and others in authority. The earliest of the ideas imbibed in this fashion retain through life a considerable compelling power even though they may have been abandoned by the conscious mind. Where rejection or modification takes place, it will usually be found that the authority of the parents has been displaced in whole or in part upon some cause or hero whose tenets or opinions now carry more weight than the original beliefs. Nevertheless the latter are not destroyed but continue, through unconscious agencies, to struggle for a renewed supremacy.

The codes thus absorbed may, or may not, correspond with those held by the neighbours or enjoined by the local god. To attribute them to a supernatural source does not in fact, though it may seem to do so, give them added strength. What does affect the mind are firstly the behaviour of leaders and colleagues past and present—not only their goodness, but even more their power to compel the minds of other people. The second factor is the benefits found to be derived from one's beliefs. Estimation of these will vary with the common sense of the individual and his personal demands upon life.

To this we may add that whereas a morbid conscience will administer cruelly even the best of codes, a sensible, tolerant and reliable Super-Ego encourages its owner to collect a rational, kindly system of beliefs—provided that the society in which he lives makes this possible.

Before going on to discuss communal codes we may note that all these facts, taken together, suggest an important question.

That is, whether every child should not be taught a definite system of morals to learn at school. To be effective, the teaching should be carried out in a spirit of mercy and understanding, and given by people whom he is able to admire and love. The contents of any such code we have still to consider.

CHAPTER 7

COMMUNAL CODES (1)

It follows from what has been said in the last two chapters that morality of some sort is found wherever we find human life. This occurs because the mind of man is of such a nature that it imports into family relations the concepts of guilt and obligation, and of right and wrong. These are the moral concepts proper, and they are extended, through the agencies of experience and instruction, to the community and its claims, and then to ideals which may go beyond the laws, customs and opinions of the community.

To these facts we may now add another—that men live in groups, and that unless the egoistic impulses of their members were controlled groups could not survive. If a non-moral group could ever form, the last victor would soon die surrounded by the bodies of his victims. There is no possible collection of human beings whose members do not accept some obligation to do what is right and refrain from what is wrong. What is thought or felt to be right and wrong will vary within limits which we shall presently consider, but it is likely to have two aspects, my duty to my neighbour and my duty to achieve some personal ideal—to be the sort of man or woman that I think it right to be.

Both are important to the community, but public opinion is chiefly concerned with the first. It is the duty to neighbours which is supported not only by conscience but by social penalties. These run from loss of love and esteem, through public disapproval and disgrace, to the most savage punishments which human ingenuity can invent. And behind these lie the continuously operative laws which we may describe as the biological sanctions of morality—the conditions under which alone that particular community can exist.

Some readers may be expected to deny that morality has two aspects. They consider that my duty to my neighbour comprises the whole of morality, or they may narrow this still further to the duty of the individual to his community. These are important objections which must receive an answer; but before discussing them I propose to say what little needs saying here about communities and their moral codes.

The descriptive side of this subject belongs not so much to ethics proper as to anthropology. It is to the literature of that science that students must turn if they are interested in the extraordinary beliefs that have been taken for moral truths. Again, the development of human morality has attracted both historians and sociologists.[1]

Since no one is likely to deny that moral codes have varied widely, or that they have changed, these topics had best be left to specialists. But it may be as well to say something, since only a psychologist can have access to all the relevant facts, about the factors that account for their peculiarities.

These factors are of three main kinds. The first are physical —geographical, if you like. The second depend upon the need to restrain universal but inconvenient human impulses. The third are the irrational phantasies to which the minds of men are subject. Unfortunately they are not the least important.

Most of us, nowadays, are aware of the influence on morals of physical conditions. Climate determines what crops shall be sown ; and the richness or poverty of the soil, the abundance or absence of fish and game, play an important part in determining both the temper and the customs of a community. It is a subject upon which much work remains to be done—underfeeding for instance may make peoples apathetic, or more than usually chaste and bitterly quarrelsome. Physiologists and dieticians are needed here to co-operate with social psychologists. But the important fact for the moment is that such correlations exist, and that they influence ideas about what is right.

It is necessary to enlarge upon this. Pictures come readily to mind of smiling Polynesians, wreathed with flowers, and of dour and ascetic Highland clans raiding their neighbours' cattle. We remember, too, the link between clothing and temperature, and tell ourselves that the presence or absence of skins or fabrics upon various areas of the human body must have had an important influence upon sexual behaviour and even standards.

Nor are the readers of this generation likely to underrate the effect of more narrowly economic forces. Everyone knows that the distribution of slavery in the United States corresponded with the economic needs of the white population, and that this coincided neatly with the views most Americans held upon the moral justifications of slavery.

Similarly, as soon as the growing complexity of modern

---

[1] The best general book on the subject is L. T. Hobhouse's *Morals in Evolution*.

machinery created a demand for a semi-educated working class, thousands of Englishmen became conscious of the right of the poor to a suitable education. And I was interested to notice, just before the war, some examples of the opposite tendency. Certain industrialists had thought it best to organise their factories in such a way that all the intelligence needed was centred in the technical and administrative staff, while manual operations were so simplified and divided up that they could be performed by morons. So far as my own limited experience goes, those who preferred this plan were soon found thinking in terms of docile masses and of leadership. The rights of their fellow-citizens had vanished from their minds.

No one will deny the importance of climatic and economic factors. The danger is perhaps that they will be over emphasised. Many people are too apt to suppose that all our moral ideas derive from the various forms of pressure exercised by the physical environment. And even when these influences are undoubtedly at work, most of us tend to simplify unduly the chains of cause and effect.

In the Pacific, for instance, different tribes live in practically identical surroundings and have reached much the same stage of economic development. Yet nothing could be more opposed than their types of culture. The cannibals, or so I am told, are all haunted by the same ghosts—dead men, with immense eyes, who smell of rotting flesh—but their institutions have little in common. Nor can one sort them out into Polynesians and Melanesians, and give all the flowery wreaths to the first, and the black magic to the second. The Maoris of New Zealand are Polynesians ; their climate is one of the best in the world ; they did not have to contend against insect pests, wild beasts or tropical diseases. They enjoyed complete isolation from external enemies for many centuries, and until order was imposed and education provided by the English, they were cannibals and among the most war-like, formidable and blood-thirsty of savage races.

Nor is the influence of climate upon clothing, or of clothing upon sexual morality, nearly as direct or clear-cut as it may seem at first. Arabs, male as well as female, wear quantities of heavy clothes even in the Sahara. Their women are smothered in veils, and closely guarded. Husbands are allowed four wives at a time and can divorce at pleasure but adultery is punishable by death, so that young men who cannot afford a wife or a slave have on the whole to lead celibate lives. This is pretty well the opposite of our own system, but what has climate to do with it?

In British West Africa tribes will be found who live under almost every variety of sexual arrangement. Again, if we take populations of European stock and Christian affiliations who have migrated to different climates, it seems doubtful whether we should find a laxer (or if it be preferred, a more tolerant) moral outlook among the inhabitants of Brisbane than among those of New York. The great ascetic religions started in hot climates, and the Esquimos are now said to be an unusually complaisant people. The close correlations which would save us all so much trouble if they existed do not seem to be there. On the other hand in countries with cold winters there is a heightening of sexual tension as the weather grows warmer in the spring. Some people thereupon begin to dream of earthly paradises in which it would be not only pleasant but lawful to indulge their desires. These feelings are projected upon dwellers in hot countries, and the whole phantasy is taken as true without further evidence.

A similar mechanism works in the case of unfamiliar nakedness, though the evidence does not show that nudist gatherings provoke ungovernable lust.

The same uncertainty will be found when we consider more strictly economic forms of pressure. Tribes living in unfertile districts may find themselves left alone to live as they please because they have no neighbours, or because those they have do not covet their possessions. In these circumstances they may develop a peaceful, friendly form of culture, find no occasion for fighting and become almost too lazy to hunt. Or they may be eaten up by witchcraft, the prey of cruel superstitions, gloomy, ferocious, warlike and hard put to it to maintain internal order.

In the same way communities living on the fat of the land may either become slothful and unwilling to defend themselves, or they may use their superior resources to make themselves powerful. It is by no means always the peoples from barren regions, leading hard lives, who set forth upon careers of conquest. These have lived often enough in their bleak mountains or deserts century after century taking not the slightest interest in what goes on around them. It is not until they are shifted by some dire calamity like a decade of drought that they descend upon the fertile plains and either conquer or are driven off. When driven off, as usually happens, the event is recorded, if it is recorded, merely as another frontier scrap.

Nor are the defeated necessarily degenerate. There is a general tendency to believe that fallen peoples deserve their fate but it does not seem to be founded upon fact. Empires and states have foundered for every sort of reason ; because they clung to the virtues of their fathers and could not adapt themselves to the changing times as well as because they were attacked at a moment when they were adjusting their institutions to new conditions and were in a state of disorganisation. They have fallen because the heirs of the great king have quarrelled among themselves ; because they were split by bitter religious controversy ; because they had suffered from a succession of incompetent rulers ; because they had been weakened by some terrible disease, or from a combination of these and other causes. Sloth and love of luxury are only two of them.

When a country falls upon evil times a great deal of anxiety is generated, as a result of which numbers of its citizens will devote themselves to the pursuit of pleasure if it is at all possible for them to do so. This reaction is naturally and intensely irritating to men of the opposite type, who feel that the right thing to do is to repent one's sins, abandon all delights, and run through the streets of the city crying : " Woe ! Woe ! " Accusations are plentiful, every round of drinks becomes an orgy, and a false impression is created which makes historians put the cart before the horse, and maintain that the city fell on account of its corruption.

Moreover this picture of the decadent and dying Empire overrun by vigorous barbarians is only one type of incident among those that make up the history of nations. Rich communities, as I said, may enjoy the exercise of power, send expeditions to conquer peoples who would not have dreamed of attacking them and develop extremely war-like frames of mind. The presence of external danger may encourage this, but it is not a necessary preliminary. Greed, by no means confined to the poor, will do just as well, or a desire to convert the heathen, or the belief that one is descended from the gods and has therefore a divine right to rule the world and make slaves of other peoples. Or a single ambitious man, to say nothing of a paranoiac like Hitler, may set the ball rolling if he happens to be in a position to start a war.

For all these reasons when people talk of climatic and economic forces and seek to describe human conduct and beliefs in terms of these they should be on their guard against envisaging them too simply.

The second set of factors to which I referred is the necessity for keeping certain human impulses in check if men are to live together in communities. It is only with difficulty that man lives peacefully among his fellows, however great his need of them may be. And all systems of morality must allow for this fact. It is because they do that the moral systems of some human groups are so much more sensible than the deities to whose authority they have been attributed. If order cannot be kept, the group will perish.

We find, therefore, that everywhere private murder is either condemned or regularised, as in the case of duelling. This is recognised as so essential that when swashbucklers become a menace private fights, even if thought to involve honour, are made illegal. When this happened in Western Europe men who had emerged from duels as victors, or who enjoyed picturing them, declared in each country in turn that to abolish these occasions for the display of courage must lead to the decay of all valour and manly virtue. Nevertheless it was done and courage survived.

In the same way we find, universally, some sort of law or custom protecting property rights. These differ widely, but there is agreement that they should be observed, whatever form they may take. Dr. Ruth Benedict[1] describes a Pacific tribe who regard dishonest cunning as the highest of human qualities. The most skilful cheat is regarded as the greatest man. And in this community as soon as the yams have been planted for the year, everyone steals his neighbours tubers and plants them all over again in his own plot. Once this has been done, however, the yams are left in peace. No doubt there is a limit to the number of times that they will bear transplanting.

Sex is another field in which we always find organisation and regulation of some sort. Where the rules are very strict there will often be recognised areas of tolerance, as when the more worldly Victorians held, somewhat uneasily, that rich young men must be allowed to " sow their wild oats." So far as I know no large community has found it practicable to leave its members free in this respect, widely as their various systems differ. Considering the importance everywhere attached to the sexual ethic, and the closeness of its ties with religion, the enormous differences between sexual codes is a fact of the greatest interest to moralists. Very large numbers of different arrangements have been found to be

[1] Cf. *Patterns of Culture*.

workable : it is much to be regretted that we do not know more about the customs of the groups which have failed to survive. But whatever the system may be most citizens regard it as the only decent system, take it for granted that its observance is healthy, and look upon laxness or a desire for change as signs of decadence.

Another type of moral obligation which is acknowledged in all human communities is the duty felt to exist towards rulers. Even where wide civil rights exist and government is based upon consultation and consent, someone must carry out the functions of leadership and obedience is incumbent upon the individual. It is possible that the ruler himself may be tied by a set of obligations no less rigorous than those imposed upon his subjects. But this will not be held to affect their duty to him. Anarchy, like Free Love, has never worked anywhere yet.

The distinguishing marks of the moral ideas which derive from social necessity, as of those which flow from climatic and economic causes, is that they are more or less rational. Where they are not, they fail to be rational largely because the necessary facts are not known, of if known are not understood. Reginald Farrar in one of his books mentioned a district of China in which it is forbidden to climb the mountains. The reason for this ban was sensible enough, once it is believed that climbing the mountains annoys the gods who live in them, and that the gods will retaliate with destructive thunderstorms. If some expedition to the mountains had been followed by a ruinous storm, villagers depending on their own harvests could not be expected to take any further chances.

Where such mistakes are frequent the community suffers, since a knowledge of the real sequences of cause and effect is vital to gaining control over natural forces.

This brings us to the third set of important factors in the formation of moral codes—the irrational fears which affect so much of human conduct. I have used the words " this brings us " because climbing mountains may be thought a sin even without any false deductions based upon past visits. Thunderstorms, in the unconscious mind, stand for father-in-a-rage, and climbing great heights, on account of its unconscious symbolism, may be regarded as a challenging, insolent and impious act, likely in itself to provoke retribution. One chief or priest in whom the idea of such behaviour roused strong feelings of guilt might imprint his own superstitious feelings in the minds of all his followers.

Irrational fears may be proper to man as a species, or they may be the product of abnormalities in individuals. It is the universality of certain of these fears which explains why the family crimes, patricide, matricide and incest, and their derivative, regicide, are considered far more horrible and unnatural than slave-raiding and cornering food. The reader may object that this is by no means irrational—family life is the basis of society, and whatever destroys it will therefore arouse a special horror. I think this argument is refuted by the fact that only recently, and in certain societies, have children had any civil rights at all. They could, and can, be exposed at birth—as they have been by the million—killed, or sold as slaves or prostitutes, entirely at the discretion of the father.[1]

In China of old to sell a daughter in order to provide means of honouring one's ancestors would have been considered a virtuous thing to do and was lately so considered in Japan.

This complete difference of attitude to the rights of the dead and the living, the past and the future, can bear no relation to the biological needs of any conceivable community. It can only be explained by the fact that the boy's early fears group themselves round his parents, especially the father, and that he has no corresponding sense of duty or responsibility towards younger children. It can be taught him, but as a rule not without some difficulty, and the fears to which it gives rise will never go so deep.

The idea that children have rights seems to have some correlation with the degree of social freedom enjoyed by women, but I must admit that I have not studied the question thoroughly enough to make the assertion with confidence. It appears to hold for the modern world in so far as it is civilised, but the last word rests with the anthropologists.

If many widely accepted moral obligations have anti-social effects, the reason lies in the irrational character of most of our natural fears. The Aztecs sacrificed so many of their youths and maidens to their bloodthirsty gods that they weakened the structure of their civilisation. National unity and confidence in the older generation must have been hard to maintain in such circumstances. Again large numbers of people are to be found in every community, including our own, who will impoverish themselves and their families in order to provide gorgeous funerals for their dead. Wealthy Chinese would often exhaust their fortunes

---

[1] That infanticide is not the result of over population seems clear when we remember that female children were exposed in Ancient Greece.

in this manner. This behaviour was not a mere convention but felt as a moral duty of the first order. To bury with him all his most valued possessions might be rationalised as providing the dead chief or father with what he would need in the spirit world, but the base of these excesses was and is that funeral rites and feasts appease the revengeful ghosts, both by showing them how deeply they are mourned, and by virtue of magic powers inherent in the accustomed ceremonies.

Another example is the Islamic belief that those who are killed in battle go straight to Paradise. This is defended as rational on the ground that it encourages valour. But a tendency on the part of soldiers to throw away their lives when there is no need may be a weakness in an army and not a strength. One would suspect therefore both a suicidal tendency, and the existence of much repressed hatred for the young in the old, who doom the youth of their tribes to frustration and turbulence by buying up all the most attractive women.

In fact the more closely we examine the moral codes of mankind the more clearly we see that they are everywhere shot through with fantastic beliefs which can only be explained by reference to the unconscious wishes and phantasies of the human mind. That is not to say that they have all been so explained—the necessary work has still to be done. But no amount of ingenuity can account either for their form, or for the tenacity with which they are held, unless and until unconscious processes are taken into account.

Often enough—in fact one might say as a rule—the internal and external factors can be found working side by side. Where this is so, it is surprising how often the moral stress falls just where we should not expect it—on the irrational side. For example where a community is faced with a perpetual scarcity of water, or depends upon a single well, we should expect to find that the gravest offence was to steal water or pollute it. It is far more probable that the gravest offence would be to fail to play one's proper part in the magic rituals which are thought to maintain the supply of water, or propitiate the goddess of the well.

Further, these rituals have not uncommonly been so elaborate and wearisome, taking up so much time and perhaps consuming so much raw material, that they have constituted a perilous drain upon the resources of the community. Europe in the early middle ages, to take a familiar instance, was bled almost white by the tribute levied by a church which preached that the love of money is the root of all evil, to say nothing of the rich man, and the camel, and the needle's eye. But it took centuries of resentment and the backing afforded by a religious schism, before even some of the countries affected found courage to repudiate this exhausting tribute.

On some biological necessities, then, communal codes will agree—or the community which has failed to think correctly will die out. As soon as there is any relaxation of this pressure they are found to vary so widely that the differences seem fantastic even to students of anthropology. But this does not alter the fact that they are the results of economic forces, the behaviour of neighbouring groups, and the ideas and feelings of individuals powerful enough to start important traditions.

If we start from this description of social morality it will lead to some interesting results. To begin with it provides one scale by which to judge the moral codes of groups, one method of determining which are worse and which better. We can judge them by results. It would be useless at this point to narrow these results to their success in producing good human beings living in good societies, for this means little or nothing until agreement has been reached about what is meant by good in these connections. That has still to be discussed. But we can say with certainty that codes which lead to the extinction of the society which uses them are bad.

At the moment nobody takes any further interest in the moral and philosophical ideas of the Fascists and the Nazis. They are under an eclipse. Still, any possible twist of the human mind is of interest to students of human nature, so it may be worth pointing out that even this crude way of judging moral codes proves that those ethical values are wrong. They are wrong because they must bring disaster upon the groups which adopt them. The glorification of force, fraud and cruelty ; the denial to the mass of the people of justice or any security of person or property, the principle that the ruler is above right and wrong are, in the long run, unworkable. So is the systematic attempt to prevent any combination among the ruled by fostering continual suspicion and making every man believe that his neighbour is probably a spy. It is necessary to the continuance of such systems, but in the end it destroys them. These principles, put into practice, eat away the general confidence, the goodwill and respect for the rights of others, upon which societies depend for their survival.[1]

[1] In May 1942 Dr. Goebbels felt obliged to remind the population of Berlin that " courtesy and kindness are necessary for peaceful intercourse between men." It was a sad comedown.

Inculcate them, call them virtues, carry them out on a large scale, and the fear and hatred produced will be so great that internal conflict can only be averted by external war. For in default of friendly feeling danger from without will be the only cement which can bind the social fabric. It has been said hundreds of times, and with truth, that the man who sows hatred can only survive upon a diet of constant success. When no further worlds remain to be conquered, no possibility is left but civil conflict. If Hitler, for instance, had overthrown all the remaining countries which opposed him he would have been forced to go on conjuring up visions of enemies who must be exterminated, until at last some group near enough to him to kill him felt itself in vital danger. This course would have been forced upon him not only by his internal terrors, but by the sequence of events.

It may be as well to point out that no religious doctrine can do more than deny the philosophies of violence. It cannot disprove them. If I say that cruelty and treachery are contrary to the law of God, it is open to my opponents to answer that God is a myth and that they believe in no god but might, or the state, or the old German gods, or in no god at all. The most passionate insistence that they are wrong takes the argument no further. But only a suicidal race would embrace a creed which they believed would end in their own destruction as a group. In fact the strong suicidal tendencies which exist in both Germans and Japanese seems to me to have played an unconscious part in their drives for world conquest.

It is unnecessary therefore to look for any element of supernatural direction in the customs and standards accepted by communities. They are as much a part of man's response to this environment as is protective colouration in animals. Unfortunately our moral ideas, if we take the human race as a whole, are not so well adapted to their purpose as Polar bears to ice and snow or the caterpillars of the cabbage moth to cabbages. This is due to the complex and flexible nature of the human mind and in particular to the strength of its irrational elements. To demand explanations before the facts are known, to attribute inner fears to external causes, to believe what one wants to believe in despite of fact—these and a dozen other ingrained human tendencies produce mischievous and nonsensical results.

So much then for the origins of communal moral systems. The next question that calls for discussion is the very different point raised at the beginning of the chapter:—whether the communal code is the whole of morality. It is fashionable at the moment to describe it as the duty of the citizen to his state, or at most to his fellows, from this it would follow that personal excellence considered as a moral goal is not a thing apart, but depends upon the contribution made by such excellence to the good of others.

This belief stands at the opposite pole from the old doctrine that the first duty of man is to save his soul, to achieve some transcendental relation with his god, or to abolish all desire. It is a natural reaction from the egoism of these doctrines, but it goes too far. For without entering into the question of whether it would be well for us to confine our ideas of right and wrong to behaviour which can affect other people, it is easy to show that we do not. In Chapter 4 I said that when the child's conscience is finally established he becomes possessed of two new internal governors. One was what we call conscience in its prohibiting aspect, and the other an ideal of personal goodness which it was his duty to achieve. This idea is part and parcel of our moral make-up, and it cannot be resolved entirely into " how my character is going to affect other people." Children do not feel it incumbent upon them to become good sports, little ladies, tough guys, dauntless heroes, virtuous heroines or even merely good children in the nursery sense of being truthful, tidy obedient and uncomplaining, as part of any wider conception of duty. They feel quite simply that they ought to be these things. It is the sense of belonging to a community which is later and derivative, and this is why it is so often lacking in people who have nevertheless some title to the adjective virtuous. If we look at the relation the other way round, who ever asked a villager to conceive of morality as his duty to the village? And yet this may be the only group which has real significance for him. We may desire him to be a good and faithful workman for the sake of society, but he wants to be one, if he does, because he wants to preserve his self-respect and happiness in his work. And most observers would agree that such a wish forms far the safer basis of the two. It is final ; whereas to work for the sake of society may lead to asking for whose sake society is working—not always an encouragement to faithful toil.

That human beings should form and pursue personal ideals is inevitable. It is desirable that these ideals should conform to the ideas of the age, or be what we subsequently call " in advance of them," but this will depend upon moral training. And even when a man comes to reflect upon his beliefs, question his ideals and trys to find a satisfactory ideology into which they may be fitted, there are reasons for thinking that " duty to oneself " may still retain a place. Taking us at our most civilised, it is not difficult to find examples. The first that comes to mind is the obligation to achieve intellectual integrity, to face facts, put aside personal interest, longings and prejudices, and bend all one's faculties to the discovery of truth. This is the ideal of the scholar and the scientist. It has often produced results of the greatest value to society, but is felt as a rule by the most gifted individuals as a duty to pursue the truth for the sake of truth and nothing else. Such an attitude is naturally disliked by most governments and established authorities, for it cuts at the roots of all forms of absolute power. Even the common man will regard it at times as not only dangerous but wicked.[1]

There is some excuse for this feeling, since power is in fact dangerous unless controlled by wisdom and goodwill, and means of harnessing even the goodwill that exists, and making it effective over a wide enough range, are still to seek. Nevertheless the pursuit of knowledge, taken with an unequivocal demand that that knowledge shall be as exact as possible, have become vital to the maintenance of civilisation. Whether we like it or not, no course seems open to us but learning to use our knowledge well.

In the same way an artist may feel that he has a duty to strive for the perfecting of some form of expression which nobody likes or understands but himself. He may hope in his heart for posthumous glory, but he would be the first to insist that he does his work to satisfy his own standards and not for the sake of humanity. I fancy that the consensus of opinion among artists would be that this is a nobler and better attitude than the attempt to paint in such a way as to afford the maximum of pleasure to other people or even other artists.

Again, sex is a sphere in which a great many of us feel it right to live up to personal standards without regard to the advantage of our neighbours. In England for some time past there have existed large numbers of healthy young women who would like to marry if husbands were available. This has been an admitted social evil. But their existence would not sway the mind of a man who thought it his duty to remain celibate. In fact, in a society in which a great many men have married with-

---

[1] Cf. the flood of letters which reached the Press attacking science after the first use of the atomic bomb.

out much taste for it in order to perpetuate a family, there must be few who have been influenced by these wider and far more important, national considerations. I do not know of a single case.

The same principle applies to other acts of self-discipline. Men who give up smoking "just to prove to myself that I can do it" often become very irritable and unjust to their wives. They would not be believed if they tried to excuse themselves by saying: "My darling, I have done this for your sake, so that in the long run you may have a more virtuous husband."

Another set of facts show that morality is not regarded as consisting only in my duty to my neighbour. This is the degree of heinousness which we attach to offences. One example is the case to which I have already referred, of a man who runs over another because he is driving carelessly. My duty to my neighbour is not to kill or injure him, except in war or in self-defence, and in the second case only if it is necessary to secure my own safety. But how differently do we regard careless drivers and the deliberate murderer, even when the victim is a scoundrel! It cannot be said that the community stands in more danger from murderers than from careless drivers. Here the figures of deaths on the roads and by murders are conclusive. The reason lies hidden in the fact that we are more deeply afraid of our unconscious desire to kill those who stand in our way than we are of actual killing.

Finally, large numbers of people regard their duty to their neighbour as part of their duty to themselves. They assist him not to make him happier or better or not only for these ends, but because they feel morally obliged to do so. Kant went so far as to make this state of mind into a moral absolute: duty must be performed for its own sake and for no other end. And a similar vein of thought will be found to run through a good deal of Christian teaching.

It is possible to argue that though such states of mind exist, their goodness or badness must be judged in the long run by their external effects. The individual dies, taking his ideals with him: society lives on.

There is a good deal to be said for this contention. Whether it is finally correct seems to me to depend upon whether or not good states of mind are regarded as good in themselves, or only in regard to the future. Some philosophers have held that only states of mind can be called good or bad, and that they possess these qualities irrespective of the accidents which may happen to the universe. When life on a world dies out, they would say, there is still meaning in saying that it was or was not good.

This is an ultimate question which may be left to philosophers, since the answer makes no difference to behaviour. What has importance for ethics, and therefore moralists, is that men have and always will have personal ideals, that they attach great value to these, and can be moved in many matters, if at all, only by taking this fact into account.

CHAPTER 8

COMMUNAL CODES (2)

In the last two chapters evidence was given to show that man can do right without relying upon supernatural sanctions. The conscience of the old-fashioned Confucian atheist is as rigid and scrupulous as that of the old-fashioned Nonconformist and, as we shall see later, his moral code is as high.[1]

But this does not involve the belief that the morals, either of individuals or communities, are not affected by religion. Ethical codes are the result of complex interactions between our environments and our inner impulses. And one of the strongest factors in an environment is often a religion or a church.

To attribute certain commands to a god may not ensure that they are more closely obeyed but it may alter the spirit in which they are carried out. The especial barbarity of religious wars is due partly to other causes, but partly to the idea in the minds of the victors that gratitude to one's own god demands the overthrow of his rivals, the destruction of their temples, and the killing of those who refuse to change their faith. To feel that the rooting out of infidels is a blessed work will almost certainly make one root them out more thoroughly than if one merely killed until one was tired of killing and felt like a rest and a drink.

Secondly, actual fathers and human rulers live in the real and contemporary world. Unless they are mad their sayings and doings will to a certain extent be adjusted to reality. Even if their children and subjects have introjected false and alarming conceptions of them, their day-to-day behaviour can act as a corrective. Most fathers treat their children with some commonsense and a considerable degree of kindness. And in many cases the values they teach will be more sensible than they are themselves—this depends upon the traditions which they were taught. But once the conception of godhead is superimposed and ideas of right and wrong are taken as coming from a supernatural source, the link with present reality is lost and unconscious, irrational factors have far more scope. Gods and spirits are imagined and

[1] A book by Lady Hoosie called *The Pool of Chien Lung* is interesting in this connection because it gives a picture of two Confucian ladies which will remind many readers of their sainted great-aunts.

worshipped in the first place because they are assumed to control the natural forces before which the savage finds himself helpless. And this belief continues even in the teeth of growing knowledge about those natural forces. A good many clergymen during the recent war have talked about " God's weather " and represented the deity as sending storm or calm in accordance with His view of our deserts. Sickness is sent by God, He decides upon the day of our death. In short we are in His almighty hands at all times and for good or ill. Since this world is the scene of many catastrophes —floods, droughts, fires, famines and pestilences, for which none of us can rationally feel responsible, the day to day behaviour of the deity is not of a reassuring nature. And the more perfect he is believed to be, the more necessary it becomes to show that all these things are good for us or thoroughly deserved. In this way guilt is piled up and terror is piled up and resentment inevitably engendered. As a result God may have attached to him tastes and policies which real fathers, left to themselves, generally overcome. A liking for human sacrifices is one of them. Eternal damnation is another. The god may be presented as a god of love, but it becomes very difficult at times to remember this aspect of his nature in view of his actual treatment of the faithful.

The effects of such irrational fears has already received some attention, and will be mentioned again later in the present chapter.

The ever-present tendency to turn love into fear underlies so much of human misery that it has been put first in order.

Most readers will probably feel that a more important influence on conduct is the fact that religious movements tend to develop into organised churches. It is true that we can hardly exaggerate the part played by these institutions in shaping human behaviour. The function of a church is not only to preach and guard its religion, but also by reasoning, threats and promises to guide the consciences and influence the daily lives of its congregations. Even when the form of the church is democratic, as when each group elects its minister every year, the goal remains the same. It is to steep the mind of the believer in religious concepts until his every act and thought is governed, or at least affected, consciously or unconsciously, by the church's teachings.

This ideal has sometimes been achieved: for the pious Hindu almost everything is a religious observance. For the devout Christian it should be an offering to God. But even when it falls short of complete success the influence of organised churches has stamped men's minds with an uneffaceable pattern and correspondingly deflected their feelings. Whatever the nature of the thoughts and behaviour suggested, these results must be thought by the churches to be good. No other judgment is possible, given their premises.

To a psychologist on the other hand many of the states of mind which are thus encouraged seem to be thoroughly bad. This raises several crucial moral questions.

Once we begin to examine the actual teachings of the great religions, we find that most of them present us with at least two different strains of doctrine. One is the system of ideas upon which they were based originally: another—or others—will be introduced when a sect becomes orthodox and begins to exercise social and political power. This may not be true of the Mahommedan faith, which rose to an influential position during the lifetime of its founder. It is certainly the case both with Buddhism and with Christianity. Successful religious movements tend to develop in certain respects along similar lines. The message of some sage appeals to forces in the human mind for which there is not, at the time, a satisfactory vehicle of expression. He is followed by disciples for whom his message, or his personality, or both, mean a new vision and an expansion of understanding. If the age is ripe for it the movement will grow, and the fact of its growth will add to its attractive power. First those who enjoy novelty, and then those who like to be in the fashion will tend to join it. Miracles and divine inspiration will be attributed to its founder. While it is in opposition to the prevailing system it offers a rallying point to the discontented: as it becomes dominant it provides a career for the ambitious. (The Christian Church was in fact the only career open to talent during the whole tenure of the feudal system.) When the church triumphs and becomes an orthodoxy, its doctrines will be taught to all and sundry, whether or not they are of the type who would have embraced them if left to their own choice.

As churches grow, then, the type of believer changes and new currents of thought and feeling are introduced. Gentle idealists may initiate religious movements, but they do not sweep them into power. That must be done by men of a harder sort, zealots and those who are able to organise as well as teach. Temporal power begins to seem desirable because it enables one to sway the lives of millions, to ensure that the truth and only the truth shall be taught, and to protect God's treasures and the persons of the faithful against the predatory foes who prowl about them. The more mighty the church the greater the temptation to engage in politics and even to sanction the use of the sword. Such a change of front is almost forced upon a body which feels the need for organisation and must exist in an unsettled world.

Christianity could hardly have survived, and would certainly not have attained its dominating position in Europe, if it had remained a group of persons who despised wealth and power and whose instinctive reaction to aggression was to turn the other cheek. The Church of Rome has always found room for such people, recognised the value of holy poverty, and encouraged meekness, especially in relation to the spiritual authorities. But it was the princes of the church who inherited the earth, and this for a compelling psychological reason.

Granted that a church is universal and must include all sorts and conditions of men ; granted too that there exists a sincere desire to weaken and discipline men's worldly instincts, the most practical method of dealing with human longings for wealth and splendour and authority is to switch them from the individual's own life on to that of his church. This need not be done deliberately : a church, particularly if it be organised as a hierarchy will affect the behaviour of its adherents in the same way as any other great institution which claims an over-riding devotion. In particular it will provide a means of gratifying vicariously those desires and ambitions which the flock must renounce for themselves as sinful. If the follower must be obedient and poor, he will find satisfaction in the fact that his church is rich and powerful. If he may not use his private judgment, he can regard as a father the priest who judges for him. We are all familiar with this mechanism in the field of politics. There the insignificant man, who will never be able to indulge his longings for position and the exercise of authority, often finds comfort in belonging to a strong and warlike nation. The less liberty he possesses as a person, the more freedom to do as it pleases he will demand for his country. There is no need to labour the point. In the same way the whole diocese will spring to defend the rights of the church against some indigent fellow who is trying to avoid paying 17s. 2½d. which he owes her. Many of the people concerned would have forgiven the amount at once had it been a personal debt.

In short an institution which claims the allegiance of large numbers of men of different types can use their loyalty to raise the level of some types of virtue in its members, so long as it does not itself exhibit too much of the virtue in question. Princes of the church with their pomp and licence eased the longings of millions.

Whether this process is desirable cannot be decided *a priori*. Its effects can be judged only in the event if they can be judged at all. The church which sucks into its coffers much of the wealth of the faithful may or may not make a better use of it than they would have done. It may create vast hordes of mendicants, arm Crusades, or set up hospitals and seats of learning. Even then the Crusades will rid the neighbourhood of bellicose knights and their retainers, and the schools may encourage a taste for sophistry. The net effects of these redistributions of energy, feeling and desire cannot be assessed, though it would be hard indeed for the church itself to question them.

These are not the only changes in values which result from success in converting multitudes. It has already been pointed out that the relentless inner conflicts of many Christians demand a God of wrath and vengeance whose main task is to punish them for their sins. This is generally said to derive from " Old Testament theology " but the conception of God as a tender shepherd is found as often in the Old Testament as a God of fear is found in the church of Christ.

So diverse are the minds of men that no one creed can satisfy them all. Particularly when under pain of damnation each type must twist it until it provides an antidote to the anxieties characteristic of the type. This tendency accounts in part for the fact that so very few sects are really monotheistic. Either trinities or saints or major prophets ease the rigours of conformity. Such divinities or semi-divinities embody different ideals, or different aspects of the root ideal, and especial devotion can be offered where each believer finds it most helpful. The fighter can dedicate himself to the Lord of Hosts, the man or woman to whom the mother means more than the father can turn to the Holy Virgin or some female saint. The same need will often be catered for in the church's institutions : the discipline of the Poor Clares, the Trappists and the Order of Jesus alleviate different fears.

This tendency is not peculiar to Christianity. Buddhism, originally a simple doctrine which taught men how to escape from the cycle of birth and rebirth by meditation and the renunciation of desire, soon collected almost as many demi-gods as the Brahminism which it set out to reform. Protestantism, even with a Trinity, has been obliged to tolerate a large number of sects each with its own peculiar point of view, in lieu of saints with their peculiar functions. Even Islam is not entirely united.

It is largely for this reason that we find in most churches tendencies which run directly counter to the teachings of their founders. It is also the explanation of many of the shifts in religious values. Owing to the influence of some Head Priest or Pope, or under pressure from the world outside, one of these psychological groups gains strength until it is in a position to influence the attitude of the body as a whole. Without any fundamental alteration in dogma there can be catastrophic changes in moral attitudes, even though the dogma is supposed to be both the source and guardian of the attitudes.

Several examples of these tendencies will occur to readers who are acquainted with the history of any great religion. The three I propose to describe, very briefly, are the promulgation of religious intolerance, the denial of intellectual freedom, and the endorsement of asceticism, by the Church of Rome. They are chosen because we are still suffering from the effects of all of them, and because most readers will know something about them already.

About the first two it is unnecessary to say much. Every educated man knows that deities, in the beginning, were tribal or territorial gods. This conception was held even of Jehovah, whose domain extended originally only to the land of Israel. It was considered right that a man should worship the gods of his people and his country, and when he emigrated adopt if he preferred it those of the community which he joined. Even the Jews felt free to make this choice. It was not until long after the death of Christ that the Christian Church invented the doctrine of exclusive salvation, which involved the belief that all rival gods were evil spirits and demons. Before the rise of Mohammed the Middle East held hundreds of different religious groups and sects who managed to co-exist in peace and comfort.

The belief that one's own god was the only true god and all others not only rivals but powers of darkness, seems to have been an inheritance from Hebrew thought.[1]

Of itself it would encourage the view that the worshippers of idols shared in their wickedness and must be killed or tortured until they were converted in order to save their souls. But many have believed that their god is the only true god without resorting to religious persecution. For this to become feasible two things are

---

[1] I am told by Hebrew scholars that the words : " Thou shalt have none other gods before Me " really means that no other gods may be worshipped in my temples. Even if this is accurate it may not have represented the general opinion.

necessary—a tremendous head of underlying hatred, whose origins will be discussed in a moment, and the power to persecute successfully. These temptations do not assail small unorganised groups.

Lecky says that during the Dark Ages " a literature arose surpassing in its mendacious ferocity anything that the world has ever known " on the subject of infidels and their deserts.[1] It is certain that the Christian virtues of pity and mercy were straitly restricted to co-religionists.

As soon as the position of the Church was so firmly established that it need no longer fear pagans as serious rivals in Europe, the abuse, the threats, the frightful punishments, were used against doubters and heretics wherever these emerged. Complete credulity was demanded and very largely obtained from the laity and inferior clergy: religion, or what was taught as religion, dominated the minds of men as even Hitler was not able to do, in spite of all his efforts. The methods adopted were not unsimilar to his, but lack of communications, in every sense of the word, made them more effective.

By means of drastic censorship learning was stamped out, libraries were burned and works of art destroyed. For centuries the population of Europe was illiterate; even the middle classes kept their accounts by cutting notches in sticks. Reading and writing were allowed to be taught only in monasteries and to a few exceptional priests, who were subject to the severest penalties if they used their knowledge for anything but orthodox propaganda. To praise the monasteries now because " they kept learning alive during the Dark Ages," is to ignore the part played by the Church in the destruction of learning. It was not until the seventeenth—indeed in some parts of Europe the nineteenth—century, that the ground thus lost to ignorance and superstition was retaken.

Nor have the effects of this terrific crusade against freedom of thought even yet been entirely destroyed. Today, and in this country, a great many people still believe that to doubt the truth of Christianity is wicked, and that the case for unbelief should not be stated in public. Many more feel that to attack religion is in the worst of taste, besides being unfair to those who derive comfort from their " simple faith." This tendency seems at the moment to be increasing rather than diminishing.

I have selected this instance of the destructive power of

[1] *History of European Morals from Augustus to Charlemagne*, Chapter 4.

bigotry because the facts are readily available to anyone who cares to look them up, and because we know enough of the civilisations of Greece and Rome to deplore the damage done and the losses incurred. Even so we cannot measure its extent. Nobody can estimate what Europe has missed through this policy, carried out steadily for eleven centuries.

The devastation wrought by the followers of Mahommed was probably greater, but it is impossible to say by how much, as almost nothing has been saved from the wreckage. We can guess at what was lost in Persia, but we know little more than the names of some of the kingdoms and empires in the Middle East which established civilisations, produced and accumulated treasure of literature and art, only to be wiped out by wasteful war and the rage of religious fanaticism. The Catholic Church was in no way exceptional in the attitude it took either towards learning or such principles as freedom of thought. It is an attitude likely to develop in any rich and hierarchical church which believes that its gods are the only true gods and its interests therefore the only important interests.

The third example that I mentioned—the establishment of sexual asceticism—needs closer attention, for the chains of cause and effect are more complex, and its new influence of great importance. By asceticism I mean not discipline of the sexual instincts—that is unescapable if order is to be maintained—but the beliefs that sensual pleasure is dangerous if not wicked, that the flesh should be mortified whatever the effects of this may be, and that sexual continence is the most desirable mode of life.

I think I am right in saying that all qualified psychologists of any of the modern schools of thought are agreed that to make an ideal of complete sexual abstinence is not the procedure of a normal man. It appeals naturally only to people in whom an excessive amount of guilt has been attached to sex during the early years of life. Others who adopt it do so either under the influence of some leader who attracts them for other reasons, or because they have been terrified into it by their teachers and parents. To attach a feeling of deadly guilt to sex is easy enough, for the sexual instincts, in man, take many years to fulfil their growth, and must pass through complex phases before that growth is complete. The earlier of these phases are neither recognised nor understood by those in charge of children, and it is widely believed that to encourage guilty feelings in connection with pleasureable bodily sensations is the proper thing to do.

Once this foundation has been laid, any subsequent shocks or strains, whether or not they seem to be directly sexual, raise the total level of guilt and anxiety to a point at which it is felt as intolerable, and will warp the mind in some way or another.[1] To develop a morbid horror of women, so that they are regarded as evil temptresses, to become so much afraid of sex that one is afraid of life and desires to escape from the world, to fail to grow beyond the homo-sexual phase through which we all pass in early adolescence, to become incapable of intercourse, are some of the things which may happen in such a case.

Unfortunately for the world, Christianity soon became infected with these views. The New Testament seems to us now essentially a body of teachings meant to be used in daily life. Our Saviour went about among the people, talked with them, visited their homes and sympathised with their joys and sorrows. It has been pointed out again and again that his parables and teachings refer to everyday matters, and are designed to make men realise the spiritual significance and value of common things. Christ loved children, blessed a marriage, allowed women to join his disciples, and never showed the slightest contempt for family life.

St. Paul on the other hand disliked and despised women. His writings—which have little in common with the Gospels—are the earliest authentic records of the Christian Church, and did much to form and petrify its beliefs. But the great wave of violent asceticism which swept over the Churches during the second century came undoubtedly from Asia, though in the general absence of information about the earliest history of Christendom we cannot trace the path its influence took. It resulted in the monastic movement, and in the belief that the road to salvation is through chastity, prayer and fasting, and the renunciation of all the pleasures of the world and the flesh. So great a hold did these ideas obtain that by the end of the century the Egyptians were boasting that at least half their population had embraced the religious life.

The social forces which lay behind this change of feeling have often been analysed. The barbarity and uncertainty of the times, the disorder into which the Roman Empire was falling, made the shelter of the monasteries seem well worth the price that had to be paid for it—at any rate to a certain type of man. But the world

[1] "The Aetiology of Hysteria" and other papers (Sigmund Freud) *Collected Papers*, Vol. I.

has after all passed through many periods of distress without producing a flight from life upon so vast a scale, and the force which produced it was in fact terror of the most poignant and searching kind—terror of sin and eternal damnation. Those who fled in this way from the dangers and responsibilities of ordinary existence imagined that they fled in obedience to the will of God and in order to save their souls. This belief enabled them to desert their families without a qualm or a thought for the helpless women and children left to fend for themselves. It may be noted that most earthly fathers would discourage such behaviour—indeed we know that the father of the Buddha begged him to do nothing of the sort.

Christianity, then, soon became a religion based upon the idea of guilt, remorse and personal expiation of the most drastic kind. Belief in the Vicarious Atonement lost its consoling power. When taught by people who are themselves filled with dread and haunted by the conviction of sin, such doctrine strengthens every neurotic tendency in the mind. All neurotics accumulate an appalling amount of cruelty and spite, while the frustration of their deepest instincts gives rise as well to bitter envy. It was no wonder that persecution seemed desirable. For not only did the heathen escape the fear of hell during their lives, but according to the Church's teaching they avoided its pains as well. Those who have had no chance of accepting Christian doctrines will spend eternity in purgatory, but are spared the everlasting flames and the lakes of burning pitch. To the unconscious minds of the guilty who thought themselves damned, they must have been objects of the most galling envy. To offer them the chance of salvation under pain of death would be doubly delightful, since if they refused the offer they would go straight to hell.

It may be added that the disproportionate number of wars fought by Christians all the world over is itself sufficient evidence to show that, as taught, their religion has encouraged rather than prevented the generation of hostility in mankind. These are the main reasons why, during ages in which ascetic doctrines prevail, men turn either to savage and useless forms of self-punishment, or to equally savage attacks upon their neighbours.

Self-punishment is useless because however strongly the penitent may feel driven to resort to it, it does nothing in the long run to produce either charity towards others or peace of mind. It may or may not be followed by a short period in which tension is relaxed, but no punishment can remove the original frustration.

On the contrary the suffering it inflicts is unconsciously resented in its turn, and in its turn engenders fresh guilt and fresh anxiety. The morbid mechanism moves in a vicious spiral.

During the dark and early middle ages Europe was occupied with thoughts of death and doom to an extent which now seems to us fantastic. In church after church the Dance of Death or the terrors of hell were depicted with all the force that can be given by gnawing fears. It is not surprising that manners were violent or that the grossest carnal sins were common. Pleasure, as we shall see later, is an antidote to fear, and guzzling and heavy drinking in particular alleviate sexual deprivation. When the whole world of sex has become a nightmare one form of mortal sin becomes no more heinous than another. The bad monks who were so hated by their contemporaries deserve a great deal more sympathy than they have ever been given. None of us can say that in their places we might not have reacted as they did.

In such circumstances, reason, which should have precluded the whole monstrous misconception, is employed in tortuous attempts to show that evil is good and to prove the impossible. It is because these conceptions underlay to a greater or less degree the whole of the thought and feelings of those times, that this spirit seems to us so alien and remote. Only the touch of the neurotic which there is in all of us enables us to maintain a link with them. It is easier for a modern man to follow the mind of an early Chinese philosopher than that of a Christian mystic of the same date.

Lest the reader should think that the whole of this argument is a gross exaggeration, I will give one example of the forces at work during the period when asceticism dominated Europe.

Generally it was admitted that there are degrees of virtue, and that those too weak to embrace absolute chastity might marry if they chose to take the risk. But family affection, which alone makes domestic life tolerable, was regarded as a snare to entrap the soul, the whole of whose love should be centred upon God. Numerous legends were current of penitents who were ordered to drown an only child in order to prove that they did not offend in this way.[1]

---

[1] Lecky quotes from Tillemont the case of a man called Mutius who wished to enter a monastery. He abandoned his possessions and, accompanied by his son, a boy of eight, he asked for admission. "The monks received him, but they proceeded to discipline his heart. 'He had already forgotten that he was rich ; he must next be taught to forget that he was a father.' His little child was separated from him, clothed in dirty rags, subjected to every form of gross and wanton hardship, beaten, spurned, and ill-treated. Day after day the father was compelled to look upon his boy wasting

There were hundreds of similar legends in the monkish chronicles, and it is possible that not a single one of them was true. What is true is that men like Mutius were held up to universal admiration and thought to set an example of the highest Christian conduct.

It will be objected at once by any fair-minded person that both the Christian and the Buddhist churches have produced throughout their histories numbers of gentle saints as well as aggressive fanatics and self-made martyrs. Buddhist populations indeed are sometimes, though not always, peaceful. Freud quotes St. Francis as the type of human being who is able to sublimate his sexual impulses in adoration of God and loving-kindness towards all God's creatures. But as we saw in Chapter 5 it does not follow that the rest of mankind are capable of the same renunciation, even though they strive to achieve it with the whole of their might. The capacity to sublimate in any particular instance varies widely from individual to individual. We are beginning to understand the methods by which this capacity may be used to the full; even so it seems safe to say that so complete a change in the direction of sexual desire is possible, and will remain possible, only for a very few. It seems to be easier for women than for men, provided that they can discover a satisfactory outlet for their maternal feelings, and that these play a major part in their sexuality. Otherwise they become warped. The " faded spinster," the " soured " or " prurient " old maid, the silly creature who runs from one craze to another, are a feature of English life which we take for granted. We are so used to these spectacles that we do not stop to consider what a terrible thing it must be to find one's personality slowly twisting itself into a pattern of frustration. Courage and reticence often mask the suffering endured, though no one who has received the confidence of many women can doubt its reality or its extent.

Further it must be remembered that our contemporaries are not denied the remaining normal pleasures. They are free to adore substitutes for husbands and children, to enjoy their

away with sorrow, his once happy countenance forever stained with tears, distorted by sobs of anguish. ' But yet,' says the admiring biographer, ' though he saw this day by day, such was his love for Christ, and for the virtue of obedience, that the father's heart was rigid and unmoved. He thought little of the fears of his child. He was anxious only for his own humility and perfection in virtue.' At last the abbot told him to take his child and throw it into the river. He proceeded, without a murmur or apparent pang, to obey, and it was only at the last moment that the monks interposed, and on the very brink of the river saved the child. Mutius afterwards rose to a high position among the ascetics, and was justly regarded as having displayed in high perfection the temper of a saint." (Op. cit. Chapter 4.)

comforts, and to occupy themselves in an increasing number of ways.

Men are less fortunate. Those who really succeed in controlling their resentment, who do not fall back on some form of perversion, do not become selfish, fussy, crabbed or bitterly ambitious, may develop into gentle, kindly, absent-minded men who are widely loved. But as a rule they use up so much energy in maintaining unnatural repressions that little is left for the conduct of their lives. The wilderness or the monastery provided a useful refuge for them ; but their refuge was also their coffin.

To ask such fundamental readjustments of the rest of mankind, especially under pain of damnation is to apply a form of pressure which is certain to damage the mind. The Catholic Church now recognises this by refusing admission to the priesthood or the cloister to those who show no signs of a vocation. But this does not alter the fact that many ascetic cravings and ideas are still, by tradition, reverenced as saintly and adopted as moral ideals by people for whom they are totally unsuited.

The believer is likely to answer here that what cannot be done by man of his own nature can be done by the gift of God's grace which it is our duty to seek. To rely upon this argument is to ignore the fact that millions, when they fell into temptation, have implored that they might be preserved from sin, but grace has not been given. To say, with St. Luke, that they did not pray aright, is not an answer. They prayed as best they could.

Psychologists are agreed that the attempt to suppress completely powerful instincts and natural tendencies is likely to result in mental disease. To the devout believer this, too, will not seem to matter. He will share the opinion of a writer in *The Times* who said : " If we must become mental cripples for Christ's sake, let us do so gladly." This conclusion could only be believed by one who was ignorant of the terrible implications of mental disease, of its direct connection with the worst sins and excesses of which human beings have been guilty. A neurosis is, it is true, a defence against unbearable guilt and anxiety ; but if only on account of the hatred generated it is the worst possible defence. To set up an unattainable ideal and demand that a man should scourge himself towards it, is to do a dangerous disservice not only to him but to everyone whom he influences or with whom he comes into contact. Moral effort is required of us all, but it should be directed towards attainable goals, and take account of the actual results which it produces. This is to say that it should function under the control of reason.

Once an irrational and neurotic view of life has become incorporated into the common traditions of a sect it is extremely difficult to eradicate. And the results of mediaeval asceticism influence our minds to this day. Its social effects fall outside the scope of this volume : its moral attitudes have not yet been outgrown. Few of us are not affected by them, even though we may be convinced that they are mistaken. It is interesting, for instance, to find that a rationalist like Lecky, writing in the year 1869, repeatedly using phrases such as this : " . . . we have an innate, intuitive, instinctive perception that there is something degrading in the sensual part of our nature . . . something that we could not with propriety ascribe to an all-holy being." And it is probable that in spite of the superficial change in our attitude towards sex that has taken place within the last quarter of a century, nine out of every ten Englishmen and women have feelings of this sort lurking in the depths of their minds. We call them " the Puritan conscience." Sensuality is dangerous—to be deplored or even thrust out of mind. Such people are irritated or disgusted by the suggestion that like any other powerful force it must be understood before there is any chance of controlling it wisely.

The main reason for these feelings is of course fear of one's own sexual impulses. One is avoiding intense anxiety by refusing to admit that they need satisfaction, and to face the problem and consider it in the light of knowledge and of reason would disturb an arrangement which one may believe to be one's only possible protection.

Unfortunately, as I have said, once fears of this sort are implanted in the mind of a race many factors combine to maintain their strength. To begin with neurotics in each generation act as foci of infection, rediscover the false values anew, and preach them without external encouragement.

Historically speaking there has been more than encouragement ; there has been moral compulsion. They have been handed down from parents to children, expounded to congregations under threat of eternal damnation, and driven home with every type of argument likely to produce anxiety and guilt. Dicta such as " All sensual pleasures are displeasing to God " ; " The fires of hell are burning bright for YOU ! " ; adjurations to search the mind for the slightest vestige of an impure thought, as black to the infinite righteousness of God as the foulest deed—all these efforts to inspire terror and increase the burden of guilt, when continued for centuries leave their mark upon the human mind. Of its own nature it will feel guilty enough, and the piling on of agony only warps it. The actual conduct of those exposed to this sort of teaching is proof enough of the fact that it fails to produce perfect goodness. Christians may have shivered with fear, but they sinned all the same.

As opposed to all this, actual experience shows that everyday virtue is found most usually among people who are reasonably happy and lead normal lives. They may not spend most of their time in wrestling against the forces of evil, but that is because they are not tempted to do anything which by the standards of their community can be reasonably called cruel or filthy, and are not attempting to achieve unattainable standards. In the same way it is when laws are reasonable and administered in a kindly fashion that crime diminishes, and during eras of common sense and tolerance that we find marked improvements in general behaviour. We may contrast with this the attempts that are sometimes made to tighten up morals without at the same time dealing with the root problem of anxiety. Instances are the crusade of Savonarola, the Rule of the Saints under Cromwell, and the puritanical regulations put into force by both Fascists and Nazis when first they came into power in various countries. Such efforts lead, as a rule, either to a reaction after which morals are in a worse state than before, or to outbreaks of cruelty and violence. Fear and guilt are poisons. In very small amounts they may act as tonics, but one must be extremely careful about the dosage.

The two points that emerge from this data are first that the factors which govern the lives of churches are of a kind to produce from time to time vast and irrational changes of attitude towards moral questions. Sometimes there will be a shift of emphasis; at others actual reversals of opinion.

Secondly, the quarrel of the psychologist with many exponents of religion is not merely that they ask men to accept impossible and inconsistent beliefs, thereby damaging mental integrity. It is also addressed to the fact that many of their teachings tend to warp the emotional life and encourage morbid tendencies where they do not precipitate actual mental disease.

So much for the theologians: we may now ask ourselves whether the philosophers can give us better guidance.

CHAPTER 9

THE PHILOSOPHERS (1)

Confucius and the Greeks

One of the main contentions of this book has been that without scientific knowledge of the workings of the human mind it is impossible to form an accurate conception of ethical problems, let alone to solve them. This seems to me incontrovertible. It does not mean, however, that all previous attempts at finding solutions are valueless. The literature of Ethics includes some of the greatest books ever written, books which have inspired generation after generation and can still be read with profit and delight. Truths which can only be proved by the methods of science can, and often have been, perceived by men of wisdom. Many of the great moralists of the past not only realised the defects of the moral sanctions and systems of their day but reached conclusions which, even though their grounds were faulty, we can accept as true.

Whenever civilisation reached a certain point (with the important proviso that thought was free) thinkers arose who attempted to base morality upon rational principles. We find such men in China throughout her earlier history; in Greece and Rome between the fifth century B.C. and the rise to power of Christianity, and in Protestant Europe after the Reformation. The Chinese, it is true, did not appeal in terms to reason, but based their statements upon the authority of the past. Even Confucius called himself one who handed on the ancient sayings, not an innovator. But his conclusions and those of his followers were in fact reached by the use of someone's reason instead of being based upon a claim to supernatural inspiration or power. They are common-sense deductions derived from facts or what were supposed to be facts, and for these reasons their authors may be claimed as rationalists.

It seems natural to expect that the ideas of such men will show closer agreement than moral codes attributed to supernatural sources. And in fact they do. Confucius and the Greek philosophers, Kant, the Utilitarians and Sidgwick, all wanted men to behave after much the same pattern. They differed in particulars, some of which were important, but more about such matters as the ultimate ends which human beings pursue and the springs of moral conduct, than about the kind of life which good men ought to lead. There is no such discrepancy between personal ideals as we find between Christian and Buddhist monks seeking to extinguish all human desires, the Mohammedan warrior fighting his way towards an eternity of houris, the Hindu with his child marriage and suttee, and the Christian employer of the Industrial Revolution. The philosophers who fall outside this group, from Lao-tz'u to Sorel and the Fascist apologists, either ignore or explicitly reject the authority of reason.

This pleasing accord between moralists is not due entirely to the reasonable nature of their theories. It follows also from the fact that philosophers are philosophers—beings who place small value upon sensual satisfaction and prefer thinking to other human occupations. Learning, frugality, moderation, contempt for money, make a strong appeal to men of this type, and as a rule they feel strongly that everyone else should share these preferences. They preach moderation, but on this point they are often immoderate. They fail to realise that what appears cogent or attractive to them may seem senseless or repellant to others. Or rather, where this is realised, the masses, the common herd, the unthinking mob, are regarded as totally inferior. Kant thought that the most inspiring aspects of Nature were the starry heavens above and the Moral Law within. He may be right, but a great many people prefer a glass of wine.

I make this point because it accounts, in part, for the slight influence exercised by many excellent writers upon Ethics.

Again, philosophers are fond of Absolutes and Ultimates and tend to regard Particulars as unsatisfactory until they have been resolved into some impressive Universal. They demand, for instance, a Purpose for Life which is somehow to express and sum up the very various purposes which occupy, inspire and sometimes content individuals. And for this reason we find them often enough running away from reality precisely when they feel themselves to be whole-heartedly in search of it. Plato and his Form of the Good, Hegel and his Absolute Idea, are only two among many instances.

They tend, too, being what they are, to undervalue woman and the part played by them in the development of children's characters and family life as well. And this again is one of the reasons why their carefully thought-out systems of education have been ineffective. It may be objected that Plato did not undervalue his female Guardians—but except when with child or giving birth he ignored their feminine attributes.

So much for one of the causes of agreement between the ideals of the rational moralists. As for their disagreements—where great thinkers differ, the divergence can often be traced to one of two causes. The first is the limitations of contemporary knowledge : the second the influence of their own unconscious tendencies. There is no need to say much about the first. No man can be completely uninfluenced by the ideas of his age. We are all in danger of mistaking what is local and temporary for what is universal and inevitable. The view of an anthropologist, for instance, about life in an English village would startle, if it did not horrify, anyone but another anthropologist.

Philosophers share this disadvantage. It is due to no virtue of ours that centuries of recorded history and the spread of education have widened our views about methods of organising states. Nor does it give us the right to call Plato a Fascist.

It is not possible to say much of a general nature about unconscious personal factors. They may be looked for whenever a man who is clearly possessed of a logical mind, and not devoid of information which might have led him to a different conclusion, advances senseless, eccentric or invalid theories. Some powerful, unrecognised wish or fear has overcome his reason. Such are perhaps Confucius's obsession with ceremonial, Plato's horror of new rhythms, the Cynic's contempt for propriety and the opinion of one's fellows. Unconscious guilt is at the bottom of all claims that pleasure is necessarily dangerous and degrading, since it is a matter of common observation that happy human beings are kinder and less to be feared than those who are wretched. We all know that the man who has enjoyed a good dinner is more tolerant, dispassionate and amenable to reason than he who has come home hungry to find that his wife is out and that there is nothing to eat in the house.

On the whole we may say that philosophers are more free than the common man from the run of vulgar errors, but just as helpless as he is to realise and eliminate their deep, unconscious prejudices. They do not believe a thing just because others believe it, but are no more able than they to see through a brick wall without the special apparatus that now makes this possible.

In spite of all these influences there is a likeness, and a substantial likeness, between the ideas of the greater moralists so long as they are using their reasons. For since reason is the faculty by which man adjusts his ideas and feelings to the outer world, those who use it correctly will find themselves facing the same problems and reaching the same conclusions, provided that their outer worlds are not too different.

What then are these conclusions? Roughly—very roughly, if you like—they express what we call nowadays the humanitarian system of values, or part of it, and without agreeing altogether with Aristotle's dictum that the way to discover moral truths is by a careful comparison of moral opinions—since all existing opinions may be very largely wrong—still we may allow that such a comparison can be interesting. Therefore in this chapter and the next I propose to make one. For the particular purpose of this book it will be confined to a few leading thinkers, and to the points at which their teachings approached or fell away from what we are too apt to regard as modern or exclusively Christian doctrines. In the space available this can only be done through wide generalisations whereby the teeth of scholars must be set on edge. Scholars have the right of the matter; such a procedure is deplorable. But it cannot be helped.

The earliest and certainly one of the most influential of all the world's great moralists was Confucius. To write anything at all about the The Sage unless one is a Chinese scholar is certainly presumptuous. To begin with, the various English translations of his works differ considerably. Next, it is impossible for the unlearned to decide how much of the teaching which is attributed to him came in fact from his mouth.[1] If, after much hesitation, the promptings of caution have been disregarded here, it is because what interests a student of Ethics is not so much the historical truth about one particular man, as the popular conception of his doctrine and personality. Just as the inquirer into Christianity will concern himself with the Bible as we know it and the Christian churches, rather than with the findings of the Higher Criticism, so the codes to which the teachings of Confucius gave rise are more important for our present purpose than an exact estimate of the man himself. If his followers added their insight to his and gave concrete application to some of his general principles, it shows us what effect his doctrines had on the minds of those who adopted them.

As Confucius is still only a name to most Europeans, it may

[1] The truth can be obtained, so far as *The Analects* is concerned, and so far as it is known, from Mr. Arthur Waley's translation.

be as well to say a few words about his background and his life. He was born in 551 B.C., eighty years before Socrates, at a time when one of the greatest and longest-lived of the Chinese dynasties was breaking up. It was an age of rebellions and civil disorder, or corrupt and inefficient administration, and one in which the heads of principalities were setting a poor example to their subjects. The task which Confucius set himself was to discover how order might be restored, administration improved and behaviour rectified. With the only civilisation that he knew falling into chaos round him it was not unreasonable that he should envisage this process as a return to the great standards of the past.

The history of his life is simple. He was a scholar, a historian, and for a time a minor government official. But most of his time—like the majority of Asiatic sages—he spent wandering about China with a small band of disciples, teaching and answering questions, but searching always, after the custom of the age, for a prince who would take him as his adviser and adopt his theories. In this endeavour he failed, and when he was nearly seventy he returned to his native state of Lu and devoted himself to writing and study, a much disappointed man.

His teachings, however, lived on in his disciples, in the book of his sayings known to us as *The Analects* and the others which make up the Confucian Canon. Some centuries later these were adopted as the official moral code and an outline of them taught to every schoolboy, no matter to what religion he belonged. Later again it was decided that all officials must learn the whole Canon by heart, and this custom persisted until the Chinese Revolution of 1910. It seems to be universally agreed that it is largely to this solid core of moral teaching that China owes the stability of her culture and the power which she has shown of absorbing conqueror after conqueror and imposing upon them her customs and her particular civilisation.[1]

Perhaps the first point to notice about his teaching is that he envisaged the problems of morality in the same way as the Greek philosophers of the fourth century—namely as the double task of defining and securing the good man in the good society. These two ends he regarded as inseparable. And it is for this reason that he devoted a great deal of thought to the duties and functions of

---

[1] For further particulars about Confucius, the reader may be referred to *Confucianism and the Modern World* by Dr. Percival Yetts; the preface to Dr. Legge's translation of the Chinese Classics; *The Sayings of Confucius* by Lionel Giles, *The Greater Learning* written by Confucius's grandson, and, of course, *The Analects* itself in both its versions.

rulers. But they misjudge him entirely who suppose, as many seem to do, that his moral teachings were merely a code of behaviour for officials. On the contrary, the key-note of his doctrine was the importance of personal and individual virtue, and if he speaks much about officials it is because he believed that all good men should play some part in public affairs. For good government depends upon the goodness of those who govern.

This he taught, not only because it seemed as clear to him as it did to Plato that the security and welfare of the state depends upon wise and upright administration, but because it follows logically from two of his cardinal beliefs. The first is that virtue is promulgated very largely through the force of personal example, and the second that before a man can properly fulfil his personal obligations, he must first have purified and controlled his character.

These beliefs are so vital to the teaching of Confucius that something must be said about them. Instruction, education, he knew to be necessary. As we shall see he considered that knowledge and wisdom are the basis of the virtuous life. Men cannot be expected to know what is right without study. But the way to bring others to virtue is to practise it, first in one's inner life, then in one's family relations, and then, proceeding outwards, in all other spheres of duty.

He says in *The Analects*—from which most of the excerpts which I shall give are taken : " If a ruler show rectitude in his own personal character, even without his directions things will go well. If he be not upright, his directions will not be complied with." This is to give his doctrine in its most extreme form, and it must be qualified, here and always, by his insistence that the ruler must choose his advisers for their learning, wisdom and experience as well as for their virtue.

If, for the reasons already given, Confucius stresses the case of the ruler, he lays the same obligation to set a good example upon all those who seek to live good lives, and makes it, in fact, the main reason why men should strive after virtue. When one of his disciples asked him why this should be done he replied : " To improve oneself and for the sake of others. For by the spread of virtue from one man to another we should at last arrive at the brotherhood of man."

It is a fact too much neglected in the modern world that moral values are in the main taken over from others just as Confucius supposed. Unfortunately, as we have seen, the process is not so simple as he thought it. The influence of the virtuous may be rejected, and that with violence. Further, a certain degree of rebellion against authority, and especially the parents' authority, is essential to healthy growth. It is part of the effort which must be made by us all before we can achieve independence of mind. Lastly, in all but a world of static perfection, ability to rebel may be of considerable social value. Nevertheless, if every parent were as virtuous, as wise and loving as Confucius would have him be, the number of evil-doers would undoubtedly diminish.

In pursuance of this theory the Sage urged his disciples to make friends with the upright, the sincere, men of knowledge and experience. " In whatsoever land you live, serve under some wise and good man, and make friends with the more humane of its men of learning."

This is excellent advice for those who are attracted by the learned and the humane. Unfortunately, as we saw in Chapter 5, the possession of power, legends of great achievements, good or bad, the promise of advantage in this world or the next, the gift of " putting across " one's personality, even the ability to sin and glory in it, have commanded and always will command, the allegiance of considerable sections of the human race. A good example is essential in childhood, but the excessive reliance which came to be placed on it proved a serious weakness in the Chinese system of government.

There has been a great deal of controversy about whether or not Confucius believed in a personal God. It is not a matter about which I feel able to form an opinion. But it is certain that he did not derive morality from man's relation to God, or believe that Heaven was interested in the personal affairs of individuals or held them to account for their actions. When questioned on the subject of Heaven and the spirits he advised his followers not to trouble their heads about what they could not hope to understand. He would have disagreed completely with the Christian doctrines that not a sparrow falls to the ground without the knowledge of the Father, and that man can achieve goodness only through the Grace of God.

Confucius has held the devotion of millions not only through his teachings but on account of the nobility of his personal character. And whatever may be said about the pedantry and conservatism of modern Confucianism, it cannot be denied that his adherents, taken as a whole, have been as virtuous and as reasonable a body of men as any who have lived on this planet.

The Chinese, as a nation, are generally held to have failed in the political sphere. To accept this judgment is to ignore 3,000 years of Chinese history and concentrate on its last century. Even so, recent events in Europe and its state at the present time may make us ask ourselves whether we have done so much better. The central government of China has always tended to rely for its authority upon tradition and moral influence rather than the force of arms. When these influences failed the Empire fell into confusion. Again, moral example has never been found sufficient to prevent the spread of corruption among officials. But by those qualified to judge, this failure is attributed not to the teachings of Confucius but to the disruptive influence of negative creeds such as Buddhism, with its belief that the affairs of this world are illusory and unworthy of attention, and Taoism with its doctrines of non-interference and a return to nature.

What were the teachings of Confucius? Their foundation was the belief that the object of life is to illustrate virtue. " The life of man is his rectitude." Virtue has various aspects, but these are interwoven. The chief are wisdom, love of one's fellow-men, justice, propriety, loyalty and moderation. Other good qualities depend upon these: courage without wisdom, for instance, may be mere turbulence—a belief shared by Plato.

To be virtuous one must first acquire knowledge of men and their behaviour. Without such knowledge it is of course difficult to be just, wise or even usefully kind.

After knowledge of men, comes knowledge of facts and events. In contrast to most other philosophers and all mystics he did not speculate about absolutes and infinites, nor rely upon contemplation in its religious sense. His ends were practical. We must " seek into the roots and causes of things." "To know the order of precedence of things is to be near the goal." His disciples are to be " versed in ancient lore and get to know modern knowledge." Then they may teach.

The most important part of knowledge is, of course, knowledge of virtue. Confucius did not believe, with the Greeks, that those who know what is right will do right, but lays it down that knowledge must be followed by appropriate action. " To know what is right and not to do it is moral cowardice."

Knowledge, then, is essential. Nevertheless it is useless unless controlled by good feeling. This is the second great aspect of virtue, summed up in the word Jin, which may be translated as love of one's fellows, goodwill, humaneness. Without Jin the other virtues are empty. When one of his disciples asked him : " Is there one word upon which the whole of life may proceed ? " he answered : " Is it not Jin ? " " What you do not yourself desire, do not do unto others. "

To this last precept he attached so much importance that we find it repeated several times, once in its positive form. Elsewhere he says that Virtue in a ruler consists not only in virtuous living, but in loving the people. Again when asked : " What is a right regard for one's fellow creatures ? " he replied, " It is love to man."

In sharp contrast to this the great Greek philosophers not only failed to link knowledge to love of one's fellows, they thought very little about the importance of good feeling. Socrates said that one must be good to one's friends, or one cannot expect their good offices in return. Plato's Guardians were to love their city, but it never seems to have entered his head that they should love its inhabitants. Aristotle, while considering that mutual kindness was hardly a virtue, recognised that it is an indispensable element of human well-being, and a bond of union between members of a state. But this is a long way short of loving one's neighbour, since one may act kindly for many reasons besides love.

Christ, on the other hand, while emphasising to the full, and in the very words of Confucius, the importance of love and kindly conduct, placed no value upon any knowledge but that of His Father's will and, by implication, knowledge of Moses and the Prophets. He looked to simpleness of heart and taught that salvation may be achieved by two things : " Unless ye become as little children ye shall not enter the Kingdom of Heaven," and " Believe upon Me, and ye shall be saved." He left to Caesar the problems of dealing with human society.

This attitude, taken with his doctrine of non-resistance to evil, has left a gap in Christian thought which made room for many surprising developments in Christian practice. The Founder of a religion for the meek and lowly, sinners and the poor, gave nowhere any directions for the use of power, the conduct of states or the administration of public affairs. Had he done so, it seems hardly possible that the Church of Christ would have grabbed so eagerly after temporal power and riches, or organised itself upon so rigidly authoritarian a model. Duties to the poor became narrowed to the giving of alms, tending a few of their sick, and ensuring their religious orthodoxy. Everything else was left to the various states, whose authority was supported, for good or bad, so long as they paid tribute, and their rulers neither quarrelled with the Pope nor encroached upon the spheres of faith and morals. Christ has been spoken of as the champion of the oppressed, but he was their champion only in a spiritual sense. He never considered the problem of their rights as against their rulers, far less encouraged any notion of rebellion. It is impossible not to regret this lack of guidance.

To return to the teachings of Confucius : The next virtue that calls for comment is that of propriety. By it he means preservation of the right relations between members of families and states, decency, and observance of ceremonial. No one with wide experience of life will doubt the value of such knowledge and observance. Even etiquette has important uses. But no other great thinker has ever stressed these things as strongly, and to us this aspect of his teaching must seem not only mistaken but productive of bad results. Filial piety by which he meant complete loyalty, docility and obedience—he judged to be the fundamental virtue of home life, which leads on to good government. This conclusion he deduced from the fact, correct in itself, that the man who feels this obligation strongly will never turn against his rulers nor foment rebellion for his own advantage. Now he himself says that a ruler, even the Emperor, holds the Mandate of Heaven only so long as he continues to govern well. When he fails in this duty the Mandate is withdrawn automatically, and it becomes not only the right but the duty of his subjects to replace him by somebody better. But the completely docile child is also the completely docile subject, who will acquiesce in any government unless his father happens to have been opposition-minded.

Again, lifelong subservience of children to parents, women to men and younger to elder, entails so much frustration that it engenders very deep resentment, even if this be repressed. That it does is shown by the element of sadistic cruelty that runs through Chinese life, cropping up in their love of fantastic tortures, the institution of foot-binding, and the merciless despotism, within each household, of the old woman who survived through sheer toughness to find herself at its head. No amount of love, of duty, of conventionality, can prevent a daughter from hating a mother who slowly and painfully cripples her. And the more wicked hating one's mother is felt to be, the more damage will be done to the personality. It is no wonder that a Chinese philosopher wrote that family life is intended to teach men patience and endurance.

In the passionate desire of Confucius to secure order at all costs we have a clear case of the great thinker who is blinded by the conditions of his age. He had every excuse. The Chinese state was, so far as he knew, the only pattern of civilised living in the world. Nor could he look back upon older civilisations which had fallen into dust, only to give place to new ones. For a man in his position to watch the break-up of good government, the abandonment of right living, the decay of the arts and a growing neglect of learning, must have been to confront despair.

And, of course, had it been possible for men to return *en masse* to the outlook and conduct of bygone generations, the state might have been saved by a good ruler. But as we know now from studying the downfall of many dynasties and many empires, men do not in practice retrace their steps in this way. To adjure them merely to look back is not an effective stimulus. Only new ideas, or what seem like new ideas because they are expressed in new language, " given a fresh slant," will arrest corruption and disintegration and turn the minds of peoples into a constructive path. The times change, and ideologies must seem to change with them.

But even when all allowance has been made for his background and the limitations of his information, it seems clear that Confucius was abnormally impressed by the importance of stereotyping behaviour and in particular by the necessity for performing rites and ceremonies. One book of the *Analects* is composed of descriptions given up to describing trifles of the Master's behaviour—how he held his robe when he walked, how many bows he made and the rest of it. One of these should appeal to the English gentry—when he went hunting he never shot at a sitting bird.

Rites and ceremonies have their uses both in the life of the individual and that of the group. They rouse effective memories, and express and confirm national unity. Hitler used them to produce the impression of mass agreement and irresistible power. But their chief personal function is that they enable us to work off in a disguised form some of the impulses which we cannot endure to reveal directly. Some men will attach undue value to types of ceremonial behaviour which they find useful in this way.

Another of the major Confucian virtues was moderation ; the last is trustworthiness. A man must stand by his word, once given. According to Mr. Waley this is all that any Chinamen means by characters which have often been translated as " candour" and "sincerity." No doubt he is right. Confucius's warning to " beware of the subtly perverse, the artfully pliant and those of twisted speech " implies a condemnation of twisted speech, but it is not for me to argue the point. Telling the truth had not the prestige in the ancient world which it enjoys today ; neither Moses nor the Greeks paid much attention to it. Aristotle thought that a virtuous man would be truthful on the whole. But then his high-minded man was assumed to be in a tolerably safe position.

Socrates spoke the truth as he saw it, though he was unwittingly a twister of arguments. (It is doubtful whether Confucius and Socrates would have liked one another.) Plato defines truthfulness as a determination never voluntarily to receive what is false, but to hate it and love the truth. This, though perhaps more important than what we call truthfulness, is not the same thing. To speak the truth is not always practicable in a tyrannous society, riddled by spies and informers. Even the most fanatical believer in truthfulness would hardly have expected members of resistance movements to be sincere with the Gestapo. Indeed the Greeks as a whole, like the Chinese, seem to have admired successful weavers of plots and stratagems.

These are I think, the main aspects of Confucius's description of virtue. Apart from his mania for ceremonies and blind obedience it is rational and practical and clear. And it was found for centuries by millions of educated people to give them the moral guidance which they needed. It is customary to attack it on the ground that it does not satisfy the religious instinct. It was not intended to do so : Confucius believed that speculation about the supernatural should be checked rather than encouraged.

When we turn to the Greek moralists we find that it is much more difficult to discover what they meant by virtue or " the good." Socrates maintained that every good must be good for something, and one school of his disciples took it for granted that by this he must mean good for producing happiness, since, they thought, happiness is what all men desire. This assumption, however, is by no means certain, and others of his followers thought it almost the opposite of the truth. Socrates was extremely skilful at evading direct questions and refusing to be pinned down to definite statements.

Plato, whenever a definition seems within reach, tends likewise to slip away on to some side issue. And in this matter of the good he admits defeat as a moralist and retreats into metaphysics. In *The Republic* he says that the Idea or Form of the Good is the ideal which all knowledge implies; that it lies behind this changing world which is its manifestation, and that we can only understand it when we have perfect knowledge. Again, " it is the cause of all that which is right and beautiful in all things, producing in the visible world light and the lord of light, and being itself lord in the intelligible world and the giver of truth and reason, and this Form of the Good must be seen by whosoever would act wisely in public or in private."[1]

These two statements may be felt as inspiring by philosophers but they hardly assist us to arrive at a conception of virtue.

He is more helpful, though again not in detail, when he discusses the nature of justice in Book 4 of the same work. Here, in order to support an invalid analogy between the structure of a city—which, he says, consists of rulers, soldiers and craftsmen—and the human mind, he lays it down that the soul of man is composed of three parts—the rational, the desiring and the spirited. (By the spirited he means that which is capable of indignation, moral or immoral.)

What he calls justice is the proper relation between these parts; the rational ruling, the spirited supporting it and the desires guided and controlled by both. Justice, therefore, is the health of the mind—a man's successful management of himself. The whole mind must be governed by reason, and there must be harmony between its parts. These are the identical conclusions later reached by Freud from his very different angle of approach. They have been of immeasurable importance in the history of European thought—sometimes the one sea wall which protected reason against the onslaught of neurotic superstition. But they do not give us a practical moral code, or assist in defining virtue.

Aristotle, on the other hand, did attempt to solve this difficult question. As everyone knows he taught that virtue is the mean between two extremes. And he expended much ingenuity in attempting to show that each of the individual virtues can be described after the same manner. It has generally been felt that most of this is mere juggling with words, the outstanding case being his famous definition of veracity as the mean between boastfulness and mock modesty. The whole argument serves, in the end, merely to stress the importance of moderation. And its

[1] *The Republic*—Book 7.

main interest today lies in the fact that it helps us to measure the distance we have travelled under the influence of biological conceptions.

Once we have learned to think of human behaviour as the interaction between an organism and its environment, the conception of separate " virtues," which a man can acquire or fail to acquire, is seen to be misleading. For instance courage is often praised as the essential virtue, since upon it depends the performance of all the others. This, by itself, is untrue. Millions of people are terrified by various forms of ill-doing ; virtue for them represents safety and freedom from anxiety. Strict sexual abstinence may be practised for no reason but fear. Some of us are afraid of being dishonest and others of being unkind. It all depends upon the way in which a man's conscience works.

Next, because a human being shows courage in one situation, it does not follow that he will always be brave. Men react differently to different stimuli. The man who will charge a machine-gun single-handed is unable to make a parachute jump. The best parachutist in the unit will refuse to jump because he has suddenly become suspicious of his wife's fidelity. The courage which will take risks is not the courage which can endure, whether it be endurance of pain or of anxiety. In short, to parcel out virtues under separate names is convenient but it does not correspond to the realities of human conduct.

On the other hand the value of any particular virtue varies with the circumstances. The values of peace are not those of war. The standards of a scientist cannot be those of a poet. That is to say, conduct cannot be judged in a vacuum, but only in relation to the environment taken at a particular point in time.

Perhaps the most direct comparison between Confucius, Plato and Aristotle can be made by considering their descriptions of what they mean by good men. The Superior Man of Confucius, Plato's Guardians, the High-minded Man of Aristotle, are not intended by their authors to fill precisely the same functions, but they do give us some idea of how those authors expected their systems to work out in practice. That all were aristocrats of one sort or another is attributable to the ages in which their ideas were conceived. Permanent mass illiteracy involves permanent leadership from above ; but we may note that none of these three thinkers thought in terms of a hereditary caste. All men were eligible who had the necessary personal qualities.

Confucius, Socrates and Plato all thought of the good man

as playing a useful part in his state or his city and so practising virtue for the sake of others as well as for his own. It is perhaps a pity that we do not post up some of the things that they said in the meeting-places of public bodies and on the hoardings during elections. "He is the greatest of all impostors who, possessed of no valuable qualifications, should deceive men by representing himself as capable of governing his country," was said by Socrates. Confucius said: "One should not be greatly concerned about being in office, but rather about one's fitness for such a position." But many of their remarks on this subject might have been made by either.

Similarly Confucius's "When the possibility of making a profit is seen, contemplate virtue," might well be quoted on the Stock Exchange.

Aristotle's ideal man on the other hand lived to himself and it sometimes strikes one that he might have been called "Portrait of the Artist in His Better Moments."

Of the three descriptions that of the Chinese sage approaches most closely to the notions of the modern humanist. Confucius thought that the Superior Man should be catholic minded, have a large and generous heart, and friendly feelings towards other human beings. He would make the most of their good qualities and not, as do common men, the worst of their bad ones. He would support the right wherever he found it, have regard for virtue when others think of mundane pleasures, and reveal himself in his just dealings with his fellows, including his enemies. Confucius would not have agreed that we ought to love our enemies.

Four qualities are essential to him. In private he is humble-minded; to his superiors respectful; in looking after the welfare of the people generous and kind; in the exaction of public services from the people, just.

He seeks self-improvement for its own sake and not for material benefit: "Even if a man had all the gifts of the Duke of Chou, if he were proud and avaricious the rest of his qualities would not be worthy of notice." He has seriousness of purpose, self-control, and an agreeable manner. He is modest in his words and profuse in his deeds. "The Superior Man is exacting of himself; the common man is exacting of others."[1]

He is not contentious and does not try to worst others—

[1] Cf. St. Simon's "doux pour les autres, sévère pour soi" said of the Duc de Bourgogne, and Henry Sidgwick's conclusion that a man should seek the happiness of others and excellence for himself.

Socrates might not have alienated the bulk of the Athenians as he did if he had been taught this maxim.

If we added to this description a sense of humour and a passion for sports and games it would fit in remarkably well with our English traditions. The Greeks, of course, did add gymnastics, and Confucius agreed with them in the civilising rôle which they allotted to music, of which he was extremely fond.

Besides this the high-minded man of Aristotle seems childish. He is a person who values himself as he deserves, is only moderately pleased by honour from men of repute, and instead of loving the people, despises the common herd. He loves to confer favours, but feels shame at receiving them. He shuns all subordinate positions, cares only for great affairs, fears no one, is generally candid, though ironic with the unfortunate common herd, is free from malice, does not gossip, is careless of the small concerns of life, not given to wonder or praise, and his walk is slow, his accents grave and his speech deliberate. What a man to have about the house !

After this it does not seem to matter that when the philosopher condescends to human affairs he must realise moral perfection. It would not occur to such a man that he missed it.

Beside this picture Plato's Guardians are human. They are fit to rule the city because they alone love it, and because they have studied the realities of justice, truth and temperance. Like the good official of Confucius they regard office as a duty, not as a prize to quarrel over or an opportunity for plunder. They are lofty-minded, gracious and courageous ; in short, compact of qualities which commend themselves until we come to the important sphere of human relations. Here Plato, like all his contemporaries, was affected by the homo-sexuality rampant at the time among the Greeks. He could not realise either that this was an abnormal state of affairs, or that it was directly connected with the treachery, bitterness and continual warfare which disfigured political life. The idea that the good home is the chief source of national strength did not occur to him. His Guardians were to be bred for their work as well as trained for it, but he had no inkling of the part played in a child's development by wise and affectionate parents. And since he did not consider it necessary for a ruler to love the people, but only virtue and the city, he would not have appreciated the importance of the discovery that all loving and kindly impulses towards our fellow men are closely connected with the healthy growth of family affection

The children of his Guardians, suckled by any mother among them whose breasts were filled, brought up in batches by nurses and taken to watch battles, would have turned out a great disappointment to him and a disaster for their city.

The downfall of Greek civilisation has been attributed to various causes, among them malaria. But a contributory factor is certainly the restless enmity, forever issuing in violence, which is characteristic of the Greek homo-sexual types.

Good feeling is in fact an essential element in good government, for only sympathy and fellow feeling can give that insight into the suffering of others, that respect for their human dignity and value, which prevent power from corrupting. The people must be loved, or they will be despised, and it is a very short step from despising one's inferiors to treating them badly. In the same way good feelings towards equals must exist, or it will not be there when the times of stress demand co-operation. One must also be able to trust, and be loyal to, superiors who deserve it, or faction fights will break out even with the enemy at the gates.

From a moralist's point of view this under-valuation of good feeling constitutes the most important difference between Confucius and the Greek thinkers. This apart, a book could be filled with beliefs which they held in common.

Their methods, of course, were utterly different. Confucius laid down the law, and left his followers to reflect upon what he had said. This is one of the reasons why his sayings repay a patient study—he wished his disciples to work out their implications, and thus develop the virtues of thoroughness and perseverance, and the habit of thinking for themselves.

But this does not mean that he spun his conclusions, like Spinoza, from absolutes and his inner consciousness. He did not. His teachings were based upon a wide knowledge of history, of ancient and modern thought, and his own varied and practical experience of politics and men. Nothing in his work is more impressive to western readers than the depth of his insight into human nature and the universal application of his maxims. Nevertheless he taught as one having authority.

Socrates on the other hand argued incessantly, drawing endless analogies, it is true, but not heeding that they were largely imperfect; treating his questioners as adversaries, and seeking to constrain minds rather than to inform them. The more constructive intellect of Aristotle gleaned from this procedure the logical principle of induction—one of the most important steps in human thought, and one that was never reached by the Chinese. Plato on the other hand failed to absorb this lesson. He believed what he wanted to believe, selected his facts to suit his conclusions, and, where facts failed him, went ahead without them. For all his learning, his nobility, the beauty of his writings, we are forced to feel that he knew very little about human life and had no real respect for evidence. For him the most fascinating of all activities were the study of metaphysics, the search for the nature of goodness, beauty and temperance. Therefore those men were the best who spent their lives in this endeavour. Therefore they, being best and possessed of the most important sorts of knowledge, alone were fit to rule. But the truth is that while the study of philosophy may steady a man's principles and be incompatible with certain types of baseness, it is no guarantee of political sagacity or practical wisdom, or the ability to handle one's fellow men.

A similar contrast between Plato and Confucius appears in their pictures of the good state. Plato is concerned with its structure Confucius with the conditions of life of its population. His attitude on this aspect is best summed up in a passage in one of the books of the Confucian Canon in which he described the golden age of Ta Tung, or world brotherhood. He did not write it himself, but it is consonant with everything that he said upon the subject.[1] These dozen lines are worth consideration even by us today.

[1] Quoted from *Confucianism and the Modern World* by Dr. Percival Yetts. "Under these blissful conditions the Empire existed for the good of the people. Virtuous and able men were chosen as rulers, men who cultivated sincerity of speech and kindliness in their relations with all. The people, in extending their loving devotion to their own families, were not forgetful of the interests of others. Maintenance was provided for the aged to the end of their lives; employment for the able-bodied; nurture for the young. Tender care was given to the widowed, the orphan, the childless, the sick. The right of men to the work that suited them, and of women to good homes, was recognised. The production of goods was so organised that nothing was wasted, while useless accumulations for private use were regarded with disapproval. Labour was so regulated that energy was stimulated, while activity for merely selfish reasons was discouraged. There was no room for the development of a narrow egotism. Such was the age of Ta Tung."

CHAPTER 10

THE PHILOSOPHERS (2)

The Value of Pleasure

Since Aristotle died no moral philosopher has exercised an influence comparable with his. Kant is read only by metaphysicians ; Hume and Hobbes, Butler, Locke and Bentham have never been esteemed as are the Greeks. The arbiters of moral opinion have been on the one hand Christ and Mohammed, Luther and St. Paul, on the other reformers in fields which are sometimes far removed from that of morals. Men like the Encyclopaedists, Darwin, Marx and Hitler so altered the direction of human thought that the currents of moral feeling were deflected. Nor was this effect invariably intended or foreseen.

From all the hundreds of issues which have occupied moralists during these two thousand years, I am picking out one and one only for discussion. This is the function and value of happiness and pleasure. It has been chosen for three reasons :—because it has a strong practical bearing upon our lives ; because until it has been decided many other enquiries must remain confused or in suspense, and because modern psychology enables us, for the first time, to understand the nature and bearings of the problem.

Is pleasure the only good, or a good at all ? Is it the ally or the enemy of virtue ? What are the relations between happiness and pleasure ? And is it true that we always seek pleasure whether we know it or not ? The answers to these questions are of radical importance.

The last is the easiest to dismiss. Every competent thinker is agreed that men seek other ends as well as pleasure, and further that pleasure is not even the principal goal of human effort. Long before any real research could take place into the factors which govern human behaviour, it had been realised that it is only after an action has been found to give pleasure that it can be performed for the sake of the pleasure it gives. Therefore many actions done for the first time are done for other reasons.

It is true that children are born with a tendency to grasp

immediate pleasure and to avoid pain, and that this tendency persists in the unconscious mind throughout life. But unless checked and corrected in the field of conscious behaviour it would lead to an early death. Infants are protected from it by the fact that they respond to few situations, and to those few with definite reactions common to all healthy members of the species. These will be persisted in through a considerable degree of pain. The baby continues to suck even when his mouth is sore, and screams at a terrifying noise even when he is punished for screaming. In short much of our behaviour is the result of instinctual dispositions by which we are driven whether we like it or not, and the pleasure which some of it brings is only an added inducement to repeat it. We fall in love because we are made as we are, and even when we resent the fact, and know that it can only bring us sorrow. In the same way, men do not become chronic drunkards for the pleasure of drinking more and more beer, although they may think they do. Fundamentally they drink because intoxication, while it lasts, blunts the fangs and claws of conscience. If this were not so we should all, when beer was available, be compelled to struggle perpetually against a temptation to drink too much.

Nor is this all. To minds loaded with guilt and anxiety pleasure may become suspect. " I don't deserve to enjoy myself—this is only a snare—I shall have to pay for it later on." As we have seen, those in this state of mind will welcome pain, screw down the safety-valves punish themselves, develop a corresponding amount of resentment, and thus frighten themselves into feeling more guilty than ever.

If we add to these considerations the fact that in normal men and women instincts which concern the preservation of the species are often more powerful than those which tend only to benefit the self, we shall have reasons enough for deciding that pleasure is not and never can be the only object of desire. But since the springs of our actions are often hidden from us there will always be those who believe it. As we all know it formed the basis of the first system of ethics to be published in England after the Reformation—Hobbes's *Leviathan*—and many will continue to argue that they would only save a drowning child if it gave them a kick to do so. It is true that they are not, in the main, people who would run much risk in order to save drowning children, for the doctrine forms a convenient cover for greedy and selfish behaviour.

To say that men seek other ends than pleasure is not to deny that pleasure is the only good. A great deal of human striving is directed towards foolish and unworthy objects, and to realise that we do not always pursue pleasure or even happiness does not debar us from believing that it might be better if we did. In fact this doctrine has had some very notable adherents.

Aristotle himself believed that all men seek happiness, and Epicurus stated that happiness is the only good and pain the only evil. According to both of them, happiness was to be obtained through a rational choice of pleasures. But one must admit that this doctrine only appealed to either because, being philosophers, they felt that the pleasures and pains of the mind are far more important than those which arise from the body, and maintained that the search for wisdom produces a state of mind which is the highest form of human well-being. (The same belief was held, more logically, by the Stoics and Cynics who denied the value of pleasure.)

This somewhat naïve attitude reduces the question of whether pleasure and happiness are good or bad to a theory without much practical importance. Nevertheless the point was argued by all concerned throughout its endless implications until the Church of Rome, centuries later, put an end to independent discussion.

But since the desire for pleasure, whatever we do about it, whether or not we repress it or associate it with guilt, will always activate the human mind, the controversy was bound to re-emerge as soon as thought was freed. By this time, however, the problem had changed its aspect. Earthly pleasures had become suspect to the Christian mind. If not positively dangerous and degrading, they were booby-traps placed on the road to heaven ; snares which distracted the soul from its only proper preoccupation, the means of salvation.

Nobody assumed any more that the best life consists in the search for truth and wisdom. On the contrary, such activity was regarded with suspicion unless the conclusions arrived at were strictly orthodox. To the vast majority of men the doubter, the persistent inquirer, seemed more wicked than the frank sensualist or the straightforward criminal. He was an offence to God and could not be harboured safely. By the beginning of the eighteenth century philosophers had gained a considerable degree of freedom —though Leibnitz is said to have turned his First Monad into God with a view to placating the church. But even they could not escape the effects of this change in the intellectual climate. In their works the best life is not discussed. It is no longer felt that educated men will do what they see to be right, so that our main task consists in thinking clearly until we have found out in what the good consists. The spiritual life as envisaged by the Christian fathers is a life of conflict, and it was in terms of conflicting forces that the new systems were worked out.

Secondly, the minds of Europeans were now soaked in the conception of the fall of man and universal sin, and with them the belief that only through remorse and suffering can sins be purged.

Thirdly, there was a general recognition of the power and importance of conscience. As we have seen, its functions were not yet understood, but its right to a certain authority was admitted.

The main result of this change of outlook was to place the pursuit of pleasure in the dock. As long as the search for wisdom was held to yield the best and greatest pleasure this could be avoided, but to the Puritan conscience to look askance at pleasure seemed common sense.

To us, their descendants, there appear to be certain grounds for this belief. We all know that certain pleasures are harmful, and that those who spend much of their time hunting after personal pleasure, even of a mild description, seldom lead what seem to the rest of us really virtuous lives. And since for centuries the odium deserved by some of its forms had been extended to all but a very few " innocent " pleasures, pleasure as a whole, and even " earthly happiness " found itself in the opposite pan of the scale from virtue. For the " innocent pleasures," though widely praised by all, are not by most men found to satisfy the whole of their natural instincts.

The opposing principles were therefore no longer ignorance and wisdom, but duty and conscience on the one hand, with pleasure or the more complex idea of self-interest thrown into opposition to duty. This was the general feeling, a feeling which still nags at the minds of most of the inhabitants of Britain.

Minds nourished upon the classics, however, could not remain content with it. They felt that pleasure, if not the only good, must be allowed a place among things that are good in themselves. And if pleasure—or only happiness—be a good, it cannot be wrong to seek it. Much of the thinking on this subject consisted, for this reason, of attempts to rehabilitate happiness at least, and to show that in moderate amounts and with adequate safeguards it is not incompatible with virtue.

This was no easy matter, especially for those who had been

taught to accept as final the authority of conscience. Morality meant for them that a man must do what he feels to be his duty. And this, unfortunately, only too often involves the renunciation of one's own well-being. But as writer after writer pointed out, from Clarke onwards, man did not make himself, and is so made that he must desire his own happiness. Therefore he has a right to expect, if he has done his duty, that a corresponding happiness will be his reward. Otherwise, as Kant puts it : " moral ideas would lose their compelling power." Or as we should say : the universe would be fundamentally unjust. Therefore duty and the pursuit of happiness—or self-interest—have somehow to be shown as interdependent and harmonious at bottom.

Little but historical interest attaches to most of the solutions put forward. They are based upon psychological entities which do not exist—innate ideas, boniform faculties, infallible moral intuitions, unnatural affections, natural ideas of propriety—invented by each thinker in order to balance his system and make it plausible. Stripped of their complications the more important of these theories fall into three main groups. They overlap, but, can be brought without, I hope, too much injustice, into the following classes :—

(*a*) The good are always happy and the evil are not, even though they seem to flourish.

This is flatly contradicted by the experience of mankind, and may be classed as wishful-thinking. Even those who indulge in it would shrink from the assertion that the amount of happiness experienced by each of us corresponds to the amount of virtue that we display. For this reason the theory does not appeal to philosophers—virtuous men, on the whole, who do not seem to be exuberantly happy. Bishop Butler came near to it when he talked of " the happy tendency of virtue in this world." But since it seemed clear that the search for happiness (called by him self-interest) must be guided by reason if it is to be successful, and since what is reasonable cannot be wrong, he was driven to the conclusion that we should follow self-interest, if reasonable, rather than conscience urging virtue. To use his own words : " If there ever should be, as it is impossible there ever should be, any inconsistency between them," self-interest must be preferred. We are not responsible for our own natures, and " our ideas of happiness and misery are of all our ideas the most important to us."[1] He did not state in so many words that reason must be the ruler

---

[1] Sermon 2.

of the mind, but on his premises he should have done so. Perhaps it was asking too much of a Bishop.

(*b*) Pleasure is the only good, and it must therefore be right to seek pleasure and get as much of it as one can.

As a moral doctrine, this breaks down at two points. The first is that unless we are prepared to admit that all forms of pleasure are equally good, we find ourselves judging it by a standard which is not merely its pleasantness. " Good " and " bad " mean something other than a mere quantitative measure of enjoyment. And morality is concerned not with enjoyment, but with the notions of good and bad.

Secondly, starting from this doctrine, there is no escape from an attitude of utter selfishness. And selfishness, whatever else it may be, is not what we mean by virtue. If I do not desire to seek the good of others, this theory cannot show me why I should.

Bentham tried to demonstrate that we secure our own happiness by adding to the general stock, so that " vice is a miscalculation of chances." Mill in attempting to bridge the same gulf was forced to rely upon a " natural feeling of unity with one's fellows " which he admitted to be absent from the natures of many men. Where Mill and Bentham failed it is unlikely that anyone else will succeed. " The greatest happiness of the greatest number " is an excellent motto, especially for governments, but it cannot be deduced from the statement that happiness is the only good.

The third solution is by far the commonest. It is the adoption of supernatural sanctions. If you believe that pleasure is the only good, you can, like Locke, believe in a divine Law-Giver who sees to it that those who obey his law gain most pleasure from it in the long run. Or, like Kant, you may reach the same conclusion from the opposite direction.

Kant considered that the moral law is self-sufficient, and that duty must be done for its own sake and for no other reason. Nevertheless this behaviour would not be rational unless an ultimate harmony exists between merit and happiness. And since he could not face the thought of an irrational universe, he allowed that we must posit both God and immortality in order that the injustices of this world may be righted in the next. This " felt want " he held to be the only evidence for the existence of either God or immortality.

No clearer example can be given of the man who clings to

dogmas which he would otherwise reject on account of their supposed influence upon morality.

This reinstatement of happiness as respectable was a valuable achievement, even though the methods used were open to objection. Happiness is a good, in spite of all the efforts made to persuade us that it is not. The Buddhists, the followers of Lao T'zu and the Stoics—to take only three examples—held or hold that the good man, the man set upon securing salvation, must free himself at every cost from the clutches of desire. Only by this means can Nirvana, communion with nature, or freedom from pain be achieved.

Christians believe—or should—that all desire must be directed towards doing the will of God. In theory this leaves room only for accidental happiness such as that gained from a fine day. And even that must not be allowed to preoccupy the mind too deeply. Any longings which conflict with God's will must be cast out, stamped out, and atoned for in suffering and shame.

This doctrine seemed logical enough until scientific study of the human mind began to show the effects which follow from such attempts. They may appear to succeed, but the surface of success covers an abyss of failure. Nature cannot be cast out with a pitchfork, nor primitive impulses got rid of by trying to destroy them. They must instead be adjusted to the requirements of civilised life by long and complex training. It would be absurd to pretend that we know in detail just how this can be done. Every human being is in some respects a case apart ; some of the most important factors in moral growth seem to be beyond our existing power of control. Nevertheless we have now some considerable knowledge of the part played by pleasure in the moral life, and until this knowledge is understood and used efforts to make men better than they are will not be likely to succeed.

The rôle of pleasure is complex. The word itself covers feelings of many different kinds, which serve both conscious and unconscious ends.

One type is connected with endeavour. Man has been described as a machine for making efforts, and healthy men and women enjoy physical and mental effort up to a point, and are apt to become bored and restless if nothing is required of them. Even the tension produced by danger can feel pleasant so long as confidence is not too deeply undermined.

Under the same biological heading fall the pleasures of

success, the elation and satisfaction which follow achievement. These, sometimes thought of as " manly " pleasures, are frowned upon only by ascetics and one or two classes of abnormal persons. They are in fact the sweeteners of work which make life on this planet tolerable. We can put up with the rejoicings of the burglar who has got safely away with the swag when we consider the artist and the virtuous apprentice. Effort and achievement are necessary for the survival of the species, and we can say that though they are not much admired by men in women—except in connection with cooking—their general value would be admitted if one bothered to think about them.

Most of the trouble which is stirred up by the notion of pleasure is roused by a third class—the specific delights which accompany the gratification of particular instincts. To enjoy eating, hunting, fighting, making love, may be natural, but should it be thought of as right ?

Except among those who condemn all pleasure the commonest answer would be I fancy : " good in moderation." Both to the philosopher who has studied Mencius and Aristotle and their doctrine of the Golden Mean, and to the man in the street, the word " moderation " sounds attractive and reasonable and soothing. It saves further thought. Nevertheless as a standard for the goodness of pleasures it works badly. Rapture is not wrong in itself ; most of us like to see it in children to whom we have given a present, young lovers, a mother with her baby, or any human being faced by overwhelming beauty. A life is poor indeed which has been empty of such emotions. Again, the V.C. often goes to the man who is transported by the lust of battle. To enjoy eating so much that you can enjoy boiled salt cod can also be a valuable asset.

Moderation in pleasure, therefore, is not an end in itself. What is good or bad is not the feeling, or the amount of it, but the activities from which it springs. Further, to say that a thing is good in moderation is only to say that it is good in such amount as is found to be good. We do mean something, and something important, when we praise moderation, but we are referring then to the value of self-control. The concept should not be applied to the capacity for feeling pleasure.

On the other hand it is true that experience of pleasure may become a part of a process which, as a whole, we must condemn. What is felt as pleasant tends to be repeated, and not all that gives pleasure is good. The obvious instance is the taking of pleasure in cruelty, of all states of mind the most shocking and repulsive to normal man. We shall return to this example in a moment. But even here, to suppose that the sadist is a sadist on account of the pleasure he gets from inflicting pain, is to put the cart before the horse.

In spite of this disadvantage, the specific pleasures must be considered good on balance, not only because we like them, but because the part they play in human life is one of reassurance. Rightly or wrongly, man does feel in the depths of his mind that while he can experience pleasure the worst will not happen, that if life allows him enjoyment he cannot be so bad after all. And this effect is more marked in the case of the normal " animal " pleasures, than in that of puruits which we think of as civilised. In fact pleasures both lessens guilt and assuages anxiety. And since the deadliest and commonest mental poisons are excessive guilt and anxiety, it is a curative agent, and one of the utmost importance.

Most of us would agree, I imagine, that happy men are likely to be less quarrelsome, less greedy, less envious, suspicious, bitter, and actively cruel, than similar people who have been starved of enjoyment. On the positive side, they are more ready to be kind, more willing to be just. And since pleasures—particularly those connected with the affections—are the ground of happiness, they are good not only because we desire them, but on account of their civilising effects. Even those who fear pleasure, if they realised the part it plays, would admit that it is one of the conditions of important moral virtues.

Many people find it hard to believe this, so it may be as well to deal with the commoner of their objections. One is that pleasure is dangerous, and gives rise to anxiety.

Next, a good many actions whose consequences are evil are also productive of immediate pleasure. The classic instance is taking drugs.

The third objection is the fact that most of us know or have read of people who have, we think, been ruined by too much pleasure : people without capacity for steady work or an adequate sense of duty, who waste their lives in frivolity and dissipation, or sink into crime.

About the first of these I will only repeat that to teach human beings to be afraid of pleasure will create in them the most bitter unconscious resentment. This resentment, at the cost of a lifetime of struggle, may be stifled and kept from doing external harm, or, in rare natures, successfully masked with benevolence. Far more often it issues as hatred, which remains hatred however easily one may convince oneself that one wishes to pain only the guilty, and these in order to do them good. The Inquisitors were convinced of their own righteousness. Few of us share this opinion.

Another bad result of fearing pleasure is that feelings of guilt tend to spread until they have covered almost all activities that serve as safety-valves for impulses which do need control. Freud has said, for instance, that the best outlet for the sexual impulses is given by art. To paint, model, compose, or play an instrument, to decorate or carve, satisfies, in part, the creative side of the sexual urges, just as enjoyment of the beauty afforded by works of art can be a substitute for some of the sexual pleasures. In normal people it will not be a complete substitute, but then, only neurotics would wish that it should.

It is, therefore, unfortunate that just because this connection exists the puritan who fears sex, hates and disapproves of beauty. Instead of welcoming it as something which he can enjoy, he fears it because it flowers in the desert which he is determined to keep in that region of his mind.

To help him in this endeavour he makes up myths. Artists are thought of as especially immoral, and places where they congregate likened to Sodom and Gomorrah. He would rather see his son lying dead at his feet than have him pursue this evil way of life—the symptoms are familiar to every Englishman.

It is, of course, true that some artists and art students are immoral—that they live with their models, or other women, or are unfaithful to their wives. But this does not mean that they are moral men who have been corrupted by painting. On the contrary, they are men whose sexual impulses are so strong that even painting cannot work off the whole of them. Tie them to some " respectable " occupation which they detest, and such men may become more furtive but will not be more virtuous—unless virtue is to be judged by the number of occasions on which intercourse takes place. Here opportunity is undoubtedly a factor.

On the other hand it must be admitted that a famous man who flaunts his promiscuous life acts both as an example and as a magnet. Sinners who would have offended somewhere else find it more agreeable to do so in his neighbourhood. Some who would not have dared to sin find that he gives them the courage. All this is true. But against it we must set the effect which great works of art have had upon the lives of millions, their power to enrich our minds, refine our feelings, enlarge the narrow boundaries of the self, unite men in common sympathy, assuage suffering and illuminate dreary lives. To put it shortly, art is one of the basic civilising forces at the disposal of mankind. By lessening frustration it lessens hatred and anxiety, by affording pleasure it increases goodwill. To point out that art is an aid to virtue is extremely irritating to many artists who make Art supreme, and like to look down upon virtue. But the statement is true all the same.

Before leaving the subject, we may as well note that the " manly " types who need, above all, outlets for aggression and are able to tolerate their own sexual desires, regard art not as a lure to vice but as effeminate and debilitating. Their myth is of " long-haired artists hanging round in drawing-rooms "—the unconscious contrast being robust behaviour in bed. Here again, it is just because art does enable men to sublimate sexual urges, that they despise it.

To return now to the second reason given for regarding pleasure as dangerous—the degrading pleasures.

These exist and it is a very great pity that harmful actions do not always produce violent and immediate pain. In that case only neurotics would perform them. But this does not mean that the pleasure they produce has not a useful as well as a harmful effect, but only that the whole business is bad on balance. The pernicious vices generally—and this includes sadism—are not pursued for the pleasures they afford, but in order to gain relief from inner conflict. Their victims do not drink themselves stupid, beggar themselves at cards, indulge in sexual perversion, merely for the joy of doing these things. On the contrary, they may hardly enjoy them at all. They are driven by compulsive forces into a spiral of behaviour which becomes more and more disastrous and helps them less and less. But the process was entered upon because it did give a little help in a situation that was felt as intolerable. Drink and drugs, for example, bring elation, or relief, or oblivion, and not all the misery and degradation which may follow can be feared, by the man who takes to them, as he fears his conscience. Like the neurosis, they are defences against what is felt as intolerable, and though onlookers see that the shelter they give is illusory, the sufferer himself cannot face the thought of enduring life without them.

These statements may become clearer when we consider the third objection I mentioned—the sight of irresponsible pleasure seekers. This is, of course, only a milder instance of the vicious behaviour we have just discussed. The results are less tragic but the essential mechanism is much the same. Even here what is bad is not the pleasure gained—which helps these people —but their continual need for it. Healthy human beings do not need and would soon weary of, one distraction and sensation after another. To be always hankering after something that will give one a "kick" is a morbid state of mind. Most of us refrain from getting drunk every day and from sexual promiscuity not because we have a severe, though victorious, struggle with temptation every time we pass a pub, or see an attractive woman (or man), but because we do not want to get drunk, and have other things to do besides making love. In addition most of us have ideals to satisfy in both these connections. In short, we are not the victims of insatiable cravings. And where constant stimulation, constant reassurance, constant proof that one can still enjoy, are such pressing needs that life must be spent and wasted in their service, the real evil is the antecedent misery which sets up these needs, and not their temporary alleviation.

Even the gold-digger, the girl who sells herself for expensive clothes and a car and a diamond wrist watch, is not a proof that cars are evil and should be destroyed. She is lacking in self-respect and in respect for her womanhood, and longs for luxuries because they become part of her picture of herself and thus lessen her sense of unworthiness. The fur coat and the wrist-watch give her a feeling of safety, and place her on the level of other girls whose goodness fills her with envy and despair. If she had felt from the beginning that she was reasonably good, such objects, though desirable, would not have seemed worth winning at all costs.

Therefore pleasure is a good not only, as the philosophers recognised, because we are so made that we do desire it, but because we are so made that it helps to keep the mind wholesome. The problem with which it confronts us is not how to abstain from it, still less how to root out all desire for it from our minds. These are impossible tasks. What is needed is so to handle human beings that their desire for pleasure retains its natural forms, and so to arrange their environment that reasonable satisfaction for these is obtainable.

As we have seen, in this matter people differ greatly. Some can gratify many of their instinctive urges through such "civilised" channels as games, art, going to the movies or the pursuit of knowledge. Others demand a much greater proportion of direct satisfaction. These types tend, of course, to despise one another, but they will always be forced to co-exist. Except by the use of a terror which would warp his mind Sir Toby will never be weaned from his cakes and ale.

CHAPTER II

METHODS AND CRITERIA OF A SCIENTIFIC SYSTEM OF ETHICS

In the preceding chapters an attempt has been made to do four things. The first was to demonstrate that none of our existing moral systems possesses either the certainty, the clarity, or the consistency that its supporters have expected us to assume. The second was to show that morality does not proceed from religion, but from psychological and social necessities, and need not depend upon belief in religious dogma. The third and fourth were to give a brief description of the actual origin and development of moral beliefs, and some examples of the teachings of leading moralists.

All these discussions have been in a sense not only critical but destructive. But they have not been merely destructive. To realise how the mind works when it builds the system by which it controls its primitive impulses is to provide ourselves with knowledge essential to constructive progress. And it is because this basis of knowledge has hitherto been lacking that so many moral theories and customs have failed of their purpose, and that so many treatises on Ethics seem to be beating the air.

Clearly, however, all this is only a first step. Unless it can be shown that modern knowledge will help to show a way through the tangle of conflicting beliefs which are called eternal ethical principles, there is nothing to put in their place. The next task is therefore to demonstrate this possibility, if it exists.

First, what is the problem? It is not, I suggest, to find a set of moral absolutes, or a first principle from which, once given, we can deduce practical details by a series of logical theories. The search for absolutes is fascinating, and so congenial to many minds that there will always be human beings who embark upon it. We may wish them the best of luck. But so far this inquiry, carried on though it has been whenever thought was free, has proved sterile. Everyone can agree that the good is what ought to be sought and promoted, and that our duty is what we ought to do. But no thinker has yet found an absolute definition of the good which was not open to objection, or with one exception, satisfied more than a small minority of inquirers. The exception is the doctrine that good is what Gods wills us to do, and we have already discussed a few of the difficulties which attend upon this definition. And surely these difficulties are inherent and the problems which they present insoluble ? Unless there be a fresh and unambiguous revelation who is to decide in what the will of God consists ?

The search for an absolute, then, may be left to those who will not accept anything less. So far, all the absolute goods which have been presented to man for his acceptance have been either empty or too simple—too simple because they do not account for all the facts. " The only good is happiness " is too simple, even if the general happiness is meant, for it omits the concept of excellence which plays so important a part in most men's notions of morality. It is a matter of common observation that men will die for their country without once saying to themselves, or feeling, that it would have made them unhappy if they had stayed at home in a reserved occupation. Nor are they acting for the general happiness, but for a large variety of ends which they think right or good.

On the other hand the conception of duty for the sake of duty will seem empty to many people, since it is impossible to tell from it what one's duty may be.

The problem for those who seek a scientific basis for morality is still, I suggest, that to which the ancient philosophers addressed themselves—the two-fold problem of deciding what we mean by the good man in the good society and, when that has been decided, of finding the best means of producing both.

If this statement of the problem be correct, we are confined to a limited field of inquiry. We must think in terms as of men as they are ; improved perhaps, but still recognisable. We must realise that we are dealing with this planet and with only a portion of its history. We are not trying to lay down moral rules for the universe or any beings other than ourselves. And this for the simple reason that we should be without the necessary starting points for thought. It is possible to conceive of creatures upon some other world who live in a nutrient medium, perpetuate themselves by fission, do not combine into groups, and yet have developed minds. Without any of the problems that arise from shortage of food supplies, sex or neighbours, what sort of morality can we imagine for them ?

As for mankind in the future, we have some ideas but probably not enough to justify us in judging their behaviour. If the earth dries up, or freezes, or falls slowly into the sun, who can say how our descendants will adjust themselves to these conditions? Practical morality deals with concrete problems, and only so long as these remain similar to those which confront us now, can we be sure that similar methods and principles will suffice for their solution.

The problem then is limited though, in all conscience, wide enough. But before attempting to close with it and give a concrete content to the notions of good men in good societies, it will be an advantage to clear away one difficulty which has held up several philosophers.

That is the vexed question of whether actions should be judged by their motives, or by their results. Here modern psychology is immediately helpful, for it enables us to say at once: "By their results." It is now widely realised that human motives cannot be fully known, and that they are known least of all to their owners. They are always complex, and always partly determined by factors inaccessible to consciousness. Nobody quite knows why, at any moment, he does what he does. And often enough, when he thinks that he knows all about it, he is yet completely deceived as to his motives.

It seems therefore both impracticable and unjust to judge an action by a factor which cannot be fully determined.[1]

An action, therefore, must be called good or bad in accordance with its consequences, and with these alone. For example: if voluntary hospitals are valuable, even though only as stop-gaps, then to subscribe to them is a good action, no matter why it is done.

The doers of the actions, on the other hand, we are entitled to judge by the whole of our knowledge both of what they do and of why they do it. In considering whether a man is virtuous or not, it is only just to consider his intentions. If he means to do well but errs in ignorance, he will be thought better than a man who does not care what happens if only he gets what he wants. But however good a man may suppose his intentions to be, if he consistently does harm he will be thought either a complete fool or a Jonah, or a hypocrite or a neurotic, according to the knowledge and bias of the observer.

This is yet another reason, therefore, for disagreeing with Aristotle, Kant and the many theologians who have held that duty

[1] Kindly Christians often feel and say that a man can be judged only by his Maker. All the same, daily life requires us both to make moral judgments and to act upon them. The maxim remains useful as a corrective of intolerance.

METHODS AND CRITERIA OF A SCIENTIFIC SYSTEM OF ETHICS 139

must de done only for its own sake, and that an action is not virtuous when any other motive plays a part. The first point of importance is that the right thing should be done. The second is that the doer should be a person who acts, on the whole, from motives, however mixed, which tend to produce right actions. (Two of these are dislike of useless suffering, and love of truth.) The willingness to perform a duty merely because it is a duty is only one of this class of motives. Moreover it is an attitude which can become extremely dangerous in fanatics or people who will not face the fact that they enjoy giving pain. Hitler was convinced that he was the saviour of Germany, if not of all mankind.

The point may seem academic, but in judging between moral codes it will be found extremely useful.

Next a few words as to methods. When I said that our field of inquiry is limited to the world we know, it was as much as to say that the method used must be inductive. That is, instead of starting, like many moralists, from an absolute principle and then trying to deduce from it how a man ought to behave and what he ought to think right, it is better to begin with such facts as we have and to do our best to build up valid inductions from them. One such group of facts is that we are members of a species living in groups, that each group has its official moral code, and if complex contains sub-groups which obey amending codes. It is also a fact that these codes conflict in very important particulars, and another that none of them has succeeded in making more than a few men virtuous though some have succeeded better than others. One more example of a relevant fact is that we are beginning to realise why these attempts have failed because we now know more about the effect on man of his environment, what men and women taken in the mass can be expected to renounce and to achieve, and what happens to them when more is demanded than they are able to perform. And since these are facts they must all be taken into account by anyone who seeks to decide the objects and norms of what we call moral behaviour.

The code or codes which we require must then take account of facts, but this is not enough. They must also be adequate, workable, and satisfy the requirements of reason.

All these statements require definition and comment. It will perhaps be as well to start with the last, since some readers may think it odd that a psychologist should insist on the importance of reason. A widespread belief exists that modern psychology is one of the forces which has " debunked " the faith which the philosophers placed in reason. And people who have not read Freud for themselves, or have dipped into his books and paid attention only to what shocked them, or to isolated passages which seemed to provide an excuse for obeying impulses commonly thought to be wrong, are often heard to say that he sanctions the prevalent dislike of reason.

Nothing could be further from the truth. In the first place all Professor Freud's own work was based upon a close and scrupulous use of reason. No scientist has been more careful to point out the difference between fact and theory ; between theory and a mere hypothesis intended to provoke further research. No great thinker has ever been more willing to alter his conclusions if fresh facts seemed to call for such emendation. Nowhere does he ask, even tacitly, for faith, advance his vast knowledge and experience as a ground for accepting his beliefs, or rely upon such mental processes as " insight " and " inspiration." On the contrary, he repudiates them in so many words with the statement : " There is no appeal beyond reason."[1]

Secondly, the picture which he draws of the human mind is governed throughout by biological conceptions. He sees it as a developing organism, subject to the laws of cause and effect, making quantitative as well as qualitative reactions to its environment. It is true that no means exists at present of measuring these quantities. We can only say, for instance, that the result of a mental struggle will be determined by the amount of energy at the disposal of the various forces arrayed on either side—primitive urges, conscience, reason, memories and associations both conscious and unconscious, habit and the rest of them. We cannot state those amounts ; though here psychology is no worse off than many other branches of biology. And if a means of taking accurate measurements ever is devised, it will facilitate the use of Freud's methods. He himself made a good many attempts to dovetail his findings with those of physiology, though this is a field in which the next great advances must come from the physical side.

Thirdly, in his analysis of the mind he allots an extremely important place to reason, no less than that both our consciences and our conscious minds should be subject to the primacy of the intelligence. Reason should be our governor. This, he says, is the psychological ideal.[2] He could not have spoken more strongly. And in fact all his great discoveries were made by insisting that

[1] *The Future of an Illusion*, page 49.
[2] Op. cit. page 83.

mental events are facts, by tracing their causes and proving their effects.

This attitude, from which he never departed, is hidden from the casual reader by two things. The first is that Freud was often obliged to point out that a great deal of what we believe to be pure reasoning is in reality only finding excuses for beliefs that we hold because we want to hold them. And it has been deduced that in saying this he was decrying the use of reason. The deduction, of course, is invalid. To say that we often misuse our reason is not to say that we are justified in doing so, or should not make any effort to use it correctly. No amount of misuse can affect the statement that reason, correctly used, is the only reliable guide to truth.

The second cause of misunderstanding is the fact that Freud does not often use the word itself. He talks instead of the " reality principle," by which he means that the mind should adjust itself to the real world, to facts, instead of remaining under the power of its wishes and phantasies. He uses such terms as " evaluating " and " working over " instead of " reasoning about it until a matter is seen in its proper proportions," but reasoning, thinking over, is what he means. And when he is describing the causation of neurotic symptoms he makes it clear that the use of reason is one of the guardians of mental health.[1] In certain cases it prevents neuroses, and it also plays an important part in their cure.

These arguments we are now in a position to buttress by another important fact, unknown until criminals had been subjected to psychological observation. When this happened it was found that the outstanding traits of the anti-social types are hostility to their fellows and impairment of the sense of reality. It is the second of these which concerns us here. Habitual wrongdoers are seldom content to offend and rejoice in it. Instead they rely upon systems of false beliefs which protect them from the attacks of conscience. " Everyone else does it, so why should not I ? " " If they don't bother to watch their things they must expect to have them stolen ! " " I shall be able to put the money back before it is missed." " The world is well rid of such a scoundrel ! "

These hypocrisies vary from semi-truths to statements incredible to the normal mind, as when we have Bjerre's murderer explaining that he did the postman a favour by bashing his head in, since walking the streets in all weathers is no life for an old man. Again, a sailor who had tried repeatedly to kill his wife

[1] Cf. " The Aetiology of Hysteria," *Collected Papers* Vol. 2.

informed the magistrate (and the author) that she was going with other men in order to deck herself with jewels and fine clothes. The unfortunate woman possessed in reality only threadbare garments : her husband's accusation was false in every respect.

The important fact referred to is that when these types are analysed their ability to believe such comforting lies is found to spring from nonsense being forced upon them in childhood. Teach a child—especially in the guise of truths which must not be questioned upon pain of sin—beliefs which conflict, or seem to him at variance with his knowledge of reality, and the authority of reason will be undermined. He may begin to disregard it to please himself as well as when his parents and teachers tell him to. When this occurs it will no longer protect him from the false excuses which disguise and encourage a lowering of moral standards.

This sequence of events explains in part why children brought up in narrow religious homes and schools show a high proportion of delinquents.[1] Reason is, in fact, not only the sole sure guide to truth, but the strongest guardian of virtue. It is the reasonable man who realises that even people he does not like have rights as well as he ; that the world does not owe him everything he wants the moment that he wants it, and that he must not always place on others the blame for his own behaviour.

It is natural therefore, and not in the least surprising, that a psychologist should stress the importance of reason, particularly when in search of a scientific moral code. The title would be a misnomer if it did not imply that any such code must be rational. That is to say, it must be consistent, based upon facts and, while taking account of feelings, seek to guide rather than to conform to them. It must invite and be able to withstand criticism, and nowhere demand for its acceptance what are known as acts of faith.

If the reply be made that a moral code is useless unless men have faith in it, I would point out that the word "faith" is commonly used to cover two different mental activities. The first is a state of confidence which may or may not be justified. We

---

[1] (See page 6.) The other main factors which produce this result are the hostility engendered by constant frustration of natural childish wishes, and perhaps by constant punishment, and the feelings of guilt which arise out of failure to achieve the impossible standards demanded. The result tends to be discouragement, despair and a need for approval at all costs. Such children seek out low companions as soon as they are free to do so, partly in order to pain their parents, but chiefly to escape from the stigma of inferiority and unworthiness. " Alf and Jim can't look down on me ! "—and their knaveries are first accepted and then followed.

can feel faith in a leader, or in the accuracy of our sums, especially when we have looked up the answers. This is one meaning. The other, that intended by the words " acts of faith," is the acceptance of beliefs without adequate grounds, or in the teeth of the available evidence. We have already seen that once beliefs have been adopted in this manner they are usually supported by feelings of exaggerated confidence. It is on this account that the two senses of the word are often confused, and that the second activity benefits from the usefulness of the first.

Normal life is impossible without confidence, even if much of it is not fully justified. It is impracticable to be forever reconsidering all one's opinions and decisions. Once decisions have been made, action is more likely to be successful if carried out in a confident spirit. The same principle applies to trust in leaders No leader is perfect, but they cannot be changed continually, and as a rule will do better work if they enjoy the loyalty of their followers. Evidence for the truth of both these statements must be fresh in all our minds.

Again, a general confidence in one's own ability to perform a reasonable task, or to behave reasonably well, is an important constituent of self-respect. As against this two points must be noted : the first is that unwarranted faith is useful only after policy has been settled and in those who are not responsible for the guidance of affairs. Decisions should be taken on grounds of fact, and not on " intuitions." One of these facts may be the amount of confidence available, just as the state of a patient's mind may rightly affect the doctor's choice of treatment, but that is another aspect of the question.

Secondly, faith in the sense of trust is an emotional state which cannot be produced to order. Men can be frightened, or mocked or even bribed into suppressing their doubts, but they cannot be blamed if these stimuli fail to work.

Blind confidence may therefore be valuable. But one field in which it has no value at all is the field of truth and error. Here it is always harmful, and a considerable part of scientific procedure consists in applying checks in order to eliminate its influence. As soon as men desire ordered and consistent knowledge " faith " is recognised as nothing but a form of prejudice.

We see this at once when we consider some of the commonest acts of faith. Take the belief in patent medicines, especially those of what may be called the magical class. Millions are spent on them every year. The " drawing-power " of the advertisement, or the skill of the pedlar and his clever patter ; the desire of sufferers for an easy cure ; their fear of the doctor who may tell them that they are seriously ill ; reluctance to miss an opportunity ; perhaps the mere itch to spend, all conduce to an eager or shamefaced purchase. But once the customer has the sense to ask : " Why should I buy your iodine locket to cure my rheumatism rather than gold earrings, or the embrocation in the chemist's window, or some adder's fat, or—cheaper and easier still—half a potato to carry in my pocket ? " the spell is broken. And it is worth noting that the vendor will not reply by asking directly for an act of faith. He seeks instead to recreate a favourable atmosphere, conducive to faith. So we get : " The gentleman asks us, my friends, why he should buy my locket ? Well, ladies and gentlemen, I have nothing to hide ! I am going to tell you straight away why he should buy it ! Because it is a genuine wonder-working locket—the only certain cure ! I tell you that hundreds and thousands of men and women are going about cured today which they never would have been without these Wonder-lockets. . . ." He may believe what he is saying, or flatter himself that he is a skilful liar, but what he is after is some show of evidence.

This procedure is not changed materially when what is offered is not a patent medicine but a truth which is said to transcend the bounds of reason. Then we shall be told to have faith, but what is actually brought forward is a series of inadequate reasons. For all inducements, all appeals, have grounds of one sort or another. When the bounds of reason are really transcended each man must dwell alone with his ineffable certitudes. Faith is mentioned, therefore, as a cover for the weak points in these appeals.

As with the pedlar, no propagandist asks for faith in general, but always for faith in his particular teaching. To him no alternative is worth considering. But why should anyone follow him in this ? If he can give no evidence why A should be believed rather than B, why should we make up our minds ?

When it comes to the point of controversy he will in fact adduce grounds. And they will turn out to be of three kinds and of three kinds only. The first is the ground of authority, either that of the speaker, of his leader or his fellow believers. The second is the superior virtue or effectiveness of his doctrine ; the third is that the convert will in some way benefit from its adoption. If no ground is given why faith should be felt, why should anyone try to feel it ? And to tell a man that he is wrong to doubt is, of course, to beg the whole question.

As to the first of these contentions, whose authority are we to take ? If good reason can be given for preferring the authority of this man to any other, then we are being asked to judge by evidence and not by faith. Such statements as " Your fathers believed this, and how much better they were than you are ! " is either true, true in part only, or untrue. Perhaps I am what I am because my fathers held foolish beliefs about bringing up children. I must judge between these possibilities.

When superior virtue or effectiveness is claimed for a doctrine the position is at bottom the same. If proof can be given of superiority, why demand faith? If not we are being asked once more to accept the authority of the speaker. It is the same argument over again.

The last ground is that of profit : the convert is to receive some benefit from his adherence to the new doctrine. Such benefits may be objective If so, they can be demonstrated. Or they may be incapable of antecedent proof, as when a man is told that once he has experienced the mercy of Heaven or felt himself to be in tune with the Infinite, nothing else will seem to matter to him, and that the way to these states of mind is through the belief in question. If this were merely an invitation to experiment, it would be legitimate. There may be men who can adopt beliefs in order to see how they work out, and their testimony would be valuable. But it would only be testimony to the fact that certain pleasing states of mind are procurable through particular systems of belief, and it is hardly necessary to point out that pleasant feelings, whatever relief or delight they may bring, are not a test of truth. Our forefathers set much store by the idea that man is a special creation not descended from any lower animal. A good many people feel in touch with unseen forces when they foretell the future by looking into dirty tea-cups. Nothing, apparently is more delightful or reassuring than to imagine that one is God or Mr. Winston Churchill. Yet none of these beliefs is true. It is not a virtue in us, but one of our most dangerous faults, that we prefer comfort to truth.

In short, acts of faith when recommended as a method for attaining the truth, are wanted only to conceal weakness in arguments.[1] This may be denied by believers on the ground that

[1] In the review in the *Sunday Times*, 23rd May, 1943, it was revealed that some critics of Miss Dorothy Sayers's broadcast series " The Man Born to be King ", said that Singapore fell because it was broadcast. Another writer to the B.B.C. declared : " They made possible the victories in Africa." Both showed faith in the efficacy of broadcasts. Who is to choose between them ?

innumerable conversions to their form of belief have taken place on other than rational grounds. The fact is undoubted. Such conversions are known to every religion, every movement and every ideology. Whether they can be called acts of faith is another matter. They occur when very strong desires, often unconscious, urge a man towards the opinions in question, but other forces nearly equal in strength have prevented his yielding to them. Then some trifling occurrence tips the scales. Once this has happened the convert feels a sense of freedom, elation and utter certainty which seems to him proof that his new belief is true. In fact it represents the relief which is felt when an exhausting inner struggle is ended.[1] He made no act of faith ; a state of faith supervened upon a release of mental energy.

The mere fact that they occur in all religions shows that sudden conversions, however inspiring, do not prove that the conclusions reached are true.

These well-known facts about faith and reason have been repeated here because of the efforts which are being made today to confuse men's minds on this issue. The late Archbishop Temple went so far as to say that men must learn to believe without evidence. This is a lesson which no human being has any need to learn. We are born wishing to believe what will bring immediate solace, and only too often this wish has its way with us.[2]

Beliefs which rest on faith will be shared, in the long run, only by classes of people who are anxious to adopt them. A scientific moral code must be based upon something which is common to human beings as such. Reason, and reason alone, meets this requirement. It is not, as Kant and others thought it, the distinguishing mark between the minds of men and those of beasts. That position is shared by conscience. But it is a universal faculty, capable, if unhampered, of uniting those who use it. If a man or woman cannot see the force of the argument that if A be greater than B, and B greater than C, then A must be greater than C ; we regard him or her as mentally defective or as mad. Further, when two normal men agree as to facts but differ about the validity of an argument, we assume that the fallacy in the reasoning of one—or both—of them can be discovered, and agreement reached. Insoluble differences exist where the facts, or their degree of importance, are in dispute, or where prejudice is so strong that the disputants are blinded. In short, within the

[1] Cf. De Sanctis, *The Psychology of Religious Conversion.*
[2] The best non-psychological discussion on faith and reason known to me is that contained in *Some Dogmas of Religion* by Dr. J. Ellis McTaggart.

sphere of reason men find themselves under a common obligation to think in certain ways and agree upon certain matters. Complete agreement will not, as a rule, be reached on issues which arouse very strong feelings, but feelings vary from man to man, place to place and time to time. Reason remains. And when feeling sinks truths become established.

We must therefore stick to facts, and to arguments based upon facts and in accordance with the weight of the evidence. The facts in question will be those connected with human behaviour and aspects of the environment which affect that behaviour.

To return to the other criteria mentioned—it was said that a system of morals must be adequate. Any ethical method which is to be useful must cover all the issues which are regarded as raising serious moral problems. As an example we may take sexual morality. If we agree that our sexual impulses need control, then the direction and nature of that control must be indicated in sufficient detail to satisfy our practical needs. If they do not need control, then this position must be justified.

Under the last term, "workable," two different things are included.

The first is : "able to be put into practice, without defeating its own ends, by the great majority of normal human beings." About this there will be a good deal more to say, for the gravamen of the charge brought by psychologists and sociologists against existing codes is that they are, in certain respects, so ill-adapted to human nature that to obey them will in the end do more harm than good. Not only is it a fact that moral codes which are too strict or too lax arouse intolerable anxiety and resentment, but we find that serious individual character faults as well as neurotic symptoms are directly traceable to ill-advised moral directions. Here we begin to see the value of the conclusion that actions must be judged by their results. To order men, on any ground, to behave in a manner which will in the end make most of them worse instead of better, is evil and not good. If kindness is regarded as a virtue, then we must regard as bad such causes as tend to produce cruelty. And this will be true whether these causes take the form of social and economic conditions or moral restrictions, or the absence of moral restrictions. I have chosen this example because many people regard cruelty as wholly evil, so that there is no need to discuss any alleged benefits, or to choose between qualities which are more useful in some circumstances than in others.

By a workable system I mean one fitted to the actual circumstances in which people have to live. We have all seen that it is a mistake to preach the values which lead to an attitude of peace at any price to a nation which stands in imminent danger of attack by people who believe in war. On the other hand during major wars there is a tendency to exalt the virtues most valuable in war, and to undervalue the men and qualities which are useful only in times of peace. These tendencies will always operate, but a satisfactory moral system should take account of such waves of feeling, and enable us to understand and to control them.

Another example is of a different kind. Suppose it to be agreed that for several men to share a wife is an immoral state of affairs. Still, if it be true, as to which I say nothing, that in the highest districts of the Pamirs it takes the labour of several men to support one woman and her children, have we a moral right to insist that these family groupings are sinful? If so, must the population be evacuated in order to preserve their virtue, or converted *in situ* to virtuous living, when the woman and children will starve?

It may be thought that the most important consideration of all has been omitted. That is that a workable ethic must be one that will be obeyed. It must be based upon sanctions that will induce men to respect it and to live up to it, so far as they able. This is true, but as we have already seen, in the enormous majority of cases the sanction for all systems of ethics alike is acceptable authority. During childhood this is the authority of the parents or their substitutes. Later it is the authority of leaders, but leaders who are chosen for reasons many of which are not realised by the choosers. Whether attempts are made to obey any code will depend to a very small extent upon the content of the code. Whether these attempts are successful depends upon circumstances, the characters of the people involved, and what the code is trying to make them be and do. All this has been discussed already. Codes are, for the most part, accepted on authority and in a spirit of blind faith. But this does not mean that we should be content with this state of affairs. Another factor does enter in, and will, it is to be hoped become more and more influential as time goes on, and that is the factor of rational criticism. In so far as men are trained to think for themselves, in so far as they become aware of their own prejudices and learn to face them, in so far as they learn to confront moral problems without undue anxiety, it becomes more likely that they will insist on a rational system of morals.

The Jesuits used to say that if they might have a child up to the age of seven what happened later on was unimportant. This was true enough when it was said. What was thought to be the whole civilised world accepted, in theory, the same moral laws, and it is easy so to treat a child in the first seven years of its life that it becomes incapable of independent and constructive thinking upon moral issues.

The situation which we face today is entirely different. In the first place alternatives abound, and most intelligent young people are curious about some of them. Secondly, an increasing number of the world's inhabitants are taught some form of science, or are interested in science and respect it. Now science can be taught so badly that students who can repeat by heart hundreds of, say, chemical equations, have never been taught its fundamental principles and methods, or the respect for evidence which is the first virtue of a scientist. But on the whole a scientific training does tend to make people dislike sheer nonsense, and does also encourage them to use their intellects without fear of committing a sin. Human beings who have scrutinised their moral codes and found them reasonable have a very strong additional ground for doing their best to live up to them, and a ground which will remain steady under their feet. It is precisely the reasonable man who is not carried away by temporary waves of feeling; who is able to look ahead and consider the results of his actions; who can adjust himself to changing circumstances, and ask himself whether behaviour can be truly virtuous if it seems likely to result in widespread misery. Nowhere is reason both more necessary and more fruitful than in dealing with the fundamental strains which are caused by moral doubts and conflicts.

CHAPTER 12

THE GOOD MAN

These preliminaries having been dealt with, it remains to give a definite content to the notions of the good man and the good society. The problem today is wider than that which confronted the ancient philosophers, who concerned themselves with ruling classes and with the good government of states. It is wider because in democracies good leaders are not enough ; it is necessary to take account of whole populations. Indeed, for the moment, thinkers are especially concerned with the less privileged classes and groups, with both their needs and their rights and the best methods of securing these for them. To say that they should be skilful and docile no longer disposes of them. In addition to this we realise, as our forbears could not, the complex effects of social and political institutions not only on men's fortunes but on their characters and behaviour. And for this reason we not only study more deeply the basic organisation of our groups but we expect a great deal more from communal activities.

Thirdly, a group is now judged not only by its internal condition, but by its conduct as a neighbour.

So far has this process gone that there exists a general disagreement on the question of which counts for more, the hen or the egg, the individual or the state. Some feel that once the right institutions are set up the New Man will emerge automatically ; others that if only men could be made virtuous it does not much matter under what system they live. But most of those who have some knowledge both of affairs and of men, who know something of history and something of education, agree, I think, that good institutions have often failed for lack of men of intelligence and integrity, and that really bad institutions and traditions, if fastened on to a superior race, will tend to degrade them. Effort is needed at both ends : any improvement in either field will react on the other.

We have therefore two things to describe and not one, but two things so closely interrelated that it is impossible to judge them accurately unless both are taken into account.

If morality is very largely governed by the fact that human

beings tend to live in communities, then the good man must be a useful member of his group. If any particular man fails in this adjustment it may be that he is to blame, or the fault may lie with the customs and institutions of his group. Many criminals are driven to crime by circumstances over which they had little or no control. In fact the situation may be such that the first social duty of good men is to change these surroundings, whatever the cost may be. But even when the cost is very high, for example a revolution, those prepared to face it will probably feel that their duty is still to the group, though its present well-being must be sacrificed to the future. They are working for their descendants and for the better state which they hope to build from the ruins of the old.

There is, then, no real exception to the rule that the good man must also be a useful citizen. Hermits and solitaries are regarded today as examples of selfishness rather than of virtue, and the good man must not only be well conducted in his private life but of some positive value to others. It is not enough to love one's neighbour ; one must also, on appropriate occasions, be of service to him.

However closely human beings are related to their groups, when discussing the qualities which constitute goodness it is necessary to start with either the one or the other. And, no doubt in part on account of my bias as a psychologist, it seems to me that the more important definition is that of the good man. That state is, surely, good which provides for all its citizens the best life which the circumstances make possible. It guards them from those dangers against which the individual is helpless ; develops their faculties ; affords scope for the exercise of good qualities ; maintains law and order, and gives such guidance, care and succour, takes such steps to promote the general prosperity, as seem necessary at any given time. And many of these activities cannot be planned, let alone carried out with success, until their effects have been considered ; that is, unless those responsible have some notion of what sort of citizens they are intended to produce. Hitler, for instance, wanted ruthless barbarians or docile slaves, and the steps he took to secure them were very successful.

Further, communities can only act through the bodies and minds of their members. And though at any given moment a state may be rich and strong and possessed of a great art and a great literature, this state of affairs will not last very long unless its present population are prepared to use, care for, and perhaps defend their heritage, even if they do not add to it.

The state or nation may be a symbol for which men are prepared to die, setting it above their own welfare and that of those they love. But this does not mean that, in the end, communities can be judged as good or bad apart from the human beings who compose them. A state, for instance, may have efficient institutions with which its citizens are completely satisfied. Nevertheless if they are warlike it may be a curse to everyone else within its reach.

First, then, the good man. Superficially the good man may be of many different types. There are differences of gifts, which should flower into differences of function, and different sorts of adjustment made necessary by external circumstances. There will always be among human beings leaders and led, men of thought and men of action, and clever and the dull, the orthodox and the rebel. Different capacities involve different duties, and each sub-group should be helped to develop the qualities which it most needs or is apt to lack. As circumstances vary, so of course will the demand for these types and their services change. We must look for qualities which lie deeper than the obvious virtues, and realise that a successful community will contain numbers of different, though it may be hoped complementary, types.

There is one thing, however, which we may agree that all ought to have. It is not a virtue, but it is so valuable both to the individual and the group, that it may be thought to impose a number of moral obligations. This is health. The good man whom we must endeavour to produce should at least be healthy. And by healthy I mean sound both in body and in mind.

Many readers may at once object that health has nothing to do with morality, that many of the most virtuous men and women have suffered from very bad health, and that it is a common occurrence to find that a bout of sickness leads to moral improvement. Religious men are sometimes taught to think of illness as a trial sent by God to give us pause and make us consider our eternal salvation while there is yet time. Believers in transubstantiation see it as a working-off of sins committed in a past life. If these explanations be disregarded as unproven, we are faced with a recognisable evil, welcome only to certain types of mind. Among them are those who unconsciously consider themselves so wicked and dangerous that they can only feel safe when wretched and disabled ; those who use illness and its attendant helplessness as an escape from life, and those—overlapping the others—who must at any cost give trouble and cause anxiety to those around them. But all of these, disliking rivals, approve of health in others.

Most of us can agree that health is a good, and a good for whose sake we should be prepared to accept certain duties. Social institutions and customs—and even moral codes—must be of a kind which do not injure health but on the contrary help to promote it. And individual actions which prejudice the health of others must be regarded as bad except in special circumstances.[1]

Health, mental, moral and physical, is certainly not the only attribute of the good man, but it is extremely important, and a universal requirement, and therefore I propose to begin with it.

No doubt this sounds a very dull, trite, uninspiring and even sordid way to begin. A thing may be true and even important, but that does not make it a worthy or interesting moral ideal. "The healthy body in the healthy mind" calls up pictures of solemn young men waking the whole house with their alarm-clocks in order to do early morning exercises, and advertisements of enormous biceps. It sounds limited and selfish and a side-issue that ought to receive attention but leads to nothing but itself. Many sick men and women have been saints; many geniuses have been sick men. Moreover the care of the sick is a noble occupation, good for the characters of the thoughtlessly healthy, while too much interest in his own health turns a man into a bore and an egoist even if it does not make him ill.

All of these criticisms have some force if we consider only physical illness. A diseased body does not always debar a man from leading a useful life, or from the display of virtue, though society would hardly be justified in encouraging sickness on this account. But only one of them holds true when we consider mental sickness—for we can dispose of the hypochondriac by pointing out that he is not a healthy man. Too much attention paid to one's health is a symptom of existing illness, and only as part of a vicious circle the cause of fresh illness. It is, however, true that geniuses have sometimes been mentally ill, and this point will have to be dealt with.

As to the rest of the arguments; the main reason why the maxim sounds trite is that it has been accepted as true for centuries during which nobody knew how to maintain healthy bodies or even in what a healthy mind consists. Nothing is more baffling and disappointing than an obvious truth about which one can do little or nothing. But once the science of medicine began to

[1] Cf. The disregard of the health of adult civilians during the late war.

prove its worth, the subject ceased to be dull for those who possessed the knowledge necessary for effective action. Doctors and nurses may lead strenuous lives but they are not bored. They do not find life purposeless, or complain that they lack an ideal. And as soon as the possibility of raising the general level of health is recognised by the community, as a rule it is felt to establish a claim upon the good-will and resources of all decent people.

Even those who will not agree that a chance to be healthy is one of the rights of man, often recognise that illness is a drain on society. And they would admit that a state whose members are healthy is better than a similar group whose members are not.

So much for the physical side. It is when we turn to mental health that its importance as an attribute of the good man becomes clear. For mental illness, even when slight, besides being a frequent cause of physical disease affects a man's whole personality and moral character as well as his ability to cope with life. In the long run it is the greatest cause of human misery.

This may sound absurd : I will try to show that it is not.

It sounds absurd because the very conception of mental health is hazy to most of us. We have a few vague ideas about being morbid and being mad. But our native horror of madness is so great that most of us prefer, with a great deal of excuse, to know nothing about it. There are no links at all in our minds between the notions of goodness, kindness, the ability to do what one believes to be right, and the notion of mental health. We do not think of cruelty and abnormal greed, lust for power, inability to feel human sympathy or to love unselfishly, in the same way as we think of rickets, as diseases due to mal-development. Or if we do relate them to bad example and bad training we do not draw the conclusion that the way to prevent such evils is to produce human beings with healthy minds. Yet once it is accepted that the way a child is treated, and the examples which are set before him, and the emotions which are produced in him by his environment, do affect the development of his character, this deduction is unescapable.

What then is a healthy mind ? There is no simple definition ; the state is as difficult to define as physical health. Writers are apt to use such terms as " normal " and " well balanced " which get us no further than : " well grown and possessed of sound organs which function well." To talk of absence of deep-seated conflicts, or harmonious development of all one's powers, is suggestive but inadequate. Health is not a state which can be defined except by a tautology. It is however possible to describe the leading traits of a healthy mind and to say something about the permissible limits of variation. In practice most of these characteristics are closely interrelated so that the order in which they are taken does not matter.

To begin with, the healthy man will possess sufficient energy and aggression to tackle the problems of daily life with what is, in the circumstances, a reasonable degree of success.

Since work is a condition of life on this planet and has to be performed by most people, he will be able to do useful work and to take pleasure and pride in this exercise of function. Not all work, of course, is suitable for everybody, or can give pleasure to everyone. Some is too painful or monotonous to be enjoyed by anyone at all. But most healthy men can adapt themselves to work of various kinds, and feel satisfaction in doing it well. Some on the other hand have only one gift, and if they are to avoid the misery of frustration must pour all their energy through this single channel. When the gift in question is valuable to the community, and the performance is of high quality, we value or should value them highly. Such men are exceptions, but they are not necessarily unhealthy. Geniuses are often cheerful and robust. It is truer to say of them that they are people whose health depends upon the continuous and perhaps successful exercise of one particular form of sublimation or defence against anxiety. Let them do what they want to do and in the case of some men, appreciate their efforts, and all will be well. Sometimes, on the other hand, not enough of the dangerous energy can be got rid of in this way, and the defence against anxiety fails. Then the genius is "decadent" or "morbid", since his work will be affected by this failure. Whether it is still of value to the community, or constitutes a danger to the health of others, will depend upon the stability and common sense of those among whom he works. Healthy minds can face what is morbid and admire its good qualities without any ill effects. On the other hand no artist has a right to display his sores and then blame the public for disliking them. This digression has been made because many people are inclined to admire morbidity on account of its supposed connection with genius.

To return to aggression, the force which enables us to perform work and conquer difficulties : it must be there in sufficient quantity for the the job of living, but it should not be harnessed to a love of destruction, nor coloured by hatred except when directed against serious evils. The healthy man will hate meanness and cruelty, and he will not enjoy either wanton destruction or the giving of pain.

Secondly, his social and family feelings will, roughly speaking, be appropriate to the circumstances. He will be able to like those of his fellow creatures who are likeable, feel friendship or affection for congenial spirits, love his children, and his parents in so far as they deserve it. He will experience both affection and passion for a woman of suitable age. He will be able to find happiness in love and value the love of others. In fact he must have a friendly attitude towards other human beings who are not inimical, and be sexually normal.

Conversely, he will not suspect or fear people whom, given his information, he should know to be harmless, or seek to protect himself from his enemies by blinding himself to the threat they constitute and offering them love instead of seeking to defend himself from them.[1]

Thirdly, he will be able to tolerate equals and acknowledge the rights of others. And in those respects in which independence is desirable he will be able to stand on his own feet, without incessantly asking for external support and encouragement. Nor will he yearn or struggle for unchecked authority, or feel safe only when in a position of power.

Fourthly, he will be able to control his primitive impulses by working them off in socially desirable ways, or facing and overcoming them upon the conscious level, instead of giving way to them completely like the lunatic, or resorting to neurotic repressions.[2]

In the meantime the healthy human being will want to be good, though that will not be the only thing he wants, and be

---

[1] As Dr. Ernest Jones points out in his paper on " The Psychology of Quislings," *The International Journal of Psycho-Analysis*, 1923, it is of the greatest importance to any species to be able to identify its enemies and adopt an effective method of defence.

[2] This is always provided that the standard set by his group is reasonable. When it is incapable of achievement, he will suffer from acute anxiety, depression, self-loathing and the rest until he ceases to be healthy. If, on the other hand, the customs and laws under which he has to live are much laxer than his private code, so that he feels alone and unprotected in the face of what he still regards as temptation, the effect may be nearly as bad. We have the testimony of many soldiers in World War I that liberty to kill and wound and destroy was not the relief which some of their comrades found it, but acutely alarming and distressing. And we know from the medical records that a good many cases of mental breakdown were traced to the sudden lifting of this important prohibition. In the same way girls have told me during the late war what a strain it could be to find themselves among companions who drank to excess or indulged in promiscuous sexual intercourse. Any idea that their officers or N.C.O.s might condone such behaviour aroused what was very like terror : " The world seemed to be turning upside down ! "

able to perform what he feels to be clear duties, and to shoulder obvious responsibilities. He will be reasonably confident of his power to behave in this way, and not worry unduly about it.

That is to say his feelings about himself will be appropriate too. Without being smug and self-satisfied he will not hate and despise himself, or be plunged into despair on account of trivial faults or actions in the past which have been atoned for or lived down. He will be able to feel of these that he has outgrown them and learned his lesson. He will not live in dread of committing sins of which he is in fact incapable. He will be able to face the fact that he is not perfect. In short, as we saw in Chapter 4, he will show towards himself the same common sense, tolerance and goodwill that he shows, on the whole, to others.

Fifthly, he will be as happy as the external circumstances allow. Neurotics are miserable—they have been defined as a curse to themselves and to everybody around them. One type of lunatic is happy, the megalomaniac, provided that the man who thinks himself God does not meet others with the same delusion. Then there is trouble. Sufferers from manic-depressive insanity pass through periods of excitement and elation which anyone can call happy if he pleases. And some physical wrecks contrive to be happy. But taken generally, happiness is a sign of health.

The objection may be taken here that many virtuous men have been intensely miserable, and that the good man need not therefore be happy. It would be possible to answer shortly that miserable men undermine not only the happiness but the virtue of others, causing exhaustion and despair in the good, and irritation or a desperate desire to get away from them at all costs in the selfish. They are bad neighbours who should be encouraged to inhabit wildernesses, and to do them justice, many of them would if they had the chance.

To this one may add that an unhappy good man may be better than a bad man, but is certainly less valuable than a happy good man, since the latter is not only a source of happiness in others, but encourages them to feel that virtue is rewarded with happiness. But in general I must refer the reader to what was said about happiness in Chapter 10.

Next, the intelligence of the healthy man must be sufficient to enable him to cope with the ordinary problems of living, and must function more or less freely in matters which come within the range of his knowledge and experience. Outside this field he will face facts up to a certain point, and control or disregard feelings which do not correspond with the facts. Healthy men do not feel that anyone who contradicts or crosses them is guilty of a deadly sin, nor that what suits their personal interests is necessarily the best thing for the world at large. They are able to realise, again up to a point, that like everyone else they are sometimes prejudiced, and they will make some efforts to overcome this tendency. It would be absurd, of course, to pretend that everyone who is prejudiced is unhealthy : all human beings are guilty of prejudice. But in his ordinary life a healthy man will show common sense. He will be what we call a reasonable man, though far removed, as a rule, from Freud's ideal of the man who is controlled by reason.

Finally, the healthy man does not need to feel that he is moved by what we call " a purpose in life." Since he is able to tolerate in himself the main biological instincts, these will provide him with goals suitable to the various stages of his growth. He will want to cease being a child and achieve the privileges of an adult ; to outstrip companions ; to support himself ; to be liked by his fellows ; " to do the decent thing " ; to be a husband and father who does well by his family and is loved by them. Special gifts and interests will add to this list. This is an imperfect world but it provides plenty to do, to see and to desire. The feeling that one lacks a purpose in life is a tragic but morbid state, usually the result of the maldevelopment or frustration of sexual urges. It is not experienced by happy lovers. Nor does the agricultural labourer, narrow though his life may seem to be, complain that it has no meaning.

The belief that one has such a purpose is valued by those who possess it. This occurs when a tremendous amount of mental energy is being poured through some particular channel and the process is found to give relief from anxiety and guilt. So long as progress towards the goal is not too difficult, and the goal itself not too far removed from the group of pursuits which bring happiness, such men will enjoy their lives. Whether they are socially valuable will depend entirely upon the real nature of the purpose. As in the case of " doing good to others," this is sometimes the opposite of what they think it.

The reader may be feeling by this time that it is easy for anyone to draw up a list of qualities which he thinks desirable and label them as the signs of mental health. He could do it himself, and be better pleased with the result. I must ask him to believe that this is not what I have done. The list is based upon wo things—the main forms of mental disease, and the commoner ways in which mental and moral development may be arrested or twisted. And the description given is that of a human being who has reached adult life without succumbing to any of these dangers.

To put it in other words, the healthy human being is neither mad, neurotic nor mentally defective, not over half-way toward any of these states. He has not developed any of the criminal tendencies, perversions, or gross defects of character which indicate major fixations or twisted or stunted growth. He has outgrown, for instance, both the baby's complete selfishness and self-absorption, and his automatic surrender to the impulse of the moment. He has outgrown the small child's complete dependence on others, and can think for himself except in spheres where he is ignorant or has been taught that to think is wrong. His love impulses have passed through all the complex phases of their growth without being seriously warped. And if any reader will take the trouble to check these statements I believe he will find that the description given does not go beyond the limits laid down for it.

This means that human beings who fail to achieve the standards mentioned, fall short of mental health. For once we accept the fact that the development of his moral nature is part of a man's normal growth, we admit that he cannot be healthy unless he is reasonably virtuous.

Before considering the limits of this conception, and what must be added to it in order to describe the good man at whom we should aim, it seems necessary to clear away one common misconception. Many people, among them some psychologists, speak and write as though there were no such thing as a definite state which can be described as mental health. They remind us that no one is perfectly normal; that what is thought sane in one place is considered mad in another; that there are infinite degrees of mental soundness.

These statements are true enough, but they do not lead to the conclusion based upon them. Men's idea of what is sane does vary from group to group and age to age. In many communities what we now class as hysterical symptoms have been regarded as heavenly graces and signs of direct inspiration. For an example we may take the appearance of stigmata upon the hands and feet of mediaeval mystics. Vicious cruelty has been taken as a sign of courage in many other groups besides Red

Indian tribes. But the fact that there are variations in standards does not make all practices healthy, however " normal " they may be considered by the group concerned ; however " normal " they may be in the sense of being ordinary. In fact the whole argument seems to be based on a confusion between these different senses of the word normal. Customs of this sort develop from peculiar factors in the environment and from the influence of peculiar leaders. But doctors do not admit that goitre is not a disease because it is due to the absence of iodine in the water-supply, or because some artists think swollen necks beautiful, or because everybody in the district suffers from it.

In practice such customs are found to be associated with other signs of mental sickness, and to have undesirable effects. Head-hunters, for instance, are acknowledged to be certainly the gloomiest and among the most bellicose of human groups. They are given to drinking themselves almost to death as soon as they get the chance, and so long as the custom continues are refractory to education. Moreover they are ghost-ridden, and suffer agonies of fear on this account. Healthy peoples do not take to habits such as these, so that they not only cause but pre-suppose vast quantities of ferocity and misery. These are the two qualities which are most closely connected with mental illness, though the fact is sometimes masked.

The statement that no one exists who is in perfect health is no doubt true. Healthy minds are more difficult to build than healthy bodies. There may be no perfect triangle in existence, but that does not prevent us from conceiving one, nor from drawing interesting and useful deductions about its properties. And since health is improvable, given the necessary knowledge and goodwill, it must surely be useful to possess a picture of what a healthy mind should be like.

There is then a sense in which we may correctly speak of mental health and assert that it must form part of any description of the good man, if by good men we mean those types of human being whom it is desirable to breed and to encourage. The number of these types will obviously be great. Nor will it ever be possible to lay down the law and say that our knowledge of them is complete. Heredity varies enormously and may always confront us with new sports. The environment is never the same for any two children, even twins. All we can say is that certain qualities ought to be encouraged in everyone, e.g., affection and a sense of justice—and that other courses of conduct are always bad, such as terrifying a child into lying or sexual perversion. In detail each child needs slightly different treatment if the best is to be made of him and he is to be happily adjusted to his surroundings. There can never be any question of rigid uniformity —that would fail to make the best of almost everybody.

To return to the good man : the next question seems to be what more he needs besides physical and mental health, and we may get a few pointers by considering the limitations of this conception.

A healthy man may possess an equipment of ideas quite inadequate for the part in life which it would be well for him to play. His interests may not extend beyond his personal affairs and those of his immediate neighbours. In this case his sympathies are likely to be as narrow as his interests. He may be devoid of culture, and work off his surplus aggression by nothing more valuable than horse-play and violent forms of sport. He will have common sense, but common sense alone does not give the power to attack and solve complex or technical or unfamiliar problems. For that both training and experience are necessary. He may be unfitted therefore to be a citizen of any but the simplest form of group.

This will not prevent him from being good in the limited sense of virtuous. But it will prevent him from being one of the types of man needed in our complicated modern states. And it is the actual world in which we live that we are discussing, not rustic Arcadias, nor flower-decked South Sea Islanders dancing on some undiscovered coral strand. The man of limited information and unpractised mind is usually suspicious of what he does not understand, and in this and various other ways a drag upon not only reform but adjustments made necessary by changes in circumstances. It is this which makes him so dear to many minds.

The good man, therefore, unless we are considering merely the docile subjects of tyrants, must also be sufficiently informed to understand the questions which he is expected to decide. For instance he should be able to judge the records and speeches of his political representatives, if any, and to understand, in outline, the laws and institutions of his country, as well as possessing the technical skills which he may need for a tolerable life. The good woman will do her work efficiently, including the job of bringing up children who will be at home in the modern world. And as well as this, in most countries, she must face responsibilities as a citizen and be trained to perform them adequately. As

Confucius said, the people have a right to instruction, though nowadays to far more instruction than he ever dreamed of. Knowledge, in short, is an essential factor in the goodness which we are trying to define. How much knowledge is needed will depend upon circumstances. Knowledge alone, however, is not sufficient without good judgment. By this I mean the power to select from one's stores of information what is relevant to particular situations, set the rest aside, and draw correct conclusions. This capacity requires love of truth, mental honesty, scrupulous respect for facts, willingness to abide by the weight of the evidence. Nor is it possible without practice, and as a rule training in clear and accurate thinking. In short, the good man must have the wisdom which Plato, together with " reason and right principle " called " the king of all the virtues." And in the world of today one might add that he must face life with something of the scientific spirit.[1]

Here I am sure that a great many people will disagree flatly. They feel that the spirit of science is cold and ugly and uncomfortable, that it bars out all the more beautiful and lofty emotions and cramps the soul. What the world needs is not more science, but higher aspirations and a more passionate yearning for the ideal. Sometimes they will add that truth is not enough, we must pursue the Higher Truths which are beyond man's understanding.

I hope I have written enough both about love and beauty to make it clear that if we respect the facts we shall place on both the highest possible value. Good feeling is the key to the good life. But even good feeling should be based upon truth if it is to produce its full effects. Not all forms of love are of benefit to those upon whom they are lavished. To love a tyrant with selfless devotion increases his tyranny, whether we are thinking of a home or of a state. To say that all our feelings should be controlled by knowledge does not mean that one undervalues either warmth or spontaneity. These are lovely, and it is a pity that they should fertilise evil, or run to waste in unprofitable ground. I would go further and say that to approach human problems, and one's own personal longings, in a scientific spirit, allows far more scope for good feeling instead of less. To ask : " What brought him to this dreadful state ?—what made him what he is ? " enables us to replace disgust by pity, and hatred by the interest which may lead to help being given.

[1] Not " as a scientist " because a great many scientists fail to carry the ideals of science into their ordinary lives, and in everything outside their special subject are content to think like savages.

The same principle holds true for our own minds. We need understanding and mercy to deal with these as well, and the ability to regard them dispassionately while we are doing so.

Ultimately the difference of opinion on this point is absolute. Either one believes that strict intellectual integrity is a virtue, or one does not. Few, of course, are likely to deny this proposition *in toto*. Most prefer to empty it of meaning by declaring that we must set bounds to the use of reason, and that special faculties such as " the religious sense " and the " super-normal " mind have a higher claim to our allegiance. They cannot be prevented from believing this if they want to. The fact that no trace has ever been found by psychologists of any such unusual faculties, while all their supposed manifestations can be traced back clearly to well-known mental mechanisms, will not affect such people at all. They need only reply that many things have yet to be discovered, and that scientists are always altering their theories. The reader who wants information on the subject may be referred to *Introduction to the Psychology of Religion* by Thouless, and to *The Psychology of Religious Mysticism* by Leuba.

Since it is necessary in this controversy to stand on one side or the other, we may affirm that our good man will place among his ideals mental honesty in its ordinary scientific sense.

The next point will be, perhaps, more readily conceded. It is the importance of " culture." A great many people who find intense pleasure in art and literature, who set great store by their knowledge of history or the habits of birds or the cross-currents of musical idiom, have no desire that these or similar tastes should be shared by the bulk of the population, and may even dislike the prospect. But in the sense in which culture means the ability to appreciate what is beautiful, to feel interest in all the manifold aspects of life and to make the best of one's own talents, most of us will probably admit that to be cultured is a valuable attribute.

What has already been said about art is true in some degree of all voluntary occupations and hobbies. Creative work gives pleasure, and its performance has such healing force that it is being more and more generally employed as a cure for mental disease. To have made something, even if only the maker regards it as useful or beautiful, lightens guilt and acts as an antidote to self-contempt. The appreciation of sound or beautiful objects not only brings happiness to the man who feels it, but leads to their production in greater quantities. And ugliness does produce depression and resentment even when it is not consciously felt.[1]

Since most daily work at the present time is neither creative nor connected in any way with beauty, the deliberate introduction of these factors into leisure occupations becomes of great importance. Culture is not a mere side-issue, a final grace which can be reserved for the fortunate or those most eager for it. It should form part of the life of the ordinary man and be regarded as an important aid to the formation of a stable character. Art at least is normal to human beings in the sense of common. The ugliness by which Europeans and their off-shoots are surrounded today is a new and let us hope only a passing phase. It is perpetuated by bad educational traditions,[2] foolish conceptions of what is becoming in a man of business, and the erroneous idea that it pays to make cheap articles ugly in order that higher prices may be obtained for anything that is not actively offensive.

Next, a man may be healthy enough and yet possess a moral code which is defective because it is limited or out of date. He may be just and kind within his family circle and yet regard all foreigners with suspicion. He may be honest in his dealings with neighbours and lack any sense of public obligation. He may have been taught that women are animals without souls and treat them accordingly; that employees are a pack of lazy, cheating devils towards whom no mercy should be shown. He may feel perfectly happy manufacturing shoddy goods on the ground that they are meant for the poor who cannot afford anything better. A healthy human being will make reasonable efforts to live up to the code which he has been taught, but he cannot be expected to improve upon it. Violent aggression, as we have seen, rouses a sense of guilt in everybody unless it is backed by the whole weight of public opinion and accorded the approval of Heaven. Most other harmful actions are felt as wicked only as the result of example and instruction.

The " good " man then, will have a full and rational scale of moral values. He may have been taught them, or he may have reconsidered the values that he was taught, realised their defects and revised them in the double light of reason and good feeling. The world regards successful moral reformers as its greatest men. But few are capable of such behaviour, and if we are thinking of human beings in general the good man or woman

---

[1] Dr. John Rickman has explained this in his paper on the unconscious connection between beauty, health and goodness.

[2] Teachers who attempt to instil cultural values into children, where any such attempt is made, are often not of types whose values children are prepared to introject.

must have had a sound moral training. And by " sound " I mean a training given in such a way that it has taken effect.

So far the good man has been considered almost entirely as the valuable man whose life and activities will be of benefit to others. Since morality is so largely a matter of one's duty to others this order is defensible. A gregarious creature cannot be fulfilling his proper functions unless he is playing a suitable part in the life of his group. But man is not wholly gregarious : he has also his private inner life, his ideal of what he ought to be in and for himself and it will probably seem to most readers that I have not yet touched upon the core of morality—personal virtue.

A healthy human being will be well enough adjusted to his surroundings to be reasonably moral—always provided of course that the environment is not of a sort which destroys goodness. Surely it is the duty of the " good " man to be more ? And what then is to be the essence of morality, if it be denied that it is duty to a god ?

Does it not consist in taking wisdom for one's guide, in adopting consciously, as permanent ideals and principles, ends which the merely healthy man follows piecemeal, and then in a systematic effort to rule one's life in accordance with these principles ? One or two examples will show what I mean.

The healthy man helps a neighbour who is in trouble because he is a kindly creature, and not merely because he himself may be in trouble some day and need that neighbour's help. The virtuous man does the same thing whether he is feeling kind at the moment or not, because he can realise that his momentary lack of good feeling is irrelevant, and recognises the particular case as an example of a general duty which on the whole he is unwilling to shirk.

The healthy man cannot be expected to run his head against established customs even when they are the cause of suffering to others. Unless his pity has been touched, his imagination stirred or his own interests seriously challenged he will be guided largely by public opinion. The virtuous man will ask himself where the real rights and wrongs of the matter lie, whether he is entitled to take advantage of custom, and what in the long run will be the consequences of his behaviour. And he will act upon the decision he reaches.

In short he will take an enlightened, that is to say a rational, view of moral problems, and be able to replace any temporary lack of good feeling by an appreciation of its general value.

At this point it may be asked : " Then why not say at once that virtue is striving to be good ? That the virtuous man is the man who always tries to do right. That is the usual meaning of the term."

If virtuous be confined to this meaning, it must follow that a man can be virtuous without being good. In the first place striving is not enough, one must also succeed. A drunkard is not considered virtuous because he makes ineffectual efforts to give up the drink, and thus adds to the miseries of inebriety the misery of failure. Moreover many human beings pursue false ideals, doing a great deal of harm to those around them in the process. It is, surely, twisting the meaning of words to call a Gestapo torturer virtuous because in order to obey his Führer and the old German gods he is forcing himself to overcome his lingering remnants of pity and humanity. Confucius and the Greeks were right when they made knowledge and wisdom an essential part not only of a man's value but of his virtue. The capacity for moral effort is very important, but it is not the whole of virtue. On the contrary we sometimes call saints those from whom good actions seem to flow naturally, without any conflict at all. We do not think of Christ as virtuous only because of the agony in the garden, but because of the whole tenor and conduct of his life.

We may therefore describe the virtuous man as one whose knowledge and intelligence and character enable him to achieve a consistently high level of conduct. This is almost the opposite of Aristotle's idea that he is a man with an established habit of good conduct. It is true that good habits are extremely useful, if only because they save a lot of trouble, but they are not enough. For one thing they do not enable their owners to face unfamiliar situations.[1]

Secondly, the question is begged by the word " established." How are good habits established—i.e., not only formed but maintained ? Because, except in very docile and inhibited persons, they flow from a good character. Many a child who has been coerced into good habits has abandoned them as soon as he felt himself free. The good man reveals himself in his conduct, some part of which will be habitual.

Where does all this bring us to ? The virtuous man will be

---

[1] A group of children were brought up by Behaviourist parents on the theory that the right method of training character is to form good habits by an unvarying system of rewards and punishments. This is said to have worked very well until the children were sent to school, when they were completely bewildered and thrown off their balance by the need to think for themselves and make fresh adjustments.

kind, just, honest, slow to take anger, merciful and resolved to do right without morbid fears about his own sinfulness. His intellectual powers will be used to face facts, learn from experience and conquer prejudices of which he is aware. In short he is pretty well what rational thinkers have always supposed him to be, minus various traits added by individual moralists on account of their circumstances or their temperaments. According to this picture of him he will not be an ascetic, nor undervalue happiness and the pleasures of this world. He will be but rarely a philosopher, and not necessarily a member of a ruling class. But he must be a good citizen in the active sense of the word ; that is, he will discharge, honestly and competently, what public duties are expected of him. And he will be more valuable if he is also a man of wide culture.

Having reached this point, are we any the better off for having described him in a roundabout way, starting from the notion of health, instead of using one of the methods by which much the same results have been reached in the past ? The method used gives, I think, several important advantages. In the first place the description is based upon relevant facts derived from our knowledge of mental health. Secondly, mental health seems to most people an unquestionable good. Some exceptions to this rule have already been given, others are found among champions of religion. They are tempted often enough to welcome guilt and remorse and anxiety in others, because these may make them converts to the creed. The lost sheep is dear to the shepherd and the prodigal son is feasted. But no good shepherd wants his sheep to stray, nor does any father hope that his sons will go to the bad because their return may some day give him cause for rejoicing. The repentant human being is not really a satisfactory phenomenon, though to feel that he is may be a great temptation.

Neurotics, and perverts too, are often found clinging to their miserable state, and preaching to the other foxes that they should cut off their tails. Since their symptoms do protect them in some measure from anxiety, they cannot bear the idea of losing them. But it will be a clear gain when an adequate knowledge of what mental health entails enables us to discount opinions which are the offspring of mental sickness.

The second advantage is that once the close link between mental health and good behaviour and happiness has been realised, the way is cleared for methods and procedures which will make human beings better behaved, as well as very much happier. These methods will be effective because they will be based on scientific data, on observed sequences of cause and effect, instead of on what one set of human beings feel that others ought to be or do. Practices which are found to hamper or distort the healthy development of the mind can be avoided and replaced by those which further its normal growth.

Such knowledge will be, of course, especially valuable in the field of education. This does not mean that every parent must be a trained psychologist. An enormous improvement in the physical health of our children has been attained without every mother becoming a doctor. It is just as feasible to spread the knowledge of simple facts about mental hygiene as about the physical needs of the young. And mothers respond to such teaching. Already some of the basic principles which derive from the work of modern psychologists have filtered through to large numbers of people who hardly know the word psychology, with the result that their children are treated far more kindly and sensibly and are far less ridden by fear than they were.

In the same way the conception of crime as an abnormality due to complex factors, even if many criminals are incurable, will give better results than were achieved by treating it as sin.

Lastly, once the great tyrants, conquerors, oppressors and successful thieves are seen for what they are—ugly cases of mental disease, or childish creatures who are the slaves of impulses which they ought to have outgrown—their glamour will be gone. When this happens they will neither attract followers nor be able to hypnotise their prey. Men will not admire the rocket as it rises both because they will forsee the coming fall, and because they will be able to realise the wretched state of these truly unenviable men—their inability to love, to keep friends, or ever to enjoy their gains; the fearful inner conflicts, inexhaustible lusts and unquenchable hatreds which beset them. The penalties paid by the wicked have been pointed out again and again by moralists. But moralists have failed to convince because appearances were against them. It is pleasant to think of powerful men doing all the forbidden acts after which one hankers, and getting away with it. But once these acts are known as symptoms of illness and the real penalties that attend them are realised they cease to that extent to seem pleasant. Who could want to be Hitler now?

The question of how free men shall choose their leaders has always been considered one of the root problems of democratic states. It will become very much easier of solution once there is a correct general appreciation of what is meant by mental health, and what is involved in its absence.

The psychological method of approach is, then, defensible, because it points the way to securing a higher standard of actual behaviour, to say nothing of an immeasurable increase in human happiness. And to achieve these two ends does seem for all the reasons given, to be the primary function of a moral system.

CHAPTER 13

THE GOOD SOCIETY (1)

For any moralist one attribute of a good society must be that it is able to produce good men. But this is not a sufficient criterion. Russia under the late Tzar was in almost every respect about as bad as a state can be. Its organisation was centuries out of date; its government corrupt, cruel, stupid and inefficient. Nevertheless there sprang from this rotting society, generation after generation, numbers of ardent and unselfish reformers, and at last a body of men who were able to make a success of the most thorough-going social revolution that the world has ever seen. In part this was due to the fact that the leaders who carried out the gigantic task, like their predecessors, had absorbed the spirit and traditions of revolutionary Europe. Driven into exile, they were able to acquire the knowledge that their own country denied them, and finally to apply an effective technique to the problems of first destroying and then rebuilding the Russian state. But the spirit that impelled them to do this came from Russia itself. They could not have succeeded if they had not found there, as well as the conditions which make for revolution, hundreds of thousands of devoted followers.

This point is mentioned because it is sometimes said that since only atrocious misgovernment will drive most peoples to armed revolution, unsatisfactory conditions should be allowed to go from bad to worse in order to produce the true revolutionary ferment. This is tantamount to saying that revolutions are good in themselves. Since men of certain types feel in their hearts that this is true, even though they would not say more than: " Well, most governments could do with a bit of a jolt " it may be useful to remind them that wars—to which they are generally averse— have been justified in much the same way.[1]

---

[1] Mr. C. S. Lewis in *The Screwtape Letters* says : " Every now and then God permits a war in order to elicit the virtues of courage and fortitude." Surely this is nonsense, as well as a very pretty example of the elementary fallacy known as putting the cart before the horse ? Courage and fortitude are considered virtues because they are of very great use, both to the individual and his group, in times of danger and distress. It is absurd, in the logical sense of the word, to justify the danger and distress because they provide opportunities for the display of these qualities.

In the first place a brave man is a brave man, even if he has no particular occasion

In the case of revolutions, it is as well to remember that most attempts at rebellion have been crushed. And no state of society is worse as a rule than that which follows the stamping out of revolutionary movements. Next, even successful revolutions have bad as well as good results. The French Revolution abolished feudalism in France and put an end to many disgraceful abuses. But it set up strains in French society which the Republic was never able to overcome, and the bitter feuds and gross disloyalties which resulted from it helped to produce the collapse of France.

Because a terrible disease demands skilful operation, we do not therefore praise diseases on the ground that they alone will induce men to submit to operations. Bloody revolutions are desperate remedies, to be excused only by desperate situations and the absence of any other means of reform. It is not to the credit of a state that it is in process of producing a violent revolution, however deeply some may admire the men who carry it out.

If this be granted, then apart from evil conditions in which the greatest need of some particular state may be for the uncompromising rebels who are often a nuisance in better times, we are entitled to judge communities partly by their ability to breed and train large numbers of ordinary good men and women. And once it is allowed that these should be happy and healthy, as well as reasonably virtuous, public-spirited and well-informed, we are far on the way to a definition of the good state. Good societies will vary widely, but all should offer social and economic conditions which ensure health, humane, efficient and honest administration and a widespread respect for art and learning.

To discuss the factors which produce physical health falls outside the scope of this book, for it is the business of doctors, politicians, economists, teachers and specialists of various kinds. In Britain this set of problems is attracting a great deal of interest, and its implications in the field of housing, medical services, nutrition and the rest are being widely discussed. It is unnecessary to say more.

On the subject of mental health a great deal more might be said, if only because to most of us the matter is unfamiliar. But Ethics is concerned in the main with aims and ideals, and with means only in a broad and general way. For instance any system

for showing it, and God must know that he is. Secondly, war elicits not only virtues, but cowardice, treachery, and sickening cruelty, together with greed, dishonesty and intrigue. It is good that the man who is being tortured to death by the Gestapo should die bravely, but what of his torturers? Would it not have been better if the crime had never been committed? If not, why should anybody try to stop any crime? Many murderers have provided opportunities for the display of courage by policemen.

of morals must depend for its practical effect upon bringing up children in such a way that they are likely to carry it out. But that does not mean that every book on Ethics should include a manual of Child Guidance.[1] It is sufficient to point out that if adults ought to possess certain qualities, then the method of education used must be one that will actually elicit or implant these qualities, where this can be done.

But there is one subject upon which I propose to say something, because it illustrates an important principle. That is the difference between regarding "social justice" as wise or politic for the moment; looking upon sound morale and stable temperaments as useful in a crisis, and regarding them as moral ends which must be pursued on the level of right and wrong. This attitude can be justified in a sentence by saying that a good man does not accept the benefits of, say, an industrial civilisation while denying the obligations which it lays upon him. But as these neat little aphorisms are unacceptable to many minds, this one shall be fortified by an illustration.

If prolonged unemployment, or the fear of unemployment, are degrading forces, and if the main task of the good state is to rear good men, then it becomes the unescapable duty of every government, no matter what its creeds and predelictions, to put an end to it. The limit to the means used can only be that they would certainly produce even worse results than unemployment.

There is a great deal of evidence from many sources that prolonged unemployment and fear of unemployment have undesirable effects upon those exposed to them. So far as I know there is not one single piece of evidence to the contrary. Moreover, they are not merely an economic disaster and the cause of privation and physical suffering. If they were, their evil effects might be averted by a sufficiently generous and intelligent system of relief. They are also poisons which attack some of the most valuable elements in the mind. No one is likely to deny, for instance, that they cause almost universal anxiety. The poor skate, so to speak, on the surface of a nightmare into which they may be plunged at any moment: the rich begin to fear the poor, and are tempted at the same time to deny the reality of their sufferings. This of itself is sufficient condemnation. But in addition, to be unemployed for any length of time is in itself a harmful experience. It undermines men's self-respect, destroys their standing and authority in their own homes, and deprives them of the most valuable out-

---

[1] What I have to say on this subject will be found in my book, *Worry in Women*.

let for their aggression. To feel that one is on the scrap-heap, and that with every day the likelihood grows that one may be there for the rest of one's life : that one is of no use, perhaps a burden on the children whom it was one's pride to bring up well and with better opportunities than one's own ; to realise that one is helpless though not to blame, is to be in a state of corrosive misery as well as intense frustration.

Whether this drives men to rebellion, illness, cynicism, apathy or to such dissipations as they can still afford, depends upon their natures and the circumstances of each case. But worklessness and the fear of worklessness are social poisons, undermining personality destroying civilised values, and forcing their victims back into the narrowest possible circle of interests. A couple of examples of how this tendency works will explain what I mean.

A generation ago education and learning were widely valued in this country among the working classes as goods in themselves, and very great sacrifices were made both by groups and by thousands of individuals to obtain the benefits of wider knowledge and a broader mind. But since the slump that followed the 1914–18 war this conception has narrowed. It is a general complaint that education is now valued solely as a means to earning one's living. An immediate job is the only end to which many parents look forward for their children, and no mental or moral improvement is considered by the side of this. It is useless to talk of the value of knowledge, of a child's gifts and capacities, to parents who are haunted by this anxiety. They may listen and even feel flattered, but their decisions will be governed by the dominant fear.

Another example is, of course, restrictive practices in vital industries. These will be justified by real and imaginary grievances, but everyone knows that they flourish in trades where jobs are temporary, or hard to come by. Fear of being workless drives whole groups of our decent, sensible British workers into complete disregard of the national interest, and something that can look very like dishonesty towards their employers.[1]

The appearance of Fascist tendencies in the middle classes was due in many cases to the same fear. It might be disguised as dread of Bolshevism, but the real dread was of losing privileges which were felt to be the last barrier against a rising flood. The real situation which confronted the young men who wore black shirts was that they found themselves in a jobless world where their

---

[1] A good book on the effects of unemployment on personality is *The Unemployed Man* by Bakke, an American research worker who was given facilities by the government to study the problem in this country.

privileges were no use to them. The Anti-Semitism, the *Führer Prinzip* and the rest of it were attached to this fear by skilful propaganda. Under a more prepossessing leader the movement would have had a much wider appeal.

Widespread and prolonged unemployment is a disintegrating force which undoes the work of years of effort to civilise populations. It should be regarded therefore not merely as an economic maladjustment but as a national disgrace. For the same reason the provision of useful work should be considered a duty of the first order. This is not a matter about which honourable men should feel themselves entitled to take sides, or from which they have any right to disinterest themselves. What we have here is a simple moral issue.

I stress this because to believe that a state of affairs is disgraceful is a stronger incentive to effective action than to feel that it is unfortunate. It is a truism to say that during the last slump all the means for providing employment were at hand; idle money, idle machines and unused raw materials. Ignorance played a part, but what was lacking at bottom was goodwill and love of our neighbour. As a nation we were deficient in the sympathy with his distress which gives insight into his problems, the incentive which makes men resolve at all costs to right a shameful wrong. Seeing what Britain has accomplished during the war, the problems we have solved, the difficulties we have overcome, can anyone doubt that means could have been found of providing work, if as a people, we had wished to find them?

It may be thought that as a social evil poverty should come before unemployment, and that what I have said about moral duties should therefore have been applied instead to the abolition of poverty. One answer is that unemployment is a cause of poverty both for the workless man and for the state which fails to make use of his labour. There is another answer as well. Customary poverty can be endured without lack of self-respect. Generally speaking it gives rise to resentment and humiliation only when it is felt to be unnecessary and unjust. Taken with its attendant evils of sub-normal health, lack of opportunity and narrowness of outlook, it should be resented on behalf of the poor by all their more fortunate neighbours. But the poor themselves, unless and until they feel that they are being exploited, will suffer it with the meekness of apathy.

Further, the abolition of poverty may or may not be feasible. That depends upon factors which are not always within the control of the group concerned—climate, soil, natural resources, inventive genius, willingness to work and ability to organise. It cannot be a moral obligation to achieve the impossible.

It is for this reason that it was not until after the invention of machines that men's consciences began to trouble them about the poverty of the masses. Occasional islands of dazzling wealth are valued even by the poorest as stimulants to ambition or material for daydreams. We are all brought up as children in rooms where almost everything is the property of adults who will not allow us to play with it. Even our toys are not wholly our own. They must be put away when we are told, and perhaps lent to other children. It seems natural therefore to all but the most rebellious that leaders and rulers should be rich while others are not. Until this state of affairs has been made to seem unjust, it will be tolerated without mental damage.

To turn from employment to work itself: Important as is the provision of work merely as a means to earning a living, it will be far more of a solace and support if it can be felt to be useful and valuable. To spend the best part of one's life making shoddy or unnecessary objects, or at some process whose place in the scheme of production is not understood, induces cynicism and an evaluation of effort in terms of nothing but money. Where the job is involved we get the attitude summed up in :—

> " We go to work
> To get the money
> To buy the food
> To give us strength
> To go to work."

It is the parent of laziness and bad workmanship.

This fact is becoming more widely understood. Everyone remembers that sending pilots down to the aeroplane factories after the Battle of Britain in order to thank the workers, of displaying completed machines to those who were manufacturing small parts, or explaining that a special lot of tanks would be sent straight to Russia, were helpful in maintaining output. But if work is to take its proper place in men's feelings instead of being regarded as a hateful necessity, much more use should be made of such methods. Pride in craftsmanship is a valuable protection against guilt and anxiety, not the invention of amateur potters,

Moreover if a man's work falls into the category of something about which he knows little, and over which he has almost no control, other spheres of interest, like politics, tend to be regarded in the same way. All sense of responsibility for other than personal affairs is lost, until only the markedly ambitious and rebellious types are willing to become active citizens.

In the same way homes of which they can feel proud, where they can point to the results of their labour and call them good, are essential to the health and happiness of women. To spend years of heartbreaking drudgery in rooms that can never look cheerful or even really clean, that give no pleasure to the eye, which one can never show off with satisfaction, and above all where children do not flourish, wears away not only hope but self-respect.

In the slums escape is only possible either by keeping oneself to oneself and avoiding all human contacts in a bitter attempt to avoid the squalor round one, or to accepting not only for oneself but for one's family what are really animal standards. This fact too, however, is now generally realised, and no more need be said about it.

When we have agreed that the modern community must protect, succour and train its citizens, besides providing them with opportunities for self-development, we have only described one aspect of the good state. It has also external obligations—what is now called the duty to be a good neighbour. But before going on to deal with that it may be best to consider another vexed question, that of its organisation. At the moment there seems to be no hope of agreement on such questions as state control versus private enterprise, the retention of some forms of status versus a classless society, and absolute government versus democracy. The last controversy is supposed to have been settled by the arbitrament of war, but wars, while decisive for a time in practice, do not produce final answers.

The first point to be judged seems to be whether any of these matters are moral issues and not merely matters of expediency. And provided that they do not interfere with the development of individuals, nor promote unneighbourly conduct, on the whole I should have thought that they must be classed as matters of expediency. This, of course, is to take Kant's view that only human beings are ends in themselves ; everything else is only a means. It follows from this that states can be judged only by their effects on the human race, either in the present or the future.

But the proviso just made still holds. Anyone who believes that autocracies must always end in wars, or that capitalism has shot its bolt and can no longer provide a tolerable standard of living for the workers, will of course feel that both these institutions are evil, and should decide that he has a moral duty to fight against them.

Nevertheless it remains true that what suits one people will not necessarily suit another : that what is required in one period will not fulfil the needs of a later age. And this holds for the future as it has held in the past. In the matter of democracy we have all seen for ourselves that a free people involved in a total war may find it necessary to surrender, for the moment, many of its most ancient and treasured liberties.

Again, Lenin seems to have believed that an ideal society would need a minimum of restrictive government. But few will deny that he was right when he decided that the population of Russia would need a generation of training and education before they could be entrusted with democratic institutions. And if we may judge from their behaviour during the election held under the Stalin Constitution, the people of Russia agreed with him at that time.

In fact, during the period which preceded the war it was frequently said that not all peoples had reached the stage at which they could make a success of democracy. During the war this idea receded into the background, but it has already been sharply recalled to our minds. History at any rate gives us many examples of attempts at democracy that have ended in tyrannies, and of reforms and salvage operations which could only have been carried out by enlightened autocrats. George Washington is a case in point. Or we may remember that the extension of the Roman Empire was resisted fiercely by the peoples it conquered and that its rule was for many good reasons often unpopular. But the benefits it conferred on its subjects were so great that we now, on the whole, consider those nations fortunate who passed under the Roman yoke.

Whether any more of such civilising work remains to be done; whether every human group has now reached the stage at which it can be left to manage its own affairs without becoming either a slum or an intolerable nuisance, remains to be seen. But though democracy is a form of government difficult to work, it may, for all that, be the form at which all groups should aim. In the first place, though a particular democracy may be no better, or worse, than some especially benevolent tyranny, no means has yet been discovered for keeping a series of tyrants benevolent. If such a method were discovered, the controversy would, no doubt, acquire new life. And in the meantime successful democratic states have two advantages over autocracies. One is that healthy-minded people prefer to live in them; the second that they are more likely, in the long run, to breed healthy-minded people. It may therefore be considered a duty to aid and encourage all groups to work towards democracy, and another to grant them democratic institutions as soon as it seems wise to do so. This may seem to be putting things mildly, but when it comes to the laying down of duties, one should be sure of one's ground.

In the same way the opposition between state control and private enterprise must surely be judged by the exigencies of the age. What is useful, and in so far as it is useful, right, at one period may easily be wrong at another. Most people are agreed that a good deal of planning and regimentation are needed if economic chaos is to be avoided at the present time. If this is so, then those who oppose or try to sabotage either the international co-operation which must be its basis, or the consequent restrictions placed upon individual nations and industries, will be doing wrong. If they act for selfish reasons, we may call them wicked. But this does not mean that all planning is virtuous or even useful.

The argument may be advanced that any intelligent planning is likely to give better results than the haphazard interplay of thousands of different ambitions and aims, hitting or missing in a general scramble. No reasonable man will deny the force of this. On the other hand it must be remembered that all restraints upon desired liberties are resented. And except in periods of emergency, or in peoples whose customs have been stereotyped over long periods, every fresh extension of control into the personal life of the individual will increase resentment. And this will be true of many types of good citizens as well as of the undisciplined and predatory. Men are not ants or bees and will never resemble those insects. But they do tend to judge general problems in the light of their own experience. Some period of confusion persuades a large number of people that close organisation is necessary if an economic breakdown is to be prevented. The planning involved, and perhaps even the detailed measures which seem desirable, are then praised, advocated and believed in for their own sakes, and erected into absolute standards for society. But once this main purpose has been achieved, the restraints imposed begin to provoke a reaction. Liberty and the rights of the individual regain their enchantment and a social philosophy is built up, or dug up, which enshrines them as the new ideal. And the new ideal gains force as the sense of frustration accumulates. On this account those who fear that the future holds nothing but some particular horror—say, complete subordination of the individual to the machine—are haunted by a bogey of their own invention. In this country it is far more likely that the reaction will come before it is really needed.

The aim, therefore, in any group must be to adopt that organisation which will give the best results in the circumstances. What they will be differs not only with the environment but with the materials of which a group is composed. An anxious human group like the Germans will accept as normal a stricter discipline than a people like our own. And, owing to the enormous accumulation of hatred which has been going on, the same tendency is likely to appear in peoples who normally prefer a large amount of political liberty.

What is true of the opposition between liberty and planned societies is true of most other political ideals. There is nothing sacred about them. They are not their own justification. They can be justified only by arguments based upon their effects.

The doctrine that forms of society are not ends in themselves is unlikely ever to be popular, since if there is a thing which most of us like to take for granted it is the absolute rightness of our political ideals. To deny this is to be placed under a continual necessity for thought and reconsideration which only those who enjoy thinking can be expected to find tolerable. This cannot be helped. But the more enlightened, the more reasonable, the more friendly human beings become, the easier it will be for them to use political institutions as means instead of exalting them into fixed ideals which must be defended at all costs and even perhaps forced upon others. Some human beings will always have a liking for change, while others cling to tradition. It is when both these parties possess the qualities named that smooth adjustments can be made as they become necessary.

If political systems and institutions are good or bad only in relation to the circumstances, are there any other qualities of states which must be considered an integral part of the notion " good " ? What about such terms as strong, stable, wealthy, glorious— can they be called absolutely desirable, granted that the society concerned be good in other ways ?

It may at first seem obvious that the good state should be all these things except perhaps the last—though a glorious past is often considered an asset even by those who most fervently hope to avoid a glorious future. But if we examine them more closely we shall see that not all these attributes stand on the same footing. Wealth in the hands of the good is a blessing, and a good society should have enough of it to ensure a tolerable life for all its members. Without a modicum of wealth a group is in practice precluded from attaining goodness of the sort that has been described. Unceasing toil from dawn to dark which produces only mere subsistence may evoke a sturdiness of character useful in war. But peasants settled on poor soils are as a rule narrow, dour, avaricious and filled with suspicion and fear of the unknown. They have no chance to become anything else, unless they form part of a larger unit which can and will expend upon them some of its surplus money and energy. The good state does depend in part upon a sufficiency of resources.

Strength and stability are different matters. Nearly everyone desires them for his own group. But very great strength has often been an overwhelming temptation, and stability should not be so complete that it passes over into stagnation. In fact the good state will possess enough stability as a whole to permit of considerable changes in its parts, without producing acute anxiety.

As for foreign states, it is difficult to judge them objectively because our feelings towards them are much affected by what we believe about their feelings towards us. Most people want their friends to be strong and stable and their enemies disunited and weak. The question of what these nations are, in and for themselves, is in normal times a secondary consideration. Before the war for instance, those of us who loathed Nazi Germany seldom stopped to consider how much the Nazis were enjoying themselves.

At the moment, of course, the times are not normal. World opinion is split between rival ideologies which very often count for more than the usual national divisions. Large numbers of people have pinned all their hopes and dreams upon some country which is not their own because it embodies, or is thought to embody, their particular creed. In this case other nations are rated as good or bad by their relation to this chosen home from home. Its friends are the believer's friends, its foes his foes. And all his other judgments are made accordingly.

In short, nearly all that can be said about such attributes as we are discussing depends upon the fact that societies as we know them exist not alone but surrounded by others, and that these others are potential enemies. In such a world the good society must not be weak, even if the necessity for remaining armed uses up men and money and machine-power that it had rather devote to other objects. One school of thought would even like to force every small state into a confederation on the ground that its weakness constitutes a perpetual danger. In fact to such a pitch have we come that to be oneself a threat to nobody is thought likely to undermine the virtue of the states next door.

We can proceed no further, then, with an analysis of the good society until we have discussed the problem of its external duties.

CHAPTER 14

THE GOOD SOCIETY (2)

International morality is needed for the same purpose as group morality—the restraint of violence. It is more difficult to achieve for several reasons, of which the first is that nations differ from individuals. We are apt to underestimate this difference in our ordinary thinking, and we have several excuses for doing so. To begin with, during nearly the whole of the recorded past nations have been represented by individuals, particularly in the field of their foreign relations. The policy of a country depended largely upon the personality of its ruler, who was as a rule appointed by Heaven, descended from Heaven, or for some similar reason entitled to implicit obedience. If he enjoyed warfare, he went to war whenever he could screw up money enough to fit out an army. So close was this identification that Shakespeare used the words " France " and " England " for either the countries or their kings.

If we add to this the fact that in the unconscious mind one's country represents either the mother or the father, we shall see why to this day states are often referred to as though they were human beings.

Nations do sometimes, of course, behave like human beings, though seldom like sensible adults. It is not talking nonsense to say that some peoples are notoriously touchy, that some tend to bully, that others are suspicious, and that several regard themselves as the only really civilised—or democratic—country upon earth. Quite a number are obsessed by old hatreds which prevent them from dealing with current problems in a rational manner. In short there are such things as national traits and methods of regarding and treating neighbours, and these may endure through many generations.

Nevertheless the likeness between a person and a group is only superficial, and the dissimilarities are numerous and important. To begin with human beings have each a conscience, a set of ideals and a code of behaviour derived from family life. These, as we have seen, differ in almost every conceivable way, so that " the national conscience is shocked " can only mean, if true, that there is a general and temporary agreement upon some particular issue. Again, human beings pass through a long period of tutelage, during which they learn a certain amount of self-restraint and some elementary respect for the right of others, even if those others are only their near relations. Human groups do not. They are self-sufficient in a sense in which no man or woman can be self-sufficient.

Another difference, more important even than these, is that individuals possess loving and friendly feelings which, if not warped, will attach themselves in turn to parents, kindred and friends, to their own country and to groups within it. In healthy persons these feelings are more or less stable. Indeed people often argue that we need only extend them to other national groups for wars to end and the brotherhood of man to be achieved.

Unhappily, not only are nations, as nations, without these primitive feelings, but the transfer by individuals of loyalty and love from groups of which they are members to other groups, is blocked by several deep-seated tendencies. Indeed the very fealty and affection which a man feels for his own country sets in motion mechanisms which hinder him from extending goodwill towards others.

We fail to recognise this because the terms we use disguise the facts. We say, for instance, that England is the natural friend and ally of France. Even supposing that the current French government agrees, what does this mean but that the economic interests of the two countries are not thought to clash, that they have for the moment no competing territorial claims, and that another power or group of powers seems likely to prove troublesome to both? In the absence of danger and fear of danger allies are not needed. All this is very different from the statement that the French and English or, if you like, their leading statesmen, must be lacking in natural good feeling if they are not united in bonds of lasting affection.

The baldness of these facts is hidden from English eyes because a small but important section of our citizens do, as individuals, " love " various entities such as French scenery, painting, literature, cooking, French friends or holidays in France. They think of this as loving " France." Such sentiments may continue through periods of acute exasperation with French foreign policy, But it is possible to be a healthy and satisfactory human being without feeling love for any foreign country. And where this emotion exists in large amount it generally involves a double dose of hostility against the " enemies " of the country that is loved, even when they include one's native land.

The absence of any instinctive growth of affection for other groups is one obstacle to the formation of universal international goodwill. Another is the very strong human tendency to get rid of inconvenient hostility by placing it outside the groups to which one happens to belong. Just as a man who dislikes killing snails will throw them over his wall into the next door garden, so inimical feelings which would rouse guilt if turned against neighbours are bearable if vented upon outsiders. Membership of any group implies restraint and therefore resentment. And in the degree to which loyalty, love and admiration are felt towards a group this resentment must either be repressed—which cannot be done to order—or projected upon something else. Various impulses combine to make the most handy objects those without the pale. They are far away ; one's feelings cannot hurt them, and, alternatively, they deserve to be hurt since they have strange customs which are not those of decent men. Nor is one a man who dislikes without cause, as may be seen from one's friendly attitude at home.

Tendencies of this sort, however irrational and repugnant to the conscious mind, can only be controlled if they are recognised. And the need to displace hostility upon distant objects in order to avoid the unpleasantness it might cause in daily life, will always be a factor in human behaviour.

For though such a projection is only a device, it is one which is very useful. Daily life is what matters to most of us, not nations overseas. This chain of cause and effect is easy to trace in time of war, when so much energy is being devoted to destroying a common enemy that only the most quarrelsome want to go on pursuing feuds at home. During the Blitz, for instance, neighbours were regarded with something like affection, and generous help was forthcoming from the most unlikely quarters. On the other hand a German aviator who landed on an open space in South London was pursued with knives by a number of women from the houses round, and would certainly have been hurt if he had not been rescued by the police.

It has often been said that the best and quickest way to unite the inhabitants of this planet would be to start a war against Mars but it would have to be a perpetual war if unity were to be preserved.

Yet another of these unfortunate tendencies is fear and suspicion of the unknown. The dog with a different smell, the albino bird, the man with a black—or buff—skin, are regarded askance. This distrust is difficult to overcome, for it has a rational element. The social reactions of foreigners differ from our own, and we do not know what to expect of them. Call an African a nigger, and he takes offence. Why should he be so silly ? To be escorted to a foreign police station is apt to alarm even the innocent, however accessible the British Consul. " You never can know what these foreigners will be up to ! " leads on to : " or what dirty tricks they will not play."

In addition to these three forces we may recall the tendency, already mentioned, to project on to one's country desires and ambitions which the individual must relinquish for himself. One of these is independence of action. " My nation must be free to act as it thinks best ! We will never be controlled by foreigners who will use us for their own ends ! " The very idea rouses acute anxiety.

Others are power and prestige, pride and not giving a damn. Glory does not count for as much as it did, but wealth counts for more. In the first place peoples are demanding higher standards of living, and governments would like to satisfy these claims ; next, millions have been near starvation for the first time in their lives, and even in more fortunate countries such as this, large numbers have felt that they could not get the sort of food which would keep them well. Such experiences rouse very strong and persistent feelings which are likely to attach themselves to negotiations which touch upon markets, trading and currency arrangements, in so far, of course, as the individual is aware of them.

With all these tendencies at work it will never be easy to secure sincere international goodwill. It is not a thing which will come of itself as nations get to know one another better. Not all peoples improve upon acquaintance ; not all travel is pleasant, and there is always the possibility that contact will only reveal incompatibility of temperament.

International morality, therefore, does not stand upon such firm foundations as that which obtains within groups. For not only is good feeling precarious and shifting, and evil always likely to be imputed, but two of the great sanctions which maintain individual morality are lacking as well. These are, of course, the backing of force which every group has so far found necessary for the enforcement of its laws, and the pressure of public opinion.

Individuals are deeply affected by public opinion even when

they set themselves deliberately to flout it. The ordinary man does not give two hoots for the opinion of foreigners. He ignores it, pities their ignorance, or resents their cheek. As for force, we are, for the moment, willing to apply it to our recent enemies if not to submit to it ourselves. But even this application depends upon continued harmony between four great countries whose traditions are largely hostile, whose ideas and customs vary widely, and whose interests can only be reconciled at a high level—the level where one considers the good of the world as a whole.

Nevertheless, and in spite of all this, once nations have to live at close quarters it must be allowed that they, or their rulers, owe one another duties. For in default of external restraint and mutual liking men are faced with the prospect of perpetual snatch and grab. Few tribes and nations have been so warlike that they did not desire intervals of peace. The victor wants to be free to enjoy his spoils, the vanquished to recover from his wounds even if only to prepare revenge. Therefore it seems likely that the first international virtue was good faith. Treaties and agreements must not be made merely in order to throw one's co-signatories off their guard. Without good faith no one can relax for an instant, and life becomes almost intolerable.

Unfortunately, however, the recognition of this international duty has not secured its observance. From the Norman Conquest onwards most of the wars which have broken out in Europe seem to have been excused by allegations of bad faith.[1]

After good faith, the virtue most in demand from neighbours seems to have been loyalty to friends, or the other members of some ideological group. Socrates denounced war between Greeks. Christian nations were not supposed to fight one another without the permission of the Papacy. Louis XIV shocked Christendom when he supported the Turks against the Austrians. The American Republic helped the French Republic: Revolutionary Russia had not a friend in the world: tyrants stand together against democracies. When war breaks out countries which cross the floor are felt to be selling their souls unless it is in one's own interest that they should do so. Then, for as long as the struggle lasts, they are thought to be seeing the light.

Here again we find good feeling limiting itself to those who can be considered as comrades.

After loyalty, clemency. A current of thought concerned with

---

[1] This statement is based upon a hasty re-perusal of Green's *History of the English People*. This may not mention all European wars, but probably gives a fair sample.

mitigating the horrors of war is found early in European history. The Romans praised magnanimity in victors although they did not often practise it. By the end of the Dark Ages knights were evolving a code of chivalrous conduct which helped to secure tolerable treatment for knights. Nobody troubled about tolerable treatment for other ranks until after the French Revolution. Now we have agreements and conventions intended to protect civilians and all prisoners of war, though they have not been as useful as their designers hoped.

Once the desire is felt to lessen the horrors of war, it is bound to give rise to the further idea that war itself is not merely a horror but a crime which ought to be prevented. But in spite of the support which it received from Christian ideals this notion made very slow headway until the appearance of constitutional governments. It seems to have been regarded as natural that war should be the sport of kings. Ferdinand and Isabella, for instance, introduced the Holy Inquisition into Spain not from religious conviction—they had resisted pressure from Rome for a good many years—but because it enabled them to seize enough money from the Jews to drive the Moors from Granada. Largely on account of this proceeding they are usually placed among the greater monarchs of history. In fact to be warlike was generally considered a virtue in a sovereign. Such princes as disliked war were thought effeminate and blamed for passing their lives in silken dalliance rather than in the stirring air of camps. Lovers of peace were despised even though the blessings of peace were acknowledged and extolled. There is, of course, something to be said for this point of view ; it is not merely barbaric. Vigour and courage are obvious virtues in rulers and the first function of any sovereign is to protect his realm. Therefore it is partly for this reason that not until the nineteenth century do we find kings and foreign ministers consulting to limit or prevent hostilities and consenting to such devices as the Concert of Europe and the Hague Court.

On the other hand it is only just to governments to remember that many wars, like the Boer War, were extremely popular, while some have been forced upon rulers who did not want to fight—e.g., the War of Jenkins' ear. Nor would Napoleon II have tried to imitate the achievements of his uncle if he had not known that the people of France would exult in being "covered with Glory."

It is not only just to remember these facts ; it is also im-

G

portant. Many peoples are bellicose, and to ignore this is to refuse to face the facts.

It has often been said that the masses are the chief sufferers in war, and never gain from it. This is not borne out by history. The chief sufferers in most wars have been the soldiers who took part in them. It is true that civilians have suffered great miseries at the hands of armed forces, whether victorious or in retreat. But what of the armies whose bones lie buried in all the great cockpits of war? How many of them have perished—along the Chinese borders, in Northern India, Asia Minor, the Balkans, Northern Italy, the Low Countries—to mention only a few? And it is absurd to pretend that none of these wars brought wealth and prosperity to the winning side, or inaugurated a period of peace to the benefit of survivors. Civilians tend to regard their troops as scapegoats and themselves as innocent peaceful creatures whom it is wicked to harm. But if all wars at all times had been hated at home many of them would never have taken place.[1]

These sketchy remarks are not intended to give even an outline of human feelings on the subject of war. Asiatic religions —together, no doubt, with defective diets—have produced some races who have not got it in them to fight. The Chinese, too, have not waged an aggressive war for many centuries. All I am trying to do, by mentioning a few outstanding tendencies, is to mark the magnitude of the change which is taking place. On this subject during the last half century the direction of human feeling has been reversed. We do believe—at any rate for the moment— that aggression is wicked and that it is the first duty of nations to keep the peace. Much anxious thought is going on as to how this can best be done, and there seems to be a general agreement among those who think that the well-being of separate groups depends in these days upon the well-being of all, so that every nation able to do so has a duty to contribute to the general prosperity.

We have reached a point at which we realise that states ought to be good neighbours. If these excellent ideas have not yet made much headway against the vast tides of resentment and selfish feeling which were released by the ending of the war this is only, though lamentable, exactly what one would expect.

The need for co-operation was felt even before the use of atomic bombs. The comradeship of war had established strong

---

[1] Cf. This conversation, overheard in a bus in 1917. *Old Lady:* " Why can't these Zeps stay over where they belong, in France? "
Soldier: " Well, that's where we soldiers are, Mother, in France."
Old Lady: " Well, that's what you're there for, isn't it—the wawer? "

currents of goodwill between the allies, whose more hostile impulses were absorbed in the common struggle. Pity for the peoples of occupied countries was another feeling which united free men, and the need for continued effort after the war a third. While the good will was there, this need could be felt as an obvious duty. The use of the atomic bomb administered a sudden and a terrible shock. All of us could see that another war would wipe out our civilisation, and there was a widespread feeling that human beings as a whole must learn to amend their ways if they are to survive. Men looked about them for the forces, the levers, which are needed to secure this new behaviour. And for the moment it seemed as though fear of the new weapon might provide the necessary stimulus.

Unhappily, tremendous shocks do not make men either more kindly or more reasonable—in fact they tend to have the opposite effect. The fear and resentment which they cause arouses suspicion, reactivates old grudges, throw men back upon ways of thought and feeling which, though no longer appropriate, are associated in their minds with periods of comparative security. All these tendencies can certainly be seen at work in the world today. We know that we cannot afford another war, but the foreign policy of almost every country seems to be sliding back to the level of taking precautions against a war which would be fought upon the lines of the last. Sub-wars are going on in China, Palestine and India. Efforts to secure economic co-operation are threatened by suspicion, ignorance and national selfishness. Fear, as usual, has proved to be an influence which does not unite, but divides. Since the new weapon is too dreadful to contemplate, we do our best to behave as though it did not exist.[1]

In the meantime our civilisation is sharply threatened, and since a society which fails to survive fails in a necessary attribute, it will not be irrelevant to the business of defining the good state if something is said about the causes of war.

During the last quarter of a century they have been discussed *ad nauseam*, but much of the discussion has been wide of the mark because so many people are unwilling to admit that the root cause of war is men's willingness to fight. Those who loathe the very thought of war deny this statement violently. They prefer to regard mankind as a peace-loving species, the continual victim of monsters driven by greed or lust for power. This is not true. If

---

[1] In this country of pressure groups not one society has been formed to urge governments to do this, that or the other about the atomic bomb, and so far as I know only one meeting has been held, and that one was organised by ex-pacifists.

human beings resembled rabbits wars would not take place. What men dislike are the consequences of wars; fighting itself has a strong appeal for them.[1]

Willingness to engage in conflict is neither an abnormality nor a sin. It is a characteristic which the species has developed in response to the problem set by their environment. Men could not have provided themselves with food, nor overcome the assaults of wild beasts and the consequences of natural disasters, unless they were extremely aggressive. If threats had not called out appropriate defensive reactions the species would have perished long ago. We who are alive today are the heirs of the victors in all these various and protracted struggles. Our ancestors knew better how to defend themselves, on the whole, than those who were wiped out early, leaving no descendants. They had learned how to discriminate between their friends and those who wished them harm, and how to deal with their enemies. Otherwise we should not be here. Normal men defend themselves as soon as they realise that they are being attacked and provided they feel that there is hope of successful resistance.[2]

If any Pacifist should be reading these pages he will certainly feel at this point that it takes two to make a quarrel, and that the answer to the threat of war is for all men to share his opinions. Fortunately or unfortunately real Pacifism, as apart from hatred of war in its modern forms, is not at bottom a creed but a state of mind which most men cannot share. Ordinary human beings do not believe that non-resistance to an evil aggressor will stay his progress or alter his character. Experience shows that they are right.[3]

[1] Cf. An article in the *Evening Standard* of November 13th, 1945, written by an airman about to be demobilised. After stating that he detested the service in peace-time the writer added: " I was much happier. It was active service, thrust upon me, terrifying but satisfying. There is no doubt that men do enjoy a relapse into barbarism. Destruction is much more exciting than construction. The threat of death is a great tonic. I have no doubt that thousands of men will never live again so fully, so completely, as they lived between June, 1944 and May, 1945. The British Liberation Army liberated more inhibitions than cities."

[2] Both these provisos were understood by the Nazis when they invaded Europe. They took the greatest care both to achieve the maximum of surprise, and to create the impression that resistance was hopeless. We all remember how they lulled their victims into security by pacts, negotiations and promises. They exhibited paralysing films of bombing in Poland. When they struck they did so with the help of parachutists, forged orders, agents spreading terrifying rumours. They did everything to ensure that the fighting instincts should be inhibited by confusion and despair.

[3] This assertion will not of course influence the mind of any genuine Pacifist. Nor indeed will anything else so long as his basic fixations remain unaltered. Further, it is because the Christian Churches are made up of ordinary men and women that it is unjust to blame them when they bless their country's forces and pray that its arms should be crowned with victory.

If man were not of necessity an aggressive creature, and if anxiety did not so often stain his aggression with hostility he would not fight. The causes of aggressive wars are therefore those events and situations which evoke and invigorate the fighting instinct until it sweeps the board and action follows.

Sometimes no great exciting cause is needed. A ruler enjoys killing and destruction, or is driven into it by paranoid mechanisms. These impulses may be shared by a warrior class. Only what is felt as a good opportunity will be needed to set them marching.

After this come perhaps situations which produce desperation. These may be natural or economic disasters, especially of a kind which compel migration. Extensive Asiatic droughts started both the Huns and the Turks on their invasions of Europe. Forced to move, they were forced to fight. Even today governments find it hard to arrange for the peaceful reception of large bodies of alien refugees.

Another source of desperation is a threat to men's religion, or to an ideology which takes the place of a religion, or to customs which are held as sacrosanct. To place a human being in jeopardy of losing his soul, or to forbid him behaviour which he believes to be the only basis of righteousness, is to arouse the keenest anxiety known to mankind. And it produces both the maximum of hostility and willingness to die rather than surrender.

Injustice, real or imaginary, is a less powerful stimulus because the whole question stands on a more practical level. In seeking to remove injustice men may pause to consider the chances of success. Other methods of achieving their aims may be tried before violence. But imaginary grievances, and old grievances once real but now without substance save in the mind will often explode into conflict. The behaviour of the Finns when they continued their war against the Allies, of the Indians who rose in support of the Japanese, are two examples of the inciting power of ancient hatreds and the extent to which they can dominate common sense.

Next we may take, perhaps, desire for loot. Raiding is part of the way of life of some groups, and it is a habit difficult to eradicate. For once established it serves many ends. On such expeditions young men get a chance of displaying their prowess. And where wives are expensive and women locked away, a raid may be their only opportunity to secure one. The males even of peaceful animal species will fight in the mating season. Further, the " greasy merchants " whose city one is sacking may be infidels as well—and so on.

From these roots—the lust for wealth, prestige and the elation which comes from achievement—have grown the economic rivalries which have been the cause of many conflicts in the past, and continue to threaten our future.

Another common mischief-maker has been desire for revenge—one war begets another. This feeling is frankly entertained by some types—e.g., *La Revanche*—and disguised from themselves by others. A great deal might be said about it, but in the end it is only a special, troublesome form of hostility which will yield, if at all, to methods which have a soothing effect upon hostility in general.

A long list could be made of other stimuli which have provoked men into armed conflict. But one more example is enough. That is bad leaders. These men are of different types. They may be paranoiacs who want a war because they feel that they are surrounded by enemies and must kill before they are killed, or fanatics who must force some creed upon the world at the point of the sword. They may be merely stupid and quarrelsome people who find themselves in a position to force some issue. More probably all these traits will be found in the same great hero, for they tend to overlap, and are often accompanied by intense ambition.

For the moment, perhaps, these types do not constitute a pressing danger. The most magnetic leader will not find many followers unless, as we say, the times are ripe—a phrase, which means, at bottom, that there is a widespread willingness to listen to him and his propaganda. And in spite of the minor wars still raging it seems doubtful whether this willingness now exists. There is, of course, a dreadful amount of hatred let loose in the world, and a very large number of men and women whose aggressive and destructive instincts will not be satisfied by life in a peaceful society. It remains to be seen how many there are, and what the extent of their influence will be. But on the whole the general longing for peace and some sort of safety and comfort seem to be so strong that it makes us practically incombustible. This state of affairs, however, may not last. War-weariness could hardly be more general than it was between 1918 and 1939, yet a great many people both in Europe and America were hoping that Hitler would declare war on Soviet Russia. Terrified of Bolshevism, they deceived themselves about the results of such an event. Hitler would go through the Russians like a knife through butter, all would be over in three weeks, and then his ambitions would be satisfied.

To return to the bad leader : the real danger seems more likely to lie in some man or men devoid of warlike tendencies who have not the knowledge without which great power cannot safely be wielded. Every important ruler has experts at his disposal, but what is the use of that to a man who cannot understand what the experts say ? Ignorant men in great positions tend to choose bad counsellors, personal friends to whom they feel that they can cling, yes—men whose flattery helps them to feel equal to their job. If the dawning feelings of international fellowship are destroyed today, in all probability this will be done by sheer economic blundering. The real enemy at the moment is economic chaos and injustice, or what will be felt as gross injustice by politically conscious and numerous groups. All falls in the standard of living are deeply resented ; if they are felt to be unjust and unnecessary they will soon be put down to enmity. Whose enmity does not much matter—a series of revolutions which make ordered government impossible are as dangerous in our present position as a quarrel between states.

We return, then, to our pressing need for competent leaders.

So far the discussion has been centred on the subject of aggression. If none of us resented loss and injustice and disappointment and starvation we should all die quietly of misery instead of by modern explosives. But men are not only aggressive ; they are mentally lazy, stupid, ignorant, corrupt. They like to live in dream worlds where things which they hate to think about simply will not happen. " Hitler has broken other pacts, but it stands to reason that he will respect our neutrality."

They are obstinate and irritable ; their patience becomes exhausted. " God knows we are willing to make a fair compromise. But it is impossible to go on month after month like this. These fellows are mistaking generosity for weakness."

They judge the whole world in terms of their own lives, and twist all that they see to fit their personal prejudices. " The British are using Lend-Lease to steal American markets."

They feel that they have a right to despise and dislike other peoples, while they expect other peoples to like and look up to them.

They love money and power, if not for themselves then for their countries. " World trade must certainly be shared out, but this particular market is an exception. " We need it to iron out seasonal unemployment." They enjoy exhibitions of power. " We are on top now and don't you forget it." They fail to see other people's point of view. " Other nations must not prepare for war, or one day war will break out. But there is no danger in our being armed, since we should never fight except to resist an aggressor."

Human frailty is a subject upon which it would be possible to write indefinitely. On the other hand, if peace be desired strongly enough, we need not, nowadays, be forced into war by external situations. No convulsion of nature is likely to be so terrible that it could not be coped with by efficient collaboration. The greed of individuals or classes or even nations can be kept in check if their own, or other governments, are determined to check it. Economic miseries can be alleviated before they produce a dangerous state of mind. Injustices can be remedied. In fact when we ask ourselves whether there is any hope of ending war we are really asking whether human beings are capable of rational behaviour.

A good many people will say at once that we have learned our lesson. Modern weapons are so terrible and the chances of being left outside a war so small, that the whole world will combine against any movement or country which threatens to start a war.

As against this it may be pointed out that most new weapons have been terrifying to those attacked by them. Both gunpowder and bombing aeroplanes were horrifying innovations. Yet we have got used to them. What can be more deadly than a volcano in eruption? Yet men have continued to live upon the slopes of Vesuvius.

The atomic bomb is admittedly more destructive than Vesuvius, but no fate can be worse for a community than to be wiped out. In the Thirty Years' War whole districts were laid in ruins and their inhabitants put to the sword. Civilisation after civilisation in the Middle East has been so completely annihilated that nothing is left of it—if that—but its name and a few piles of rubble. Modern wars kill millions instead of thousands, but to men who knew nothing of millions it was the thousands who mattered.

It may possibly be true that the new weapon is more alarming than any which has gone before it. But fear is not an agency which makes for peace. Fear disturbs clarity of thought, gives rise to suspicion, induces general resentment on account of the discomfort which it causes, and produces either hatred or a cringing attitude towards those who are thought to cause the fear. "At the moment our atomic bombs are the best in the world—but who knows when the . . .s will not catch up with us? What are we to expect then? Think of their history! And remember, there will be no declaration of war, no warning, only obliteration! Without danger to ourselves we can remove this menace to world peace—*if we act now*. The people at large need know nothing about it until the whole business is over." These are the counsels of fear, and there will always be men and women who are haunted by the thought of secret enemies preparing evil. Recollection of this war will not reassure them.

If we are to keep out of war it will not be because we are frightened, but because we are able to control our fears and refuse to be guided by them.

Nor is this enough. As long as human beings continue to indulge in wishful thinking, believe without evidence, some powerful man is sure to feel that he has bribed or converted so many of the international police, sown such dissension between his neighbours, accumulated such a store of secret weapons, that his war is in the bag. "Our new rays will blow up their atomic bombs a hundred miles from the frontier. . . ."

Even granted that populations are scared stiff of war, until they choose men to govern them who are far above the average of their fellows, another war will come. Just, kind and reasonable men do not start wars; wise and well-informed men can deal with the conditions which give rise to them. But peoples poisoned with hatred, suspicion and fear, or weighted with irrational guilt, tend to choose leaders who embody their own passions and find plausible excuses for them. Provided that the present level of human hostility is maintained, provided that its flashpoint is low enough, another war will come. The fundamental problem which confronts us as a race is therefore the abatement of existing hatreds, the prevention of fresh ones, and the control of the whole vicious circle of fear and suspicion and guilt and hostility by reason.

Freud thought that this cannot be done. In his *Civilisation and its Discontents* he says as much. If he is right, the outlook is hopeless. But he may not be right. Many human beings are sensible and friendly and kind; able to combine together to carry out wise policies. It is possible that their influence will prevail. It is possible that our present leaders will rise to their opportunities. It is possible that the period of hard work which lies before us all will use up much of our aggression and induce a sense of comradeship. We are sick to the heart of bloodshed and cruelty, and it does not seem likely that another great war will follow close upon the heels of this one. We are to have, it seems, a breathing-space. We may be able to use it to build a foundation for peace. It is by no means certain that the outlook is hopeless, and it would be suicidal to act as though it were. The more slender the chance, the more reason for making the most of it.

Whether or not we shall succeed, is no part of the subject of this book. It has been discussed at all merely to show that from whatever angle we approach the good state, whether we consider its internal functions or international duties, we are brought back to the quality of its citizens and their fitness for the part they play in the machinery of its government.

Whether what we want is better standards at home or peace abroad, the best means of obtaining it is through the moral and social and political education of our peoples. The need for this is widely recognised ; let us hope that it will proceed apace.

CHAPTER 15

SEXUAL MORALITY

That some sexual ethic is desirable no one is likely to deny. Without a code of sexual conduct social life would fall into confusion and the welfare of children be jeopardised. Someone must be responsible for them, must undertake the long and nowadays expensive business of bringing them up. And though in theory marriage could be abolished and mothers subsidised by the state such an arrangement has not yet recommended itself to the men of any civilised group. Nor does it seem probable that this will happen. For one thing, fatherhood means a great deal to men—far more than many of them realise. For another, what those who dislike to be " tied " call jealousy and possessiveness are important factors in the human mind. Next, all the evidence goes to show that a child's relations with his father play an extremely important part in his mental and moral development. And lastly, to divorce passion from affection, tenderness and the desire to protect or serve one's mate, has undesirable results. Women left without a man to love tend to centre the whole of their emotional life upon their children, which is bad for the children. What the normal man or woman wants is a home, a family and a more or less permanent wife or husband in the singular or the plural.

Anarchy in sexual relations seems therefore to be ruled out, and marriage on some basis to be necessary.

Anyone who imagines that psychologists, and in particular, Freud, sanction anarchy on the ground that repressions are bad for us, is either indulging in wishful thinking or confuses the notion of repression with that of self-control. There is all the difference in the world between the statement that an automatic, unconscious refusal to admit the existence of an impulse is a bad way of dealing with it, and the doctrine that we should give open throttle to our primitive instincts. Freud's own belief was, as we have seen, that they should be controlled by reason.

Nor can this question be decided, as many people now assume by saying that it is "all a matter of glands." When physiologists began research on the glands of internal secretion and their functions it was widely thought that they had discovered the physical mechanisms which control personality. This hope has been disappointed. Glandular deficiency or disease does disturb personality in certain definite ways, but the number of these ways is limited. The large majority of character traits bear no relation to glandular functioning. And this statement still holds for much of the sphere of sex. Diseases like acro-megaly, abnormalities like hermaphroditism, have direct effects upon our sexual tendencies. Physical causes may account in some cases for excess or deficiency of virility in males, and nymphomania or sterility in females. But every sort of perversion, and the whole gamut of neurotic symptoms, including impotence and the inability to carry children, can and do appear in patients whose bodies are normal. In these cases it is fear and guilt and hatred which have affected the sexual life.

Whatever may happen in the future, the interconnection between character and physique cannot yet be shown in detail.

Moreover, even if none of these facts existed and sex were merely a matter of glands, this would no more dispose of the need for control of sexual cravings than the statement : " It is all a matter of muscular strength " can dispose of the need to regulate the use of strength.

Some sexual code communities must have. And whether it works well or badly is of the greatest importance. It is not only a matter of preventing jealousy and violent behaviour, or of securing rights for women and children. For it is now known that all loving, friendly and social feelings spring from the same root. Damage or stifle the sexual instincts, and the whole emotional life is endangered. Those whose sexual life is seriously warped cause much unhappiness to those around them and are unlikely to make good citizens.

To give some examples : The narcissist, whose affections have been stunted at so early a stage that he is unable to love anyone but himself, may be a good worker, for he needs money to pamper the body that means so much to him, as well as to save himself from anxiety. Moreover he enjoys the display of any gifts that he may have. But he will play as a rule no valuable part in the life of his group, since other people do not interest him. Again, prostitutes who find their trade not uncongenial, are ravaged by hatred of men and jealousy of women. Homosexuals are of different kinds, but the active type " swarms with obsessions " and develops huge amounts of cruelty, which may or may not appear on the surface.[1]

Men and women who are afraid of sex either spend most of their energy in wrestling with temptations which through force of suppression have become hideous, or use it up in persuading themselves that they are sexless. All but the last of these types cause suffering to all those who love them or depend on them. And, with rare exceptions, either they are too much preoccupied with their internal miseries to care about communal duties, or they are compelled to reproduce around them the eternal conflicts which rage within.

One of these exceptions are men who are driven by an urge to "save" some portion of humanity—which represents the mother—from some other being or class which stands for the father.

Those in this state may devote their whole lives to social questions. Where they carry out their work in a temper of hatred and fanaticism we get Savonarola, John Knox and the Spanish Inquisitors. These fall within the general rule. But where the same compelling impulse to rescue is infused with a spirit of love and pity it has provided the world with some of its greatest benefactors. In the latter case the sublimation was successful; in the first the desire to save is used to excuse a discharge of cruelty and hostility.

Happy love and affection, rational regard for the welfare of others, practical interest in the well-being of the community, are attributes of sexually healthy human beings.

The second reason why sexual codes are important is that home life is one of the main factors which help to determine human happiness or misery. And it in turn is deeply affected by the attitudes taken towards sex. A good many people would deny this, or say that money and common interests are more important in marriage than a successful physical relation. All the facts are against them. The research that has been done on this subject goes to show that shared pleasure and reciprocated love allay anxiety, diminish resentment and sweeten men's attitude to life. Shared interests and enough money for a decent life are valuable, but chiefly because they help to maintain affection.

If correct ideas on this subject are important, how are they to be reached ? If we look round us, the most striking fact is the

[1] Cf. "The Nosology of Male Homosexuality, in *Sex in Psycho-Analysis* by S. Ferenczi, pp. 306, 310.

wide variety of systems evolved by groups which managed to survive.[1] There is far less agreement between groups in this sphere than in any other field of morals. And at the same time, apart from what are called " advanced circles " there is closer agreement within the group that the accustomed arrangements are the only arrangements possible. Oddly enough, however, very few people really long to extend their own marriage customs to other races. Nor do they feel this to be a duty. Most men say that moral laws are universal and absolute, but on this vital point they do in fact regard them as determined by race or country. Large numbers of practical monogamists would regret the abolition of customs which they regard as possibly regrettable but certainly picturesque. No doubt day-dreams of sheiks, harems and dusky beauties play a useful part in the phantasies of those who would not dare to behave in an unorthodox manner. In any case one of the few things for which the British Empire is seldom blamed is its policy of non-interference with sexual customs unless they involve taking life. No civilised observer feels in this way about theft or cruelty to children.

It is just as well that the general attitude should be so unexpectedly tolerant, for no means exist by which one group can force all others to adopt its sexual standards. All the same it would be extraordinary if some systems were not better than others. We have no warrant for assuming that all communities have in fact evolved the customs best suited to them, though some anthropologists seem to think so. Therefore it would be interesting as well as useful, if the advantages and disadvantages of marriage customs could be determined. And this confronts us with the question of the standards by which comparisons should be made. How are we to judge between monogamy and polygamy, divorce at will, restricted divorce or indissoluble marriage, and the host of other alternatives which suggest themselves?

The answer must be that sexual practices should be judged by exactly the same criteria as any other patterns of human behaviour. They must be judged by their results—their effects upon the life of communities and the health and happiness of individuals.

This statement is not likely to gain immediate acceptance. In the first place there exists a widespread feeling that sexual morals are a field apart, in which to sin is more wicked and to obey more necessary than in any other. In fact the very words " morality," " vice " and " virtue " have acquired in many

[1] Cf. Westermarck's *The History of Human Marriage*.

minds an almost exclusively sexual meaning. Moreover a great many people feel that sex itself is both mysterious and " dirty," a topic from which to avert one's mind, something of which to feel slightly ashamed even in its permitted forms. This attitude has been modified in recent years, but has still a very considerable influence.

It seems safe to say that all scientific students of the subject, whether biologists, psychologists or anthropologists, would agree that the attitude is mistaken. Sexual behaviour is of great importance because our sexual impulses are strong, because they are so closely connected with the future of the race, and because very violent feelings of jealousy and rage are closely connected with them. But sex is not, of itself, either mysterious or dirty, magical or disgusting. All the evidence goes to show that these conceptions are not " natural to any decent man " but due to bad traditions and faulty training. Parents who were themselves infected with these ideas have felt it their duty to hand them on to their children. But the original sources of the ideas themselves were neurotic states of mind.

Once the subject is faced in a straightforward way and the mind cleared of notions about unnamable offences and unforgivable sins, it becomes clear that sexual morality, though always important, is only a part of morality in general. It presents special problems, but all the same its codes must be judged by the same criteria as other codes, and breaches of them by the amount of harm that they are likely to produce. Included in this harm, of course, must be the rousing of ungovernable emotions either in individuals or the community. To break one's mother's heart, to cuckold a husband who will certainly murder his wife if he finds her out, to precipitate the siege of Troy, even to stir up scandal throughout the village, are all results which must be taken into account when conduct is approved or disapproved, or better still when action is contemplated. Sexual offences may have dreadful consequences, but taken by themselves they are not necessarily more wicked than such vices as treachery and cruelty.

It may be objected that if sexual morality is of great importance, we should face the fact that special sanctions may be needed to enforce it. Therefore to teach children that sex is mysteriously sinful or disgusting can be justified by results, even though it may not be true in the scientific sense of the word.

If there were any evidence that such teaching makes human beings good—and in good we must include happy, and mentally healthy—it might be necessary to argue here the general question of lying as an agent of education. In fact the evidence is all on the other side. As has already been said, the enjoyment of normal sexual pleasure is of great psychological value, and this is jeopardised when sex is associated with feelings of guilt and shame. Nor do these feelings produce the results which are hoped for them. To give only one instance from cases which might fill a book: Dr. Ernest Jones points out that girls who have been taught that this subject is taboo, and connect it therefore with wickedness and the necessity for concealment, are sometimes unable to derive pleasure from intercourse with husbands and lose their coldness only with secret lovers. This result cannot have been what their mothers and teachers wanted.

Sexual systems must then be judged by their results and by their results alone. Most people will agree that a very important result is the production of enough healthy children to maintain the existence and well-being of the group. One can of course take the view that mankind is so wicked that the species had better die out, or that life is so evil or wretched that the best thing to do is to renounce it.[1] Both these states of mind seem to me equivalent to moral nihilism, and one is therefore entitled to ignore them when dealing with questions which are closely related to the future of the race. And if it be accepted that human beings should be healthy and happy and good citizens, then it is, I think, possible to say categorically that the main object of sexual regulations at the present time should be to secure happy and successful marriages—as many of them as possible, and as happy.

By happy marriages I mean marriages in which the partners are physically well attuned; where they obtain from each other the degree of companionship which they need; where affection is shared, and where husband and wife remain together, on balance, because they want to, and not only as a duty.

I should expect all psychologists, most doctors, and indeed most kindly people, to agree with this. A happy marriage is often cited as the greatest of earthly goods. But though all civilised moral codes regard marriage as fundamental to society, even if they do not invest it with a sacred character, the all-important element of happiness is as a rule left out.

[1] Some people feel at the moment that they would like to see certain races exterminated, but this is a feeling that will almost certainly pass. Even they would agree that good communities should remain in being, and the adoption of attitudes which ensure happy family life is an important step towards the improvement of any community.

The value of happiness to husbands and wives has already been dealt with. It seems almost unnecessary to add that a happy home is vital to the mental and moral health of children. They are highly sensitive to misery and resentment in their parents, even where these are thought to have been concealed, and especially to ill-feeling between them. Tension and hostility between adults cause anxiety and even guilt among children and prejudice their later attitudes towards the whole of family life. Girls tend to regard their fathers as representing the male sex, boys to judge all women by their mothers, and a parent who ill-treats his or her partner will wake in the children not only fear of one sex and over-estimation of the other, but often a sense of grievance and bitterness towards life as a whole.

Later influences may to some extent undo the harm that has been done. But the habits and tendencies acquired by the sons and daughters of unhappy homes often preclude them from responding to the very influences which would have helped them.

Once we start to consider the rights of children we come to another consideration. One of the first requirements of a child as regards his home is that it shall be stable. Children need secure backgrounds. The break-up of families, the intrusion of step-parents, continual changes of nurses or teachers, are always disturbing factors in their lives and involve them in very difficult readjustments. The change of persons may be for the better, but even when this seems obvious the good results that are looked for do not always follow.[1]

One reason for this is that parents are the source of morality, and no two human beings have precisely the same ideas about what children should and should not do. The resulting confusion is dangerous. Another is the inaccurate ideas which children have of their parents. His daughter may adore a dissolute scoundrel, resent deeply the fact that her mother has separated from her father, hate the decent man whom she is asked to accept as a substitute, marry someone who reminds her of her father and wreck her life by doing so. This does not mean that wives should not remove their children from contact with dissolute scoundrels, but that care should be taken not to marry them, since removal may come too late.

It is desirable therefore that marriage should be not only happy but stable. That is why I have used the adjective " success-

---

[1] Cf. *The Delinquent Child*, by Dr. Cyril Burt ; the writings of Dr. John Bowlby, and all the reports on evacuated children which have been drawn up during the war.

ful" as well as the adjective "happy." Brief periods of rapture followed by estrangements, even if the sequence suits both parties, are not successful marriages. Children need both their parents, and the successful marriage must provide a good home for its children.

All this will seem obvious to any reader who is likely to have read so far, but several deductions seem to follow from these facts which are not always drawn. The first is that laws, customs and public opinion should combine to encourage happy marriages, and that conditions which militate against them should be condemned on that ground alone. If this attitude were adopted in England today it would entail a great many drastic changes. Some would be economic: most of these, such as alterations in salary scales and tax allowance, are frequently discussed. Others would be social. Attempts to keep young people of marriageable age unmarried ought to be regarded as wrong. In some forms they should be forbidden. This is particularly important in the case of classes picked for sound physique, good character or intellect, such as officers, bank clerks, school teachers and civil servants. Instead of regarding a wife and family as a millstone about a young man's neck they should be considered his right, and his desire for them a sign of healthy adjustment.

Perhaps the most important changes are needed in the minds of parents. Their attitude, only too often, is that young people should turn their minds away from marriage, and indeed the whole field of sex, and devote themselves to some career while they keep their parents company and contribute to the family earnings. Refusal to comply with this requirement is thought to show how wild, ungrateful, irresponsible and wicked young people are today.

On the contrary both boys and girls should be brought up to think of marriage as an integral part of the best life, and of success in marriage as an important achievement and a source of pride.

Nor should marriage be held out to them as a means of acquiring money, assisting one's career, getting away from one's parents, proving that one is attractive, saving oneself from burning or getting a home of one's own, and most certainly not as orange-blossoms and eternal glamour, or as a trap which you, my boy, should keep out of instead of getting caught like your poor old uncle. They should be taught to look upon marriage as it really is—a shared endeavour into which it is worth while to put every effort of mind and body, the deepest source of happiness which life is likely to offer, and the consummation of love.

The second deduction, then, is obvious : marriage should be undertaken soberly and advisedly, not wantonly nor in the spirit of " we can always divorce if we get tired of it."

Thirdly, to break up a home which might have continued on a basis of affection should be accounted a serious social crime.

If it is true that sexual customs should be judged by whether or not they encourage happy, successful marriages, then we have at least a point of view from which to discuss many of the issues which divide men's minds today. And what I am proposing to do in the rest of this chapter is to take one or two of these issues, and see whether it does or does not give us help in clearing up our ideas on such matters, and working towards a solution. As I said in the introductory chapter, it does not seem to me my job to lay down moral laws to be obeyed by the rest of mankind. Nor is it obvious that all men will find happiness through observance of the same detailed formulae. All that I am trying to do here, therefore, is to test a method.

As an example of its successful though largely unconscious use we may take the recent reform of English divorce legislation. Until the passing of Sir Alan Herbert's Act our divorce laws were based not upon any single principle but on a number of confused and contradictory factors. Among these were ancient ecclesiastical taboos, the supposed feelings of the British people if one started by assuming that they are a Christian nation, the real voting power of minorities admitted to be prejudiced, and the personal feelings of members of Parliament, a class which contains an abnormally high proportion of bachelors. No one with special knowledge of their working had a good word to say for the existing laws and they were denounced in particular by the judges whose duty was to put them into operation. All that could be predicted of their effects with certainty was expense and exasperation.

Public opinion, in the meantime, was ahead of the law. If we except those large classes who are not really free to judge the matter at all, since they feel bound by the pronouncements of their churches, most people who had studied the subject found themselves in rough agreement. They felt that divorce must be judged in the long run by what can be predicted of its effect on the welfare of the community, and in particular on marriage as an institution. Account must be taken of individual sufferings for two reasons—the first that if common they tend to bring marriage into disrepute, the second, that social institutions should neither cause nor perpetuate misery. Divorce must therefore be available in cases of real hardship, but public opinion should condemn the irresponsible use of legal facilities.

I don't think that I am going too far in saying that this was the general state of mind : in any event it was general enough to force reform against strong and pertinaceous sectional interests. And this change in opinion was produced by considering cause and effect, by judging the marriage laws as we judge other legal attempts to produce right conduct in our citizens, and by regard for the decency and happiness of family life.

From an instance of the successful use of these principles we may pass on to another where success is unobtainable. If we take the world as a whole, the most striking difference that meets us in the sphere of sexual custom is the difference between monogamy and polygamy. It is a good topic on which to try out a method, because only a small minority have very strong feelings about it and nothing that is said will have any practical effect. I do not pretend to be an expert on the subject, but the following considerations present themselves :—

In the first place, polygamy is said to satisfy the sexual desires of men and thus to be an important contribution to their happiness. This can be set aside as contrary to fact. Polygamy is accompanied, among the principal races who practise it, by concubinage, household slavery and prostitution. If there is now no slavery in India it is because the British have abolished the custom.

Next it provides every woman with at least a share of a husband, and the chance of becoming a mother. This is an argument, and it is upon this ground that one was asked at Forces' Brains Trusts whether we ought not to legalise polygamy after the war. The question here is whether it would or would not contribute to the happiness of women.

Those whom I have consulted as likely to be possessed of real knowledge, agree that, except in China, the family murder rate is very much higher in polygamous than in monogamous countries. The motive is often jealousy, but more often still the interests of one's children. The old husband may be poisoned by agreement between the existing wives before he can contract a new marriage which threatens them all; a concubine may be removed because she has acquired too great an influence over her master. Or the victim may be a favourite son who stands in the way of a half-brother,

Another piece of evidence is the treatment of widows in India. The reason given for offering a widow her choice between being burned alive and reduced to the status of a half-starved drudge, is that it prevented women from murdering their husbands. Even if no single Hindoo woman had ever killed her husband, this shows what the Hindoo community thought of the feelings of wives as a whole.[1]

Among the Chinese many Confucians have refrained from taking a second wife on account of the suffering which this causes to the first. Other Chinese writers, not so considerate, have given it as their opinion that family life is intended to teach us patience and forbearance. In fact the literature dealing with marriage in polygamous countries is full of references to the eternal jealousies and complaints of women which destroy all peace and happiness in the home.

Another set of facts which confirm this account consists of the reasons given for treating women in such a fashion. They are animals without souls, or incurably ignorant, spiteful and silly : their talk is mere " women's babble," the love of a man should be given not to his wife but to his horse.

By the time that a woman has come to be regarded as an animal, it is generally felt necessary to shut her up in order to preserve her chastity, and to deny her instruction in order to remain convinced of her essential folly. This course of action tends to encourage homosexual proclivities, and these in their turn lead to a further undervaluation of women and their influence in family life. Where they are needed to work in the fields they cannot of course be shut up, but the general attitude still is that the wife pulls the plough while the husband guides it.

Such data as I have been able to collect do not suggest that the women in polygamous countries lead particularly happy lives. Those who have escaped from the old system and written books about it endorse this view. In fact it seems clear that the strongest appeal made by Christianity to Eastern women is that it teaches monogamy.

Wives, then do not seem to benefit by being forced to share a husband. The fact that they accept the system without question does not mean that it causes neither jealousy nor resentment. This theory is a piece of wishful thinking.

Having regard to the importance, for children, of happy

---

[1] Ideas of this kind, where they are in fact erroneous, spring from a sense of guilt, " They must want to murder us because of the treatment we give them."

mothers and a peaceful, stable, atmosphere in their homes, this fact has implications which go beyond the welfare of wives. But it might still be true that many of these, even if their status were only that of a concubine or household slave, are better off than they would have been as spinsters. Except through their suicide rate—carefully hidden on account of the loss of face involved—it is difficult to discover the feelings of concubines and domestic slaves. Enough has been said, however, to show that by using our present criteria we have an objective standard for judging a question which ends only in a deadlock if we try to pit prejudice against prejudice, custom against custom, and religion against religion.

The next issue raised is far more important for most of us ; indeed it is a close and vexing problem. That is whether public opinion should or should not support the doctrine of complete chastity outside marriage which is put forward by the Christian churches. It is a vast subject, and the particular aspect of it which I propose to discuss is whether or not it is ever advisable for young people to live together before they marry.

This is by no means a simple question. The first complexity is introduced by the fact that whereas the moralist, as moralist, has only to decide, if he can, whether the custom on balance is likely to do good or harm, as human beings most of us consider it in terms of individual cases. These two points of view involve quite different factors. For even if we assume that it would be wise for most young couples to live together for a time before accepting life-long obligations, this does not settle the point of whether it would be right for Jane and John. They may be confronted with such alternatives as wrecking the lives of people whom they love, or practising an amount of deceit which is felt to ruin their relation ; of losing their jobs or making false statements on official documents which may be tantamount to obtaining money by false pretences. The alternative preferred will depend upon the moral codes of Jane and John, but all may be extremely distasteful.

More important even than these is the question of whether they do or do not, in the depths of their minds, believe that what they are proposing to do is sinful. It is always very risky to do what one really believes to be wrong, for the feelings of guilt produced may stir up mental conflicts which destroy happiness and often give rise to neurotic symptoms or physical illness. This is more likely to happen if the public opinion with which one is daily confronted condemns the proposed behaviour. It follows therefore that those who have been brought up in circles where pre-marital love affairs are considered normal instead of wicked will escape the dangers run by those who have been trained on orthodox lines. Even where a complete change of *milieu* occurs, and John finds that all his old standards are regarded as nonsense by his new companions, he will still be wise to hestitate before he copies their behaviour. Early moral beliefs can never be sloughed off altogether, and even sound reasons for changing one's moral code may not convince one's conscience. Certainly this cannot be done by a string of excuses trumped up for the occasion.

The real question for the moralist is, therefore, which of these codes should be handed on to young people, explicitly or implicitly, and not the atttude which we should adopt towards individuals. As in every matter affecting individuals this should be governed by all the wisdom and good-feeling of which we are capable.

A good many readers will probably feel at once that what I have said decides the question. It is one thing to admit that times have changed, that young men will be young men though it is dreadful to think of what girls are coming to nowadays, and then to extend a grudging toleration ; and quite another to face the fact that times have changed and that therefore the standards that we set may need modification. The general attitude is still that the only safe line is to tell the new generation that it is a deadly sin to depart from the way of life which was followed—or not followed—by the old, and leave them to fight out their problems for themselves. Nothing could be more cruel, or less likely to produce the desired results. The consequence is far more likely to be that they lose all respect for the opinions and judgment of their elders than that they are guarded from the snares and temptations offered by the world. Young people should be taught self-control and to take a responsible view of sex, as indeed of all other important fields of human conduct, but this is not the way to do it. About the best methods of achieving this end something will be said later.

Coming back to the problem itself ; the two main issues seem to be whether toleration of sexual intercourse between young people before marriage leads to promiscuity, and whether such experiences promote or endanger happy unions.

As for promiscuity, a good deal of what is thought and said on the matter does not take account of all the facts. In men, the capacity to set up a home with one woman and be reasonably faithful to her is not a matter of virtue as against vice, but a stage in a long process of development which is reached when the mind becomes adult and the emotions mature. Healthy people can achieve it. But before it is reached most normal and decent young men pass through an experimental stage during which they are preparing themselves for settling down. They fall in and out of love, they may have several affairs, before they meet the woman with whom they are prepared to found a family and who seems to them worth the sacrifice of their freedom. These facts are recognised by most societies. It has never been found practicable to prevent young men from behaving in this way so long as they could afford it; and provided that other men's wives and "decent girls" are not interfered with, public opinion is seldom prepared to make it a legal offence.

This is not what I mean by promiscuity. That means the divorcing of sex from tenderness and responsibility, its treatment as a mere matter of physical pleasure and personal convenience. This is not a passing phase on the road to emotional stability, but a state of arrested development and stunted emotion, accompanied by a great deal of underlying hostility towards the women of whom use is made. The roots of such maladjustment go deep; the most common of its causes being what is known as a mother fixation. Such a condition is not caused by intercourse with women who are not one's wife; it is not curable either by abstinence or by marriage. On the contrary, those incapable of fidelity and unselfish love, should not marry until they have been cured. If they do they will make bad husbands and bad fathers. The remedy here is wiser handling in childhood, not the dogma that one must marry or be burned.

Promiscuous women are in a worse state than promiscuous men. Consciously or unconsciously every woman must always desire children, a home and a father for them and the love which seems to make these things secure. To change from man to man without achieving any of these objects produces inner states of self-loathing and despair and in the end hatred for the men who frustrate her deepest longings. "Men are pigs." But here again, the girl who would make a good wife and a good mother does not in ordinary circumstances become promiscuous. Those who do may be the victims of father-fixations, or may have identified themselves with immoral mothers, or may be suffering from such overwhelming guilt that only the most primitive forms of pleasure, repeated at the shortest possible intervals, can keep them from despair. These do not exhaust the list of causes; they are given to show that here again roots run deep.

Another fact that is relevant to our argument is that because the biological goal of marriage is of great importance to women, her emotions tend to attach themselves to a permanent object more readily than a man's. The love affair which was entered into on the express understanding that it was binding upon neither party, will leave the girl heartbroken when it comes to an end more often than it leaves her partner. Sex is always serious to a woman whether she thinks so or not.

But to say this, and to assert that girls should make sure that they are loved and love before they embark on sexual relations, is not to say that permanent marriage is the only permissible form of relation.

There is here a disharmony between the natures of the sexes which societies have sought to bridge in many ways. In some countries young men carry off the women of neighbouring tribes. In others they resort to prostitutes and make love to married women. In others the homosexual state is prolonged or perhaps made permanent. Or again they may fall into perversions. All of these systems have grave disadvantages and all are unfavourable to happy marriages.

These facts are generally forgotten by those who argue that young men should simply be continent. So is the fact that if a powerful instinct is forbidden its natural outlet it will find some other, generally less desirable, or transform much of its energy into a different form. The orthodox moral code forbids to unmarried human beings any type of gratification which gives physical pleasure. Only a minority of human males have ever carried out this ordinance, and it might have been better for the world if they had not.

To repeat what has already been said—it is not within the power of all men to transform their sexual impulses into general benevolence, or to work them off through creative and artistic activities. Some, not necessarily the most admirable, can do this, but not all. It is useless to say that they ought, for they cannot. The blocked instinct must therefore use up its energy in endless internal conflict or find some other external outlet. As most educated people know by this time, the most usual change is into aggression and cruelty.[1] And very few people will really admit

[1] These feelings are usually turned chiefly against themselves by women and chiefly against the outer world by men.

that this is a change for the better. They prefer to believe that it need not occur.

For all these reasons the problem of finding the best outlet for the sexual impulses between sexual maturity and marriage is not solved by demanding absolute chastity. Far more might be done to provide interests and occupations which are likely to drain off surplus sexual energy, but when such means have been used to their fullest extent the problem still exists. As far as young men are concerned it seems very much better that during their formative years they should associate with normal unmarried young women than with prostitutes or other men's wives. The question that remains to be answered then is " What of the young woman ? "

For obvious reasons, female chastity has nearly always been placed, in all but primitive communities, on a different plane from that of men. It has been enforced by every conceivable device, but usually by shutting up the girls until they have been provided with a husband, and killing them if they evaded supervision. This programme cannot be carried out in its entirety, but what men can do to keep their own women chaste has in most—not all—human groups, been done. Now women are breaking through the embargo in increasing numbers.

The main causes of this revolutionary change are hardly in doubt. They are what is called " the economic emancipation of women "—which means that unmarried daughters of all but wealthy parents are now expected to earn, and that the payment for their work belongs to them instead of to their fathers—and knowledge of birth control. These two facts have changed the situation with which we are confronted. It is impossible to keep a girl locked up if she is to earn her own living in any capacity but that of a slave. Nor will she regard a sterile relation in the same light as one which will almost certainly result in children. These points are proved by the actual behaviour of girls in countries where both these factors have been at work. Circumstances, therefore, have enabled young people to by-pass the strongest obstacles to their freedom. Those that remain—the feelings of parents, religious convictions, established customs and public opinion—do not seem to act as a deterrent. So far has this tendency gone, in fact, that most sensible people who consider the matter are conscious of alarm. We have been faced during the war with a deplorable increase in promiscuous behaviour. Young women by the thousand have consorted with soldiers whom they hardly knew, and in so reckless a fashion that large numbers of them have contracted diseases or borne illegitimate children. If this is the result of feminine freedom, then what was said about the causes of promiscuity cannot be true.

It is difficult to get facts on subjects like this, though opinions are to be had for the asking. We may be certain that some of the girls in question would have got themselves into trouble in almost any conceivable circumstances. But on the whole this behaviour was due to war conditions and will die out as these conditions disappear. Wars have always produced reckless states of mind, especially among those exposed to danger. It has always made women less strict and men more ardent. And in this war conditions were more adverse than usual to the maintenance of moral barriers. The break-up of social groups and even more of family life destroyed their strongest social sanction; the presence in these islands of millions of foreign soldiers went to the heads of " respectable " girls who had given up all hope of being able to attract a man, and loneliness in strange surroundings made many of them desperate for sympathy. All these factors made for irregular intercourse. The babies seem to have been largely the result of despairing love and excessive drinking—rather drink than love.

The real difference between this and other wars is not the promiscuity, but that many of the girls involved do not seem to be ashamed either of their babies or of their behaviour. That they should feel proud of the babies is surely a very good thing. The sins of the mothers should not be visited on the children. Moreover looking after a baby properly involves hard work, promotes self-respect and other changes for the good in character. But unless she can feel proud of her child the rather stupid and uncontrolled young woman is not likely to look after it well. As to their behaviour, the best way to prevent its repetition is to encourage their natural feelings that " all that " belonged to the war, and is over and done with. " To think of them days when the camp was full of Americans—it feels like another world already, doesn't it? You don't feel you're the same person really, do you? " This may seem an easy way out for immoral young women, but it does in many cases fulfil its object. The pangs of childbirth, the months of anxiety, the new responsibilities seem in most cases to be felt as a sufficient punishment for the past, and to ask that a young mother shall live in a state of shame and remorse and misery seems to her most unjust, rouses a great deal of hatred, especially of " the respectable," and inclines her to snatch once more at anything that is going in the way of a bit of fun.

The next question which must be taken into account is whether pre-marital intercourse was likely to interfere with the success of subsequent marriages. If it does, it seems to me to stand condemned upon that ground alone. If we could prove that the toleration of such relations deterred from marriage those who would otherwise have married and made a success of it, this too would be an extremely strong objection. At this point, I feel sure, any serious inquirer would like to see a great deal more evidence of what is taking place. It is not easy to obtain, but so far as I know no attempt whatever has been made to collect it. This is a pity. Nearly everyone has strong convictions on the subject, based either on subjective prejudice or a few individual instances which cannot be called a fair sample. Those who believe that the behaviour is wicked assume that its results must be bad. Those who have been unhappily married under the more rigid system often assume that lack of experience was the cause of all their suffering—again without proof. All one can say is that no evidence whatever seems to be forthcoming that the girls one knows who have lived with their husbands before marriage, or even had an affair with someone else, value marriage the less on that account. Sometimes they seem to value it more. Nor are they held more cheaply by their husbands ; nor do they make worse wives. One finds, in fact, what seemed antecedently probable, that those who are happy together make a success of marriage, while those who are not, do not—with the obvious provisos that circumstances are not too difficult, and that if there is a home to be run the wife can and will run it efficiently. Many of us would like more information than we now possess before coming to a final decision on the subject. In the meantime we seem to be faced with two facts. Social and economic changes have taken place which make more freedom possible, and that freedom is being used and will continue to be used. If these statements are true then what is to be done ? Is there any guidance than can be given even by those who are not happy about the position, or must they stand aside and let events take their own course ?

Those who really believe that all intercourse outside of marriage is wicked will, of course, teach what they believe. It has not succeeded in the past : there seems no reason why it should be more effective in the future. To make such a statement merely on the principle of " safety first " is not only foolish but cowardly and cruel as well.

On the other hand those whose minds are not closed seem to agree that the difficulty consists in finding where to draw a line. If marriage is not to be the sole boundary between vice and virtue what are we to tolerate—how far are we to go ? How can sincere and responsible relations be distinguished from reckless promiscuity and degradation ?

Is not the truth here that all voluntary intimate relations between human beings entail both duties and responsibilities ? Should not each fresh generation be taught that no matter what that relation may be we can never escape from our obligation to behave with justice and consideration ? The division is not between regard for the rights of others within marriage and callous behaviour outside it, but of avoiding in all sexual relations the cruelty and selfishness which are acknowledged to be wrong in family life. Freedom must not be made a cover for mean or treacherous behaviour. Or, to qualify Kant, human beings with whom we choose to form personal contacts must be treated as ends and never merely as means to our own convenience and enjoyment.

For what my own experience is worth, both young men and young women respond to this attitude ; indeed they will work it out for themselves if the right questions are put to them. And it has a restraining effect.

We are brought back again, in fact, to the position that men and women who are just and reasonable and have been shown the spheres of action to which these concepts should apply will use their liberty in a responsible manner. They will not run the risk of infecting a partner with venereal disease, nor father bastards upon trusting husbands, nor seduce and abandon helpless types of girl, nor break up a family. Sex is not a field apart where a human being may cease to be himself and the usual moral standards fail to apply. But because so many people wish that it were it is advisable to point this out. It is the hard and fast line which is now so often drawn, and the feelings of guilt which are roused by overstepping it which lead to the breaking down of behaviour once that line is crossed. " I am a bad girl now so I may as well make what I can out of it," and " The woman tempted me so it does not matter how I treat her," are only two of the results of such states of mind.

It may be added that wiser handling of children and, in particular, happier homes, would do more to strengthen virtuous impulses than any amount of preaching. The foundation of self-control in girls is self-respect and respect for themselves as women. Girls tend to turn their hostility inwards, despise their own sex and adore men. These attitudes lead to taking gratefully anything that a man will give you. They need to be replaced not by fear of hell, or the strong commercial instinct which will sometimes preserve a state of technical virtue, but by the dignity and sense of worth which makes insincere and trifling relations seem unattractive.

A girl of marriageable age should judge men as possible husbands when she is thinking of them in relation to herself. This is often said by men to be a fault in women, but it is their biological duty.

The chief agency which produces this sort of self-respect in women is a mother who has made a real success of her married life. Girls tend to repeat what they think to have been their mother's love-life, and the daughter of a happy home in which the mother was loved and respected may tolerate looseness in others but is most unlikely to choose it for herself.

Boys on the other hand should be brought up to value women as women and not, as so often happens, to despise them. The deep-rooted tendency in many children to regard girls as inferior boys impairs their chances of developing good relations with one another.

Finally, boys and girls should be brought up in sufficiently close contact to understand one another as human beings. In our small modern families this cannot always be done at home and during the holidays. Too much segregation, too much separation of their interests, especially during adolescence, leads to their regarding the opposite sex, when they do meet, almost entirely as sexual objects. Young women may be seen as terrifying goddesses, fair game or evil temptresses; young men as demi-gods or scalps or questing beasts. None of these attitudes helps young people to choose the right partner or to make a success of their married life.

It is a mistake to bring up young men in such a way that they look for companionship and the satisfaction of their emotions among themselves, and another mistake to bring up young women to copy young men. Yet to achieve this seems to be the object of most of our boarding schools and even clubs for boys. Instead of training our young people to make a success of marriage, we do almost the opposite. It is difficult to overestimate the amount of frustration and unhappiness which is due to these methods of handling them.

We must conclude then that sex is a very important sphere of human conduct, but that the good man will need for right behaviour here the same qualities as he needs elsewhere in his life. The aim of all communities should be the establishment of good homes, and these must be based, in the end, upon mutual love and esteem between husband and wife. To attain this end should be one of the main objects of education, and both laws, customs and public opinion should be judged by whether or not they promote it. Good men and women and good homes are even more closely related than the good citizen and the good state.

CHAPTER 16

CONCLUSION

If the main argument of this book be accepted, then we must agree that it is possible to give both meaning and content to the idea of a scientific morality. This content is nothing new—it is roughly what we are accustomed to call the humanitarian system of values, determined in its particular applications by reason based upon facts. Its practical aims, for the present, would be wiser, kindlier, more intelligent human beings and societies which elicit and encourage not only these qualities, but the especial gifts which enrich human life as a whole.

In order to obtain them we must seek to establish a high level of mental and physical health in populations, and train them in the use of all those means by which minds are broadened and characters civilised. Perhaps the most important of these means will be a moral code fitted to the actual needs and tasks of man. Such a code would neither create despair by demanding impossibilities, terrify by the threat of atrocious penalties, baffle and affront the intellect, nor seek to brush aside misery and injustice in this world by offering rewards in the next. On the other hand it must provide the guidance that we need in daily life whatever that life may be.

This is to preach a morality which is certainly " earthbound " and in one sense relative—both adjectives to which many people take very strong objection. The same duties will not be required of all ; the same type of virtue is not possible for all ; there are many sorts of good men and women, and various ways of organising good societies. Further, as the environment changes, moral ideas must be adjusted to these changes. Nothing could be more repugnant to those who insist on one perfection to which we must attain or be damned.

Yet in another sense the morality I have described is not relative. For each decision, and in every case, what is required is the best action made possible by the circumstances—which include the knowledge available at the time. Only the clearest thinking of which we are capable, only the wisest action, are good enough. Since this requirement is unqualified we can if we like call it absolute. But the need to adjust conduct to circumstance does prevent us from defining good behaviour by rule of thumb. " Thou shalt not steal " is an excellent working principle, yet no one would condemn starving prisoners who stole food from their guards. If we face this fact we are spared the need for a great deal of sophistry and casuistry.

Such an admission will, of course, seem unsatisfactory to many people. Precisely what they demand in morals is absolute certainty. To indicate ideals and ask for sound judgment will not do ; they crave for definite precepts which obviate any need for judgment, and prefer rules to which exceptions must be made, so to speak, on the sly, to the admission that since exceptions must be made the rules cannot be invariable. If the moral law is to be worthy of respect, they feel, it must be regarded as an immutable foundation to the universe. Each man must know without a shadow of doubt exactly where he stands with respect to propositions about right and wrong : the best that he can manage in the way of wisdom and good feeling will not do at all.

This demand is deep and widespread even among those who do not realise what it is that they are asking. One need not be a philosopher to hanker after absolute moral certainties. Most of us will own to a certain sympathy for this feeling. For one form of certainty we do require, and that is a reasonable assurance about what we ought to do as we go through the day. Nobody could cope with life if he were obliged at every moment to refer his behaviour to his ultimate moral standards. But this assurance can be provided by sensible moral training, and experience shows, as we have seen, that such a training can be based upon humanitarian values, with a reasonable amount of adjustment to the standards of one's group. If we except institutions, such as convents, where life follows in an unbroken routine, no existing system of ethics does in fact do more. And the fact that the Confucian code set out to regulate behaviour in its smallest details is rightly considered its gravest weakness, not its strength.

In practice, only a fanaticism so complete as to verge upon lunacy can secure for any human being an absence of doubt and conflict in moral matters. Of their nature they are not always easy to decide. Anyone who will take the trouble to read the lives of saints, of whatever creed, will realise that sanctity is no guarantee of internal peace. On the contrary many saints have suffered more than the rest of us from agonising scruples, hesitations, despondency and despair. Most religious authorities seem to hold that man should pass his life in a series of almost unendurable conflicts, and that peace can exist only beyond the grave.[1] Moral responsibility is a burden laid upon man, and to seek to escape from it is shirking. Nevertheless, we shall probably all agree that it is one of the first duties of parents and teachers to bring up children in such a way that obvious duties are performed as readily and easily as possible. The acceptance of moral responsibility may be the mark of a fully-developed human being, but one does not want to spend much of one's time in demonstrating the possession of this attribute.

It is true that many people like absolutes and fancy that they lean upon them, but do they in fact do anything of the sort? The will of God is regarded as an absolute, but the mere fact of asserting it as our standard gives us no detailed guidance.

The same difficulty seems to me to arise in the course of all other attempts to short-circuit discussions of moral issues. There are in fact no *a priori* links between the absolute and the finite. As a starting-point the notion of the good turns out to be empty, or to end in a vicious circle. The good is that which it is right to do, and it is right to aim at that which is good. It is right to obey the Will of God, but only on the assumption that the Will of God represents absolute good. As soon as we need to decide some particular problem we are driven back to the facts of the case and the results of our behaviour. These can be determined only in two ways—by reason, or by authority. Certain men and women prefer to escape moral conflicts by handing over the direction of their lives to others. They may be wise to do so, but it does not follow either that the methods should be universally adopted or that the authority chosen by them deserves their trust.

Children do need certainty, and they should get it from the teaching given them in early youth. Enough has probably been said about the danger of deceiving them as to facts, casting the mantle of virtue over the convenience of adults, or handing on one's own pet heresies as eternal truths. What sane, grown-up person really believes that it is wicked to criticise one's elders, or even that to tell a lie is the worst of all sins? But important moral values can most easily, and therefore should, be taught as categorical truths.

It is wrong to be greedy and unfair; to seize other children's toys and break them or bully one's little brother. Injunctions such

[1] Cf. *Belief in God*, by Bishop Gore, and the majority of the Christian Fathers.

as these need only be expanded later, and will never call for difficult readjustments.

Another objection which has often been made to the theory that morality should be empirical and based upon facts is that in this form righteousness would not be sufficiently inspiring. Men would not be induced by so humdrum a system to undergo the discipline which it imposes. Morals by themselves are cold, repellant and depressing, and so, in particular, is the use of reason. It is sometimes contrasted with the joy which is found in obeying our Heavenly Father.

If what the last sentence implies were true there would be nothing more to say. The good would be happy and the rest of us, desiring happiness, would be doing our very utmost to be good. Unfortunately common experience does not support this contention, and we are therefore forced to inquire why human beings should feel so depressed when they are asked to be reasonable in matters affecting morals.

Inspiration is no simple matter, and what particular doctrine will be felt as inspiring depends only in part upon the content or nature of the doctrine. The other decisive factors are the state of mind of the person concerned, who seeks to influence it, and the methods used to do this. To be " merely " good human beings does not appeal to some people, though it might have done if they had been differently taught. Taking them as they are, they want to feel that they long to be saints and are in fact great sinners, they want to be purged through suffering, to be pardoned, to be in tune with the infinite, to experience ecstasies. Religion, with its deep psychological basis of the father-figure, will always appeal to minds like these. Therefore, no doubt, we shall always have it with us, and the moral standards of its various churches will fluctuate in the future, as they have done in the past, between mystical phases dictated by fear, and leading to scorn of earthly values and withdrawal from daily life, and philanthropic moods which bring the faithful into closer touch with the ordinary problems of mankind. But except on the assumption, for which there seems to be no evidence, that the human race is turning back to religion, this is only another reason why those outside the churches should look for more stable moral standards.

Setting aside those whose feelings demand a wider sphere than this planet and its problems and possibilities, are we really prepared to say that to work for the good of one's fellows is not inspiring ? Many of the greatest minds have found it so. Is the service of truth not inspiring ? It brings great rewards. Illusions on the other hand may disappoint. To know the facts and to accept them is a source not only of comfort but of courage.

All men will not agree with this, and to those who cannot one can only answer that morality is no more the dependant of inspiration than it is of a particular faith. It is an inner necessity, an integral factor in our lives from which we can never free ourselves, try how we may. Joyous or unpleasant, dreary or uplifting, what we see as our duty is there to be done, and to fail badly in doing it is to injure and warp ourselves as human beings. The impulses which drive us to be moral are some of the strongest in the human mind : should we not therefore be well advised to turn them to the work of increasing justice and mercy, reason and good feeling in the world that we know, and those about us ? To increase human happiness and to lessen human hostility is an urgent task. We cannot, however, expect to make much headway with it while the very means used to promote morality are methods which both strengthen and confirm the most destructive forces in human nature.

For Product Safety Concerns and Information please contact our EU
representative GPSR@taylorandfrancis.com
Taylor & Francis Verlag GmbH, Kaufingerstraße 24, 80331 München, Germany

www.ingramcontent.com/pod-product-compliance
Lightning Source LLC
Chambersburg PA
CBHW052107300426
44116CB00010B/1566